Great Debates in Criminology

This book explores the role of theory and research in criminology. Adopting a unique and refreshing approach to criminological theory, it focuses on the great debates in criminology from its inception as a field to the present day. It explores the debates that have motivated criminological thought, that have represented turning points in theoretical and empirical trajectories, that have offered mini-paradigm shifts, and that have moved the field forward. Coverage includes:

- Classical debates, including the work of Lombroso, Durkheim, and Sutherland;
- Sociological vs. psychological debates in criminology;
- Control theory and cultural deviance theory;
- Criminal career and trait-based theory;
- Theory testing in criminology;
- Critical theories in criminology;
- Debates on the state of criminology and criminal justice;
- Policy issues in criminology.

Each chapter explores several key debates, summarizes key points, and offers a discussion of the current empirical status. This book is novel in emphasizing the role of debate in criminology and offering an enlightening synthesis of theorists and their perspectives. It is essential reading for students taking courses on criminological theory and teachers of those theories.

Chad Posick is Associate Professor of Criminal Justice and Criminology and Graduate Coordinator at Georgia Southern University.

Michael Rocque is Assistant Professor of Sociology at Bates College and Senior Research Advisor at the Maine Department of Corrections.

"*Great Debates* documents the development of criminology's critical theory, research, and policy tensions. The book provides an important bird's eye view of where we've been and where we're going. It's a handbook that should be on every criminologist's desk."

– Joshua C. Cochran, Assistant Professor, School of
Criminal Justice, University of Cincinnati

"This well-researched and highly stimulating book presents excellent reviews of great debates in criminology, including sociological versus psychological perspectives, social control versus social learning, and criminal careers versus criminal propensity. It also reviews methodological debates (e.g. on trajectory analysis) and policy implications. It should be mandatory reading for all criminologists!"

– David P. Farrington, Emeritus Professor of Psychological
Criminology, University of Cambridge

"If there is anything that criminologists can agree on is that we enjoy spirited debates about the causes and correlates of crime as well as the policy decisions that need to be made in dealing with crime. It is appropriate, then, that we have a volume that nicely presents the different points of view on key criminological and criminal justice matters. Posick and Rocque develop what I believe to be the book that students will learn from and by challenged by as they delve into the heart of the either/or views on crime, one that provides an objective presentation of the sides and their facts."

– Alex R. Piquero, Ashbel Smith Professor of Criminology,
The University of Texas at Dallas

"Posick and Rocque provide a unique point-counterpoint overview of the leading concepts and various assumptions framing major explanations of crime. In a chronological unfolding of classical statements to contemporary perspectives, *Great Debates in Criminology* leads readers through an ideologically balanced, empirically informed, and engaging introduction to theoretical criminology."

– J. Mitchell Miller, Editor of the American Journal of Criminal Justice

Great Debates in Criminology

CHAD POSICK AND
MICHAEL ROCQUE

Routledge
Taylor & Francis Group

LONDON AND NEW YORK

First published 2019
by Routledge
2 Park Square, Milton Park, Abingdon, Oxon OX14 4RN

and by Routledge
711 Third Avenue, New York, NY 10017

Routledge is an imprint of the Taylor & Francis Group, an informa business

British Library Cataloguing-in-Publication Data
A catalogue record for this book is available from the British Library

Library of Congress Cataloging-in-Publication Data
Names: Posick, Chad, author. | Rocque, Michael, author.
Title: Great debates in criminology / Chad Posick and Michael
Rocque.
Description: Abingdon, Oxon ; New York, NY : Routledge, 2018. |
Includes bibliographical references and index.
Identifiers: LCCN 2018003799| ISBN 9781138223714 (hardback) |
ISBN 9781138223738 (pbk.) | ISBN 9781315403861 (ebook)
Subjects: LCSH: Criminology—History.
Classification: LCC HV6021 .P673 2018 | DDC 364—dc23
LC record available at https://lccn.loc.gov/2018003799

ISBN: 978-1-138-22371-4 (hbk)
ISBN: 978-1-138-22373-8 (pbk)
ISBN: 978-1-315-40386-1 (ebk)

Typeset in Sabon and Avenir
by Florence Production Ltd, Stoodleigh, Devon, UK
Printed and bound by CPI Group (UK) Ltd, Croydon, CR0 4YY

Contents

            DISCIPLINE? CRIMINAL JUSTICE, CRIMINOLOGY,
            AND THEIR EXISTENCE   133

PART III
Great debates in criminology methods and policy   147

CHAPTER 8   WHAT SHOULD WE DO ABOUT CRIME?
            DEBATES AROUND POLICY ISSUES IN CRIMINAL
            JUSTICE   149

CHAPTER 9   ARE WE STILL DEBATING? CONTEMPORARY AND
            EMERGING DEBATES   167

            CONCLUSION: ON DEBATES PAST, PRESENT,
            AND FUTURE   189

            References   203
            Index   219

Tables

Foreword

Marvin D. Krohn

The most difficult task in teaching students at both the advanced undergraduate and graduate levels is bringing them to a point where they appreciate the differences and similarities between ideas addressing the same or similar issues. Most students can identify the components of theories and are capable of defining the constructs and concepts. It is when they are challenged to compare and contrast those ideas that we note deficiencies in both their understanding of the theories and the implications of the differences in those ideas. In part this is due to the manner in which textbooks and lectures present those ideas. Generally, each set of ideas or theories is presented as a unit with limited discussion of the interplay between the components. Some discussions include sections on the intellectual antecedents of theories and some have sections that contrast some of the ideas put forth in one theory to those of another theory. Yet these sections are typically very limited. It is, therefore, not surprising that when students respond to questions that ask for comparisons between theories, the bulk of their answers is comprised of describing the ideas of each theory and then a one- or two-paragraph response to what should have been the main focus of their answers.

The question arises as to whether there is a way to convey the material in a manner that encourages students to think deeply and critically about ideas. How do we get students to want to delve deeper into the nuances of theories and their differences? In *Great Debates in Criminology,* Chad Posick and Michael Rocque make a convincing case for the value of theoretical debates, not only for the advancement of the discipline but also for generating an interest in and appreciation for criminological theory.

Our interest in things, whether they be sporting events, political positions, or ideas is piqued when there is some controversy concerning them or competition between them. When ideas are presented as contrasting viewpoints our natural inquisitiveness leads us to ask the question of which set of ideas is correct. To answer that question we need to evaluate the elements of the arguments. In most cases this will require further inquiry and critical thinking. Questions concerning the acceptance of one set of ideas over the other will require an assessment of the implications of so doing. In some cases, such analysis may lead to the conclusion that some merging of ideas may be the best option. However, this conclusion can only be arrived at when a full understanding of the component elements of the debate is acquired. In the process of learning about ideas by focusing on the contrasts between them, the very type of analytical and critical thinking we hope to generate will be achieved.

The authors describe their book as being "primarily about theory, specifically criminological theory." While accurate, this is a rather understated description of its contents. Contrasting the differences among theoretical ideas necessarily raises issues concerning ontological assumptions about the nature of humankind and epistemological assumptions about how to study humankind. Issues regarding whether our behavior is determined by external forces or by a rational decision-making process are folded into discussions of the early debates among the founders of criminology (Chapter 1) as well as the debate between social control and social learning perspectives (Chapter 3). Thus the reader is introduced to these contrasting assumptions within the context of their implications for disparate theoretical ideas. In Chapter 4, the debate between Gottfredson and Hirschi, Blumstein, and others concerning the usefulness of longitudinal data is raised within the context of the study of criminal careers versus the study of criminal propensity. Whether society can be viewed as a conflict among different categories of people (e.g., class, race, gender) or one more consensually oriented is discussed in Chapter 6. Rather than taking these differences and arguing for some kind of synthesis (see Agnew, 2011), the authors try to assess which side of the debate presents a more convincing argument. Indeed, in Chapter 5, they present the question of whether or not we should even try to integrate theoretical ideas as a debate.

Given that the study of crime and criminal justice is studied from the perspective of many disciplines (e.g., sociology, psychology, genetics, etc.), the authors devote three chapters to disagreements concerning what approach should dominate our discipline and the implications of accepting one approach over the other. The question of whether we should study crime from a sociological or psychological perspective is debated in Chapter 2. After presenting a thorough discussion of Sutherland's reaction to the Michael-Adler report, the chapter flows into a discussion of developmental and life-course criminology, illustrating how the former debate is relevant to the current one. I had never seen this connection made before, but the transition from one set of contrasting ideas to the other was seamless. Chapter 7 deals with whether criminology and criminal justice are true disciplines and, if so, which approach is more descriptive of what we do. This is followed by a related discussion of what we should do about criminal justice policy issues, presented in Chapter 8.

The excitement for examining disagreements and debates in criminology and criminal justice bubbles over in Chapter 9. Here the authors introduce a number of additional debates that have emerged. Their discussion of this set of debates is more limited than what appeared in the earlier chapters, but serves to whet the reader's appetite for a more thorough examination of the issues.

I have often encouraged students in my criminological theory seminar to talk among themselves about theory because discussing (and, yes, debating) theoretical ideas is the only way to learn the meaning of these theories and the implications of their content. I reinforce this message by relating that in many ways I learned more about criminological theory in the bars surrounding Florida State University conversing with my peers than I did in classes. Posick and Rocque appear to concur, as they state that the impetus for this book was the discussions they had outside of class when studying for their comprehensive exams. I imagine their discussions, like mine, were interesting, lively, and, I dare say, fun. The authors have done an excellent job of conveying their enthusiasm for the exploration of different ideas central to criminology and criminal justice. Their ability to do so is to a large degree due to their choice of presenting these ideas in a debate format. In their concluding chapter the authors quote Jeffrey Parcher (1998, p. 1) describing debate as "a uniquely beneficial educational tool" because "argument is one of the most complex cognitive acts," requiring "the research of issues, organization of data, analysis of data, synthesization of different kinds of data, and an evaluation of information with respect to which conclusion it may point." I would add to this statement that debate also makes those ideas come to life, it makes their presentation interesting, and it makes learning those ideas fun.

Preface

This book covers what we call "great debates" in criminology. Our focus is primarily on theory but we do cover other debates related to policy and methodology. We both came to appreciate the value of debates in criminology as students. There is a reason that we believe this type of book is an important contribution to criminological knowledge and for organizing what we know about why people commit crime, how people study crime, and how this knowledge leads to public policy. In the end it is our hope and belief that upon completion readers will be able to better grasp the intricacies of criminological theory and thought and have their interest piqued to learn more.

In 2010(ish) we had the daunting task of studying for our comprehensive exams in criminology at Northeastern University. Having met the year before and establishing a close relationship, we embarked on this journey together. As we would bounce ideas off each other, talking about the nuances of criminological theory, one of us would generally say something to the effect of "yes, but remember what such-and-such said about that." We both found that articles debating the details of theoretical foundations and fundamental assumptions gave us the clearest and strongest understanding of a particular theory; and back-and-forth articles debating a topic allowed us to begin to understand the important, and very interesting!, intricacies of theories about human behavior.

In particular we were drawn to what Bernard, Snipes, and Gerould (2016) have called "The Great Debate" on criminal careers and career criminals that took place in the 1980s and to some extent is continuing today. In that debate Travis Hirschi and Michael Gottfredson (see Gottfredson & Hirschi, 1986; 1987) paired up against David Farrington, Alfred Blumstein, and Jacqueline Cohen (see Blumstein et al., 1986) among others in a series of articles and rejoinders about such things as the underlying cause of the "age-crime curve," the usefulness of longitudinal research, and whether it was necessary to label, tag, and theorize each "stage" of the criminal career. What made this debate especially intriguing to us, graduate students trying to understand the field *writ large*, was that Hirschi and Gottfredson were, before our eyes in the articles and rejoinders, developing a new theoretical approach to criminal behavior that would culminate in their 1990 publication of *A General Theory of Crime* (Gottfredson & Hirschi, 1990). In other words, these debates were not just fun reading, they bore the seeds of a new, extraordinarily popular perspective, one that is required reading for any criminologist.

In studying for comps and in our later academic work we discovered that the foundation of criminology rests solidly on debates, of sorts, between social scientists.

These debates often portended a major turning point in the field, one that would direct the course of our study for years to come. Needless to say we wondered if anyone had combined these debates into one book, with commentary of the debates, so that we could have them all in one place. When we looked we found there was no such book.

In this book we attempt to bring together important debates in criminology, providing a detailed overview of both sides. But we also attempt to do more than that. We show how the debates influenced the field. And in so doing we award a "winner" of the debates. These proclamations are not necessarily based on which side we agree with personally or professionally, but which side has garnered the most evidence and has had a longer-lasting influence on criminology. Thus the winner is not the view that is still standing while the opposing camp has faded into the mist. In fact, as criminologists have lamented (Bernard, 1990), criminology has long had a difficult time letting go of perspectives. No matter how weakly some theories are supported, they still manage to hang around.

Why do we need a book on debates? In some ways, reading a standard criminological theory text will make clear where theories disagree with one another. Reading a chapter on control theory, for example, one quickly understands that the image of humans is much different than the one offered in social learning theory. But these standard theory texts, while they do an admirable job outlining perspectives, criticisms, and empirical support, do not often discuss when theoretical camps have directly engaged with one another. How does social learning theorist Ron Akers defend his perspective in the face of a criticism by control theorist Travis Hirschi? Often these exchanges reveal much more about the thinking of the theorists and the perspectives themselves.

An illuminating example occurred in the 1990s, when Barbara Costello and Ross Matsueda exchanged essays on social learning/differential association theory. In that series of exchanges, which we detail in Chapter 3, Costello and Matsueda take on topics that would not normally receive much attention in standard textbook treatments. For example, in one of the essays Costello uses a term Hirschi had applied to social learning/differential association theory—"cultural deviance." This term seems benign enough, until you begin to unpack exactly what it means. Costello (1997) argues that, for social learning/differential association theory to be distinct from control theory, it must hold that some cultures require deviance. Matsueda (1997), in his response, disputed this notion and took umbrage at the term cultural deviance, which he suggested misconstrues the theory. And so, in this back and forth, we are treated to much more nuance than we would have if the bare structures of the theories, along with some empirical tests, were all that we included.

Thus debates illuminate theoretical perspectives. They force theorists to clarify their positions and to think about opposing viewpoints in ways they otherwise would not have. In one case, as previously mentioned, debates between well-known criminologists culminated in the publication of one of the most popular criminological theories to date, self-control theory. In 1983 Hirschi and Gottfredson published a paper on the relationship between age and crime. They made some strong claims, such as the argument that the relationship between age and crime was the same everywhere, which invited equally strong responses from other criminologists. Over the course of the 1980s Hirschi and Gottfredson would continue to engage with critics, developing an explanation for why the age effect was invariant. This explanation was based on criminal propensity, what they called "criminality" (Hirschi & Gottfredson, 1986) and eventually labeled self-control (Gottfredson & Hirschi, 1990).

We hope our treatment of the debates is as interesting as we found the raw material when studying for exams, and that we still draw on in our current work. In each chapter we include a table summarizing the main arguments and theorists involved, along with our declared winner. We are sure that there will be readers who disagree with our assessments, and we encourage this! It means that we will have done our jobs and that the issues involved are being seriously and thoughtfully considered by readers.

This current book would not have been possible without the assistance of several people. While we have been interested in working on *Great Debates* for some time, we first had to finish our exams, then graduate and find jobs. Fortuitously, now, over eight years later, we had the privilege of talking with Routledge editor Thomas Sutton about the topic. He was encouraging and supportive from the get-go. He was also helpful in developing the topic areas for inclusion in the book. We are very grateful for his insight and support. Hannah Catterall at Routledge was equally supportive and assisted us throughout the publication process. Second, we are grateful to leading scholars for taking the time to talk with us about these debates. We were fortunate enough to talk to John Pfaff, Barbara Costello, Alex Piquero, Al Blumstein, David Farrington, and Steven Barkan, who answered some of our questions and were able to provide updates to particular debates. We also want to thank Chad Bower and Abigail Westberry, who contributed to the book with insights about particular topics.

Finally, we want to thank the scholars upon whose work this book is based. Some of them are continuing to contribute to criminology, but many have left us. Marv Krohn, who graciously accepted our request to write the Foreword to the book, deserves thanks not only for contributing directly to the book but also indirectly through decades of thoughtful research on the topics we discuss. Chet Britt and Ray Paternoster, who helped spark in us a love of theory (and the importance of method), were two such scholars who left this world far too soon but with an indelible impact. We will forever cherish our chats with Chet in his Churchill Hall office on the campus of Northeastern University, our email conversations long after we had left the university, and our annual get-togethers at the American Society of Criminology conference. Ray was as kind a mentor, friend, and collaborator as we could have ever hoped for. The words of the Emperor of Wyoming (as he jokingly referred to himself) will remain with us always.

It is to these two giants in the field of criminology that we dedicate this work.

Introduction

What is theory and why are there debates?

The authors (Posick on the left; Rocque on the right) show their support for their side of the timeless debate regarding which baseball team, the Yankees or Red Sox, is superior.

WE HAVE ALL, at some time or another, engaged in a debate. Whether it was a formal debate, in a team setting, or just a discussion about which baseball team is the all-time greatest (Red Sox for Rocque, Yankees for Posick), these engagements are part of our everyday lives. Yet when it comes to fields of study, or disciplines, these debates can literally shape what we know about a particular subject and how we go about addressing social problems. As the title of this book suggests, the material we will cover includes debates, or arguments back and forth, between prominent theorists and methodologists in the field of criminology and criminal justice who have risen to prominence. Before outlining the organization of the book it is important to provide some foundation for the concepts we will be focusing on in the pages that follow.

WHAT IS THEORY?

This book is primarily about theory, specifically criminological theory. However, some of the debates we discuss center on methodologies and statistical techniques used to answer questions that occupy criminologists. Yet, generally, those methodologies and statistical techniques are being brought to bear on issues of theory. So what exactly do we mean by theory? How do we know a good one when we see it? What do debates have to do with theory? We think these questions are best answered with a story.

On October 22, 1989, in the small town of St. Joseph, Minnesota, three boys were on their way back from bicycling to a local store where they had just rented *The Naked Gun*, the police comedy starring Leslie Neilsen. It was dark as they walked their bikes down a dead-end street that ran through a large farm. That's when every parent's nightmare happened—a man dressed in black, wearing a black mask, stepped out in front of them and ordered the boys into the ditch at gunpoint. Telling two of the boys, Trevor Wetterling, aged 10, and Aaron Larson, aged 11, to run as fast as they could into the woods and not look back or face being shot, the man grabbed the remaining child, Jacob Wetterling (aged 11), and drove him to a nearby town. On the way Jacob asked his kidnapper, "What did I do wrong?" The perpetrator then sexually assaulted Jacob in a gravel pit and, fearing being caught, shot him in the head.[1]

We only know the details of what happened that night with Jacob because his killer, Danny Heinrich, confessed as part of a plea bargain in the fall of 2016. But in the interim much had happened. Jacob's parents, Patty and Jerry Wetterling, never gave up hope that they would find their missing son and fought tirelessly to advocate for children's safety. In 1994 the Jacob Wetterling Act became law in the United States, instigating the creation of a state-based sex offender registry that most of us are familiar with today. An amendment to that bill, called "Megan's Law," was passed in 1996 regarding mandatory notifications, and the Adam Walsh Child Protection and Safety Act of 2006 devised a tiered system in which the most serious offenders would be registered for life. Other state laws disallow registered sex offenders to live near schools and daycare agencies (Bleyer, 2013).

What does this horrific story have to do with theory? In the aftermath of the kidnapping, legislation it inspired was firmly, if not overtly, based on a theory of a particular kind of offending involving child sex crimes. First, the initial Jacob Wetterling Act created a sex offender registry which means that even after those convicted of sex crimes are released from prison or probation they must be registered with the state for the rest of their lives. Was this step taken to further punish sex offenders? Perhaps, in part. But it also rested on the notion that having quick access to convicted sex offenders would increase the efficiency and effectiveness of investigations when such incidents occur. It would also, theoretically, allow people to protect themselves, knowing what threats exist and where. Sex offender residency restrictions are also based on the idea that sex offenders tend to strike close to home, and thus increasing distance between where they live and activities involving children (schools, daycares) will reduce attacks.

Both of these are policies based on theories of behavior which put forth ideas about why and how criminal acts occur. Sex offenders, the law's theories suggest, are likely to be repeat offenders and so we must carefully monitor them even after they have served their punishment. Sex offenders are also likely to be caught and so, in the event of an abduction or attack, perusing the registry is effective because the offender is likely to have been someone who was previously arrested and convicted.

Further, housing restriction regulations suggest sex offenders are unwilling to travel more than other types of offenders, or that such travel will make it less likely they will reoffend. According to Mustaine (2014, p. 170), the housing restriction regulation is based on "routine activity theory (Cohen and Felson, 1979) and posits that if potential sex offenders are not in close proximity to suitable targets (i.e., children), they will not have opportunities to commit these crimes, even in the absence of capable guardians (e.g., teachers, parents, coaches, neighbors, etc.)."

These are theories of behavior and ones with real costs to people's lives. Both potential victims and registered offenders have a lot at stake with these relatively new regulations. In other words, the traditional dismissal of theory as irrelevant for the real world is rather silly, if not flatly wrong. Criminological theories are also just that—theories about behavior. They are not laws dictating how the world works. As such they can (and should!) be tested against real world data. Luckily such data exist for these new policies geared toward making us safer from predators. What does the research say? It's pretty clear, actually. Registries do not make us safer—they do not decrease sex offending and neither do notification laws (Agan, 2011; Sandler et al., 2008), though perhaps notification may reduce some offending (Duwe & Donnay, 2008). This is, at least partially, because citizens do not regularly look at registries (Kernsmith et al., 2009). What about housing restrictions? Not only are we unaware of any research that indicates such regulations reduce offending, they seem to create negative consequences for the offenders subjected to them (Levenson & Cotter, 2005; Levenson & Hern, 2007). A little-known fact that apparently has not informed such policies is that sex offenders, on average, re-offend at much lower rates than other offenders, and at lower rates than the public often believes. Levenson and colleagues (2007) found that a sample of community members in Florida estimated that about 74 percent of sex offenders recidivate with a sex offense. These folks would be surprised to learn, we imagine, that, even within 10 years, research has shown this figure is only about 17 percent (Helmus et al., 2012). And this is not their fault, the figures do not match the popular narrative!

So even when not explicitly stated, theory is all around us. Our behavior is guided by theory even when we aren't thinking about it in those terms. We lock our doors at night and our cars when we park at the store because we want to make it harder for would-be thieves to steal from us. What theory are we operating under? The idea that there are potential offenders all around us and they will, if we let them, victimize us. And that if we make it just a bit harder for them, they will leave us alone.

In this book we define theory as any statement or set of statements that attempts to explain, understand, or predict a phenomenon (see Bernard, Snipes & Gerould, 2016). Theory is an explanation that is not yet a law. A law is an explanation of cause and effect that has risen to the level of "fact," that is, it is no longer debatable. Gravity, in physics, is a law. No matter where you are on Earth, if you jump off a ladder you will fall to the ground, you will not float. In the social sciences, and particularly criminology, we do not have many, if any, such laws. For example, one of the strongest empirical findings in our field is the "age-crime" relationship. We know that criminal behavior increases after age 10 or so, peaks around age 18–24, then declines. But not all 24-year-olds slow down their offending behavior—some persist into adulthood and even to old age! Some offenders, especially those involved with committing genocide, start their offending much later—well into their 30s (Brehm, Uggen, & Gasanabo, 2016).

The subject of this book, then, quite obviously focuses on issues that are or were far from settled. Arguments remain about why crime happens, who commits it, where crime is committed, and how it is committed. None of these questions is solidly closed even today. However, where "great debates" occurred, typically one side emerged as victorious, which in this case means with the weight of the evidence tipping the scale in their favor. Of course, winners of these debates are in the eye of the beholder. But in this book we'll try to be objective and provide an assessment of the outcome. Sometimes it won't be clear, but in other cases the "winner" has everything but a medal and title belt to wear.

A RECENT DEBATE IN CRIMINOLOGY

Let's turn to an example of what we are talking about. Here we'll discuss a debate that is on a relatively new issue in the field, one that is in fact too new for us to have provided a chapter-length treatment in this book. However, the debate centers around a topic that has been the focus of much research in the last few years: mass incarceration.

Mass incarceration is the concept used to describe the United States' penal system, specifically the relatively high incarceration rates that have characterized our system over the last 40 years or so. While the incarceration rate may be declining as of late, our sheer number of prisoners puts us in rare company internationally. Including jails, the US has more than 2.5 million people locked up—no other country has even two million. China is next with about 1.7 million and then it's Brazil with less than three-quarters of a million inmates.[2] Even standardized by population, the US has the highest incarceration rate, by far, in the world (see Clear & Frost, 2015, for an in-depth treatment of these issues). And it's not even close.

The other reason mass incarceration has become such a focus of attention is that it was not always this way in the United States. In fact, in 1973 criminologists wrote a theoretical piece marveling at how stable the incarceration rate was in the country. From 1930 to 1970, they showed, the incarceration rate ranged from a low of 95.5 per

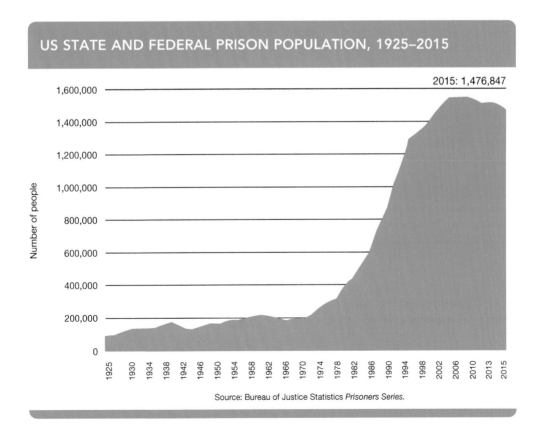

US STATE AND FEDERAL PRISON POPULATION, 1925–2015

2015: 1,476,847

Source: Bureau of Justice Statistics *Prisoners Series*.

Reprinted from The Sentencing Project (https://sentencingproject.org/wp-content/uploads/2016/01/Trends-in-US-Corrections.pdf) with permission

100,000 to a high of 131.5 per 100,000 (Blumstein & Cohen, 1973). Some notable fluctuation, but relatively stable. However, the great American prison boom seemed to begin right after publication of this article. The incline was so steep a graph of the prison increase looks a bit like a tidal wave (see figure on previous page). Even six years later, after the prison boom had begun, Blumstein argued that the data were "consistent with the general homeostatic process previously observed in the United States as a whole and in other countries" (Blumstein & Moitra, 1979, p. 389). By 2015 the rate of incarceration (670 per 100,000 people)—state and federal prisoners—was nearly seven times higher than when Blumstein and Cohen were writing.

What are the causes of this incredible and entirely unprecedented increase in the use of incarceration in the US? What are the consequences? Coming to an answer is, it turns out, far from a non-controversial task. Perhaps the most recent and popular work on mass incarceration and race is Michelle Alexander's *The New Jim Crow*. This book examines mass incarceration in an historical context, arguing that it is simply a new form of racial social control directed toward black bodies. Alexander traces the various systems of control, from slavery, to Jim Crow segregation, to incarceration. Her argument pulls no punches: she suggests that mass incarceration was a deliberate result of a set of policies that directed the brunt of the criminal justice system to criminalize African Americans. The main culprit is the War on Drugs, which was initiated in the 1970s and directed at inner cities. According to Alexander, "Convictions for drug offenses are the single most important cause of the explosion in incarceration rates in the United States" (Alexander, 2010, p. 60). In other words, her theory is that the War on Drugs became an intentional instrument used by the government to create a problem, where no problem existed, and to bring the force of the law upon young, largely male, African Americans.

Alexander's book has been instrumental in directing our attention toward mass incarceration as an instrument of racial social control (amassing more than 5,000 citations by the time of this writing). This theory is so prevalent that John Pfaff has taken to calling it the "standard story" of mass incarceration. It is accepted mostly without question. The only problem, from his perspective, is that it is wrong. In the recent book *Locked In*, Pfaff (2017) takes aim at the standard story, arguing that it actually overlooks the root causes of mass incarceration. Troublingly, most of the public think drug offending is the cause of mass incarceration over the last 30–40 years. One survey found that the majority of folks in the US believe that 50 percent of those behind bars are there for drug offenses (Lopez, 2016), yet the true figure is somewhere around 15–20 percent. While the standard story also includes factors such as longer sentences and the profit industry becoming intertwined with corrections, for the purposes of this "debate" we focus on drug offending.

Pfaff points out that, in fact, most of those who are incarcerated in the United States have committed violent crimes. The folly is assuming that federal prisons, for which a majority of offenders are incarcerated for drug offenses, represent the majority of prisoners in the country. Actually the vast portion of inmates in America are sitting in state prisons. And what makes up the modal offense for state prisoners? Violent crimes. As he argues, "A strategy [to cut incarceration figures] based on decriminalizing drugs will thus disappoint—and disappoint significantly" (Pfaff, 2017, p. 6).

So what is the way to proceed for Pfaff? It is not to tinker with sentences for various offenses, ensuring we are only locking up the truly threatening offenders. It is not to attack private prisons or to end the drug war (though of course the latter, Pfaff says, would be good in and of itself). Instead it is the recognition that our system is locking up more people who in the past would not have gotten prison sentences in the first place. And the key to that equation is prosecutors. "Yet," Pfaff remarks (2017, p. 127), "here's the remarkable thing. For all their power, prosecutors are almost completely ignored by reformers" who wish to reduce incarceration rates. They are, in a matter of metaphor, "the man behind the curtain," as Pfaff describes prosecutors in his fifth chapter's title.

Prosecutors, Pfaff argues, have tremendous power in the criminal justice system. That power derives from two main sources. First, the raw number of prosecutors in the country increased by 50 percent from 1990–2007 and so there are just more of these officials filing charges. Second, prosecutors have nearly unchecked power to charge whom they want with what they want—no questions asked. It is not entirely clear why, but prosecutors filed more and more charges during the prison boom, and this, Pfaff suggests, is largely responsible for mass incarceration.

Alexander and Pfaff have not engaged in any sort of back and forth debate, but Alexander did respond to overviews of Pfaff's work in an article published by The Marshall Project. In an email message, she said (Hager & Keller, 2017):

> Some people get so caught up in the prison data . . . that they lose sight of the fact that the drug war was a game-changer culturally and politically. The declaration and escalation of the War on Drugs marked a moment in our history when a group of people defined by race and class was defined as the 'enemy.' A literal war was declared on them, leading to a wave of punitiveness that affected every aspect of our criminal justice system. . . . Counting heads in prisons and jails often obscures that social and political history. It also fails to grasp the significance of the drug war in mobilizing public opinion in support of harsh legislation and policies for all crimes. The drug war corrupted law enforcement by ramping up an 'us v. them' war mentality, transforming local police into domestic militaries . . . which wound up diverting energy, resources, and attention away from violent crime.

Regarding the cultural shift hypothesis, we asked Pfaff whether the War on Drugs might have been part of that shift (in other words, could Alexander be right?). He replied:

> I'm sure the combative rhetoric of the "War on Drugs" contributed to a hardening of attitudes. But I also think causation runs the other way, that the militaristic rhetoric of the "War on Drugs" resonated because of trends in crime that, in and of themselves, were hardening attitudes. An example: New York State's "War on Drugs" began in 1973, with the passage of the Rockefeller Drug Laws. Yet by 1984 there were *fewer* people in NY prisons for drugs than in 1973. The number of people in prison for drugs started to rise sharply in 1984—when crack-related violence started to tear across the state and through New York City in particular. So the state declares a war on drugs, but that doesn't seem to shape more local policy until the outburst of violence tied to crack markets. And at least in NY there was an interesting symmetry: the number of people in prison for drugs starts to drop in the late 1990s, years before the Rockefeller Laws are reformed, but in step, more or less, with NY's decline in violent crime.

So who is ultimately right here? Who wins this debate? It's far too early to tell. Pfaff's book was published in early 2017, while Alexander's book has been out for the public to chew on for a bit longer. As a result the "standard story" associated with Alexander appears to have more sway with the public and has certainly been a focus of more political attention. Yet this is not to dismiss the impact of Pfaff's work. Since publication of *Locked In* his arguments have gained increasing visibility. The alternative story he tells may eventually be declared the winner and there is at least one reason why this is a reasonable guess. He offers concrete, feasible policy prescriptions based on his analysis. *The New Jim Crow* is very thin where policy is concerned. Alexander provides a laundry list in the last chapter of things that must change, but little time is devoted to how to go about such changes or what impact they might have. Perhaps this is because her book was meant as more of a conversation starter than a mass incarceration reduction recipe book.

However, Pfaff does offer—and discusses—several possible policy solutions. First, he suggests we invoke prosecutorial guidelines (as New Jersey has), which are akin to judicial or sentencing guidelines, to limit discretion. Second, states can cut the maximum sentences they are willing to impose for particular offenses. Both strategies would limit the discretion and power of prosecutors and would, assumedly, reduce incarceration rates. The last full chapter in Pfaff's book details several other reforms that could potentially reduce incarceration rates, and he is clear that to do this we will have to change the way we think about and handle those who have committed violent crimes.

We have simplified much about a complex topic. It's clearly not one thing that led to the rise in incarceration, and, as Pfaff points out in a conversation with us, "I'm not sure there will be a winner because I'm not sure Alexander and I always disagree as much as people think. I mean, I do disagree with her 'War on Drugs allowed punitiveness to grow' point, because I think violence played a much bigger role, but I think there are a lot of places where we overlap or agree." The winner, we submit, will be found in which narrative influences policy more than the other.

In the following chapters we will delve into such debates with much more detail, describing each "side" of the debate over multiple publications. The Pfaff/Alexander debate is still in its infancy and the two sides have not yet had extensive opportunity to respond to one another. Pfaff's arguments and solutions are also too new to have been properly analyzed and assessed. That is not the case for the primary debates we will discuss throughout this book. In those instances, debates involve multiple parties, multiple publications, and often direct engagement.

THE DEBATES

Criminology does not suffer from a lack of disagreements among scholars. In fact this reality is often a point of great lamentation by observers—we have too many theories, there is too much we can't settle, and so we are not a mature discipline (Bernard, 1990; Savelsberg & Sampson, 2002). Yet to us and, we imagine, many of you readers, this relative immaturity of the field, rather than being a point of despair, is actually indicative of an exciting field, one in which ideas matter and we are still in the process of making new discoveries. Of course, some of the debates we will discuss raged decades ago, but others remain just as fiery today.

We begin with the infancy of sociology and criminology. Part I of the book covers classical theoretical debates. Chapter 1 chronicles the clash between what we now think of as the "classical school" in criminology with the "positive school." Both are diametrically opposed to one another, not just in terms of what they argue are the causes of crime but also whether there are such things as "causes" of crime in the first place. Most students of criminology are familiar with the classical school, generally thought to have been initiated with the work of Cesare Beccaria and Jeremy Bentham in the 18th century. Standard textbooks in criminology liken this school to the rational choice perspective of later years. The standard textbook chronology then moves on to the work of biological/anthropological criminologists such as Cesare Lombroso, briefly mentioning that his was a "positive" social scientific perspective.

Yet most textbooks do not really delve into how these two "schools" differ on key issues, what they mean (their epistemologies), the pros and cons of each side, and where we stand as a discipline today. In Chapter 1 we'll trace this debate, which does not appear to have been engaged in directly by proponents until later in the 20th century. In Chapter 1 we'll also discuss classic debates about human behavior by sociological and psychological thinkers who continue to exert tremendous influence on criminology today. In particular we'll focus on Emile Durkheim and Gabriel Tarde, who viewed the best approach to studying humans quite differently, in ways that can still be seen today in macro/micro debates in the social sciences.

Chapter 2 will move on to the 20th century, focusing on the work of the great sociologist Edwin Sutherland. Sutherland, of course, was responsible for perhaps the first sociological theory of crime, differential association theory. Yet, thanks to the important work of scholars such as Robert Sampson and John Laub we know much more about what motivated Sutherland to claim criminology as a field of sociology. He was reacting to a report, released in 1933, which bemoaned the lack of progress criminology had made in understanding crime and crime control (Laub, 2006). In making the case for a sociological criminology, Sutherland had to show how it was a superior view to prevailing ones, such as multi-factor approaches, biology, and psychology. In Chapter 2 we'll trace the development of Sutherland's perspective and continue to track the trajectory of criminology as a field to the present. Does sociology still "own" criminology? Has criminology become a discipline in its own right? What sort of disciplinary training do most criminologists have? These are important questions that scholars continue to grapple with, and in many ways can be traced to Sutherland's work. In Chapter 2 we will also cover more recent debates centering on sociological vs. psychological approaches, including what distinguishes life-course from developmental criminology. For example, Robert Sampson and John Laub, disagree with Gottfredson and Hirschi, that life-events and social bonds matter for crime. Sampson and Laub built their own theory of age-graded informal social controls which is based on the identification of events/relationships that can act as controlling agents throughout a person's life. Their exchange with Hirschi and Gottfredson in 1995 will be highlighted in this chapter.

Chapter 3 begins Part II of the book, on contemporary theoretical debates. This chapter moves on to what we call the "seminal trio" of theory in criminology. In the 20th century three unique and ultimately competing theoretical perspectives on crime and delinquency emerged (and still exist in some form today). They are strain, social learning, and social control/bond theories. The identification of the seminal trio was first made most forcefully and clearly by Travis Hirschi in his *Causes of Delinquency* (1969). In that book he set out carefully defining, measuring, and testing all three theories against one another. Although Hirschi is often thought of as the father of social bond theory, he certainly was not the first theorist to focus on social relationships as mechanisms of social control which restrain youth from misbehavior. In Chapter 3 we'll pay particular attention to the historical development of two of these theories, social learning and control, discuss when they first engaged in conflict with one another, how they have fared over time, and where we stand today. Our conclusions here, regarding the "winner" of the seminal trio debate, is sure to be met with some disagreement on the part of readers who are faithful to one or another perspective. That these perspectives continue to be pitted against one another is a testament to their power to explain behavior and is why we refer to them as seminal.

Chapter 4 takes us up to the late 20th century, detailing the "great debates" between the criminal career vs. propensity theorists. In this chapter we provide background and context for the great debate and explain in detail the issues that were (and in some ways still are) at stake. In Chapter 4 we trace perhaps the most seminal theoretical debate in criminology to date: the criminal career paradigm. This paradigm was, arguably, initiated by the findings from the Philadelphia Birth Cohort studies which found that 6 percent of individuals were responsible for 50 percent of all arrests. In the late 1970s Alfred Blumstein and Jacqueline Cohen began arguing that, rather than focusing on who is a criminal/non-criminal, we need to delineate the "criminal career" into several dimensions, including onset, frequency, diversity, prevalence, and desistance. Into this fold came Travis Hirschi and Michael Gottfredson (1983), who argued that at all times and all places the age-crime relationship was substantively the same. They went on to argue that a focus on criminal careers, chronic criminals, and the use of longitudinal research was misguided because the causes of crime were the same at all ages, and the criminal career dimensions were just a distraction. This exchange spanned the 1980s, included numerous scholars, and arguably revitalized the field, leading to methodological and theoretical innovations. In some sense the debate is still on-going, with arguments on both sides being fleshed out in important ways.

In Chapter 5 we take a turn away from debates regarding which theories hold the most promise and discuss debates about how to best test and build theories. We cover the debate in the late 1980s and early 1990s regarding what to do about the plethora of theories in the field (what some refer to as the "cluttered landscape" of criminology). In 1989 Steven Messner, Marvin Krohn, and Allen Liska published an edited volume containing differing views on theoretical integration. Interestingly some scholars viewed integration as a way to reduce the volume of separate theories, while others argued that integration undermines each theory's core assumptions. This debate, much like the previous one, is still on-going. Criminologists do not know the best way to reduce the (mind-numbingly) large number of theories that exist, nor how to improve the sometimes quite low amount of variance such theories explain. Clearly much work remains to be done in this area.

In Chapter 6 we tackle debates in criminology (and social sciences in general) surrounding how we know what we know about the world and how we empirically study it. Traditionally, criminologists have sought to discover the facts of crime via numerical representations—quantitative data. The tradition of "positivism" revolves around measuring, differentiating, and quantifying social phenomena. In the 1970s critical criminologists began to voice opposition to this representation of the world, claiming it painted a distorted and biased view of reality. This debate between positivists and critical criminologists continues today, represented well by Jock Young's notion of the "bogus of positivism" (Young, 2011) relative to the overwhelming continued use of quantitative methods in criminology. In this chapter we will discuss critical criminology's critique of traditional criminology and traditional criminology's response. We also discuss debates between so-called "liberal" and "conservative" criminology regarding the best way to think about and reduce crime.

Chapter 7 will take a grander view of the field of criminology, rather than specifically focusing on individual theorists or theories. In recent years the notion that criminology may not be "mature" as a discipline has gained steam. Works by Todd Clear, Joachim Savelsberg, and Robert Sampson, to name a few, wonder whether criminology has its own paradigm. This debate extends as well to the field of criminal justice, where John Cooper and John Worrall as well as Peter Kraska and John Brent have considered whether criminal justice research has an organizing framework. We will generally consider these perspectives and describe the implications of each side. Because there are few who argue that criminology and criminal justice are unified, we will focus on the arguments that it is not. In addition, we will discuss what differences there are between criminology and criminal justice as a field. Programs typically include both terms (e.g., "Department of Criminology and Criminal Justice"), implying that they are inter-changeable. We examine this argument and offer our assessment on whether the two are the same and whether criminology is a mature discipline.

Part III of the book begins with Chapter 8 and covers policy and current method-ological/theoretical debates. In Chapter 8 we move beyond theoretical debates and discuss the implications of those perspectives. Policy, or what should we do about it, is a central concern of criminology. And in keeping with Chapter 7's discussion about criminology/criminal justice being fragmented or not mature, the policy prescriptions espoused by criminology have been wildly disparate. We pay particular attention in this chapter to neoclassical (deterrence) vs. positivist approaches to crime control. Does rehabilitation work? Are offenders rational? These are some of the questions addressed in Chapter 8.

In Chapter 9, the last substantive chapter of the book, we highlight some recent debates in criminology and related fields. This chapter first touches on contemporary debates over whether general theories of crime and deviance are sufficient or whether we need specific theories, such as those for white-collar crime and female criminality. Other debates concern methodological issues. For example, Daniel Nagin and Richard Tremblay argue that semi-parametric growth models are a useful tool to examine trajectories of behavior over time. On the other hand, John Laub and Robert Sampson, as well as Torbjørn Skardhamar, worry about the implications of creating "groups" from data or if it is even possible to create such groups. The method, which will identify groups by definition, they suggest, reifies such classification and implies that there are quantitative differences between people which may or may not really exist. The policy implications of such classifications are profound—and perhaps not empirically warranted. We also discuss an emerging debate in the field; how to properly define and measure desistance from crime. In this section we draw on Michael Rocque's (2017) book on desistance in which he fully specifies these issues. Finally, recent debates around the usefulness of twin studies in the exploration of the etiology of criminal behavior will be discussed as they relate to recent epigenetic evidence suggesting that it is impossible to neatly partition the origins of behavior into genetic and environmental sources.

In the concluding chapter we take stock of the debates discussed in the earlier chapters, recap what the debates meant (and mean) for criminology, and look to the future of theorizing in the field. We remind readers why these debates make for such great reading, injecting a vibrancy into the field and leading to scientific innovations. We go on to speculate about continuing controversies and future debates in the field.

We hope this journey is as exciting and interesting for you to read as it was for us to write. Theory is something to think about deeply, to discuss with others, and to be continually critiqued and revised. At whatever stage you currently find yourself in your academic or professional career, you will use theory to base your decisions and behavior. Theory is practical and influential in our everyday lives. We envision this book as a foundation for thinking about criminological theory and building upon what we know for a stronger and more unified discipline.

NOTES

1   The Jacob Wetterling story draws in part on the fascinating series by In the Dark, chronicling the case https://www.apmreports.org/in-the-dark
2   www.prisonstudies.org/highest-to-lowest/prison-population-total?field_region_taxonomy_tid= All

PART I

Criminology's founders and their discontents

Debating among criminology's founders

1

CHAPTER OUTLINE

DEBATING HAS LONG BEEN in the blood of academics. In fact perhaps the first academic discipline, philosophy, was rife with disagreements in its early years. In the 13th and 14th centuries there was considerable strife at the University of Paris, mainly centered on the work of Aristotle (Brown, Dewender, & Kobush, 2009). The website debate.org even has a page dedicated to the question of whether Aristotle was the "greatest philosopher."[1] On this website users can weigh in on interesting questions such as this. On the pro side, one commenter wrote that Aristotle "Invented logic, clarified areas of philosophical inquiry and in particular made the key distinction between natural philosophy (including physics and metaphysics) and ethics." On the no side, a commenter wrote, "No, no single philosopher is or can be or ever will be the greatest philosopher." So who won this tale of the tape? The "no" side so far wins with 60 percent of the vote.

Harsh critiques, heated disagreements, and even some animosity surrounded early work in criminology. The individuals discussed in this chapter would not consider themselves criminologists (as the term had rarely been used at the time these scholars were arguing their ideas) but rather philosophers, sociologists, psychologists, and psychiatrists. In these roles each approached the study of criminal and antisocial behavior using a different lens that often led to different conclusions on the origins of such behavior. For several reasons this made for an exciting theoretical time. The ideas themselves were new and the techniques and methods to test these ideas were new. The ground was fertile for great debates!

In this chapter we trace the intellectual lineage of what would become criminology. We start from the "beginning," with one of the so-called fathers of criminology, Cesare (pronounced "Chey-sa-rey") Lombroso, an Italian medical doctor who took to studying criminal skulls and eventually produced the first scientific criminological work in *Criminal Man* (1876). Lombroso's ideas would come into dispute, with an English physician, Charles Goring, publishing a study challenging his claims in 1913. We also take up the early debates between sociological and psychological perspectives on crime.

As it should be noted here and throughout the rest of the book, these debates generally included several individuals and even entire schools of individuals. "Sub-debates" and minutiae were discussed along with the broader issues. Unfortunately we are unable to cover *every* scholar or researcher involved in these debates, and we tend to stick to the main issues and do not wade into the minute details or sub-debates. This endeavor, to be sure, would take volumes.

LOMBROSO VS. BECCARIA AND GORING

What better place to start off our foray into Great Debates in Criminology than with the "father" of criminology (or, at the very least, the father of criminal anthropology). Lombroso was one of—if not *the*—first to use a scientific approach for the study of crime. He can be contrasted with the work of the other "father" of criminology, a title sometimes given to Cesare Bonesana di Beccaria, whose *On Crimes and Punishments* made a splash in Italy and across the world in the mid-18th century. We keep our discussion of Beccaria's work here brief, as we also contrast his ideas on policy with Lombroso's in Chapter 9.

Cesare Beccaria

Beccaria was not a scientist. He was not a sociologist or an anthropologist. His work comes closest to resembling that of a philosopher. Beccaria was trained in the law, however, so he did have some insight on behavior and the justice system in particular, but his famous book was situated firmly in humanism and enlightenment ideals (Bierne, 2006). Beccaria, in *On Crimes and Punishments*, founded "classical criminology," which drew on the notion of "a rational calculus based on the doctrine of the social contract and the belief that human action results from the exercise of free will by reasoning individuals" (Bierne, 2006, p. 4). Despite some disagreement over what exactly we should take from Beccaria's work, it is generally seen as framing the argument that crime occurs because people *choose* to do it. Humans are rational creatures who choose behaviors that benefit them and wish to limit any negative consequences of their actions. Therefore, to reduce crime, governments must raise the cost of crime so that the benefits no longer make the behavior attractive.

From this view of classical or utilitarian criminology we can deduce a theory of crime. People are rational beings and some choose to commit crimes. There are no differences between criminals and non-criminals, only this decision-making calculus differs. The classical school of criminology argued that there are no "causes" of crime in the fundamental sense, and that anyone is capable of committing offenses; mental or environmental deficiencies are not relevant. Because of this, what we need to focus on is not the criminal but the crimes. What are their benefits and how can they be discouraged, classical criminologists asked. In this way the classical school was more legalistic than criminology.

Cesare Lombroso

Lombroso ushered in what came to be known as the "positive" school of criminology (Parmelee, 1911). Positivism was an attempt to use the methods of the physical or natural sciences in the social sciences. In other words, positive social scientists believed that human behavior could be understood much like gravity or the point at which water boils. According to Rocque and Paternoster (2012), positivism as an approach to criminology has five main elements: "1) criminals are quantitatively different than non-criminals; 2) scientists can quantify or measure these differences in individual and social circumstances; 3) scientists should study the motivations underlying criminal behavior; all of which lead to the notion that 4) criminology should seek to identify the causes of criminal behavior using the scientific method; and 5) in defining the appropriate problems to study, scientists must view the world from the vantage point of scientific neutrality" (p. 606).

Lombroso and other positivists "rejected the doctrine of free will, asserting that all human action was determined by material forces" (Gibson, 1982, p. 157). Whereas the classical school of criminology largely focused on particular crimes as well as the law, positivists wanted to focus on the criminal. According to criminologist Maurice Parmelee (1911, p. xi), since the demise of the classical school in the 19th century "The treatment of the criminal is being based more and more upon his own characteristics rather than upon the character of the crime he has committed." Lombroso was not interested in abstract theory, but rather empiricism (Gibson, 1982). What this means is that he did not want to sit around with his friends in a coffee shop and discuss interesting ideas (as Beccaria had done). Instead he wanted to bring the tools of science to bear on the study of crime. He collected and analyzed data and came to conclusions about what made someone a criminal. Lombroso wrote that he sought, early in his career ("amid the laughter of my colleagues"), to utilize experimental methods in psychiatry, seeking to focus on "the differentiation of criminals and lunatics" (Lombroso, 1911b, p. xiii). This is in clear contrast to the classical school, which did not view criminals as being differentiated from non-criminals. As Rafter (2011, p. 144) wrote, "Beccaria took the causes of crime—human greed and self-centeredness—for granted."

In his preface to his most famous work, *L'uomo delinquente* (*Criminal Man*, translated by Mary Gibson and Nicole Rafter in 2006), which was initially published in 1876, we can see the traces of Lombroso's rejection of the classical school of criminology. He lamented that "judges almost always ignore the criminal and emphasize the crime." Yet we should, he argued, be focusing on what it is about criminals that propelled them to engage in such deeds. That criminals are "different" is not disputed among "Those who have had direct contact with offenders" (see also Trulson et al., 2016). Policymakers, Lombroso thought, seemed to have been influenced by the classical school, believing that free will is the primary factor around which to base justice. "Most criminals," he said, "really do lack free will" (Gibson & Rafter, 2006, p. 43; see also Caruso, 2012, for a more recent rejection of the idea of free will and what that means for public policy). So it was not a choice to commit crimes but rather something that propelled them to act in such ways. That "something" needed to be uncovered and could only be uncovered through empirical examination.

Lombroso was a medical doctor for the Italian army and worked closely with soldiers, conducting routine examinations as well as autopsies. He was also a scholar, having been employed at the University of Pavia twice, the last time becoming Professor of Forensic Medicine (Mazzarello, 2011). The scope of Lombroso's data collection was breathtaking. He collected data from "some three thousand Italian soldiers, then compared each soldier's measurements with his observable behavioral traits. Lombroso took similar measurements from some six thousand living prisoners and autopsied nearly four hundred dead ones" (Jones, 1986, p. 83). He was particularly drawn to the behavior of southern Italians who were believed to be more criminal and deviant than northern Italians. He was interested in explaining this criminality, and was particularly influenced by the work of another academic making waves during his time, Charles Darwin. However, he was unable, at first, to connect Darwin's evolutionary insights to human behavior (Gibson & Rafter, 2006; Rafter, 1992). He may not have been well-versed in biology or heredity, making his quest for causes of crime difficult (Parmelee, 1911).

The seeds of Lombroso's most well-known theory came from one of the more famous stories in criminology. According to him, Lombroso was conducting an autopsy on a criminal (a thief) named Vilella when he noticed several anomalies with the individual's skull. One in particular, a depression in the occipital region, caught his attention. This feature was common in "lower beings," especially rodents. Then came Lombroso's epiphany. Criminals were not fully developed humans. They were more like primitive man, which he called atavisms. In Lombroso's own words (Lombroso, 1911b, pp. xiv–xv):

> This was not merely an idea, but a revelation. At the sight of that skull (Vilella), I seemed to see all of a sudden, lighted up as a vast plain under a flaming sky, the problem of the nature of the criminal—an atavistic being who reproduces in his person the ferocious instincts of primitive humanity and inferior animals.

Lombroso went on to examine many other individuals—both living and dead—and applied his atavistic theory. In *L'uomo delinquente* Lombroso reported that criminals have several physical characteristics that are markers for atavism, which he called stigmata. This included everything from a protruding jaw to large ears and other features such as facial hair—which is an odd physical feature as it has more to do with personal preference than biology (Gibson & Rafter, 2006).

Lombroso referred to atavistic criminals as "born criminals." They were not necessarily responsible for their crimes as they were born inferior and driven by their biological makeup. Lombroso would go on to expand his categorization of criminals as well as the causes for crime (including extensive discussion of environmental factors) but his legacy is with his formulation of the born criminal. The theory had a huge impact on criminology. Supporters vehemently supported his perspective on inferior criminals while opponents rejected his biological theory which, at its core, was viewed as not only inaccurate but racist.

It is important, we think, to note that Lombroso did not argue that all criminals were atavistic throwbacks or that biology was the only factor that influenced antisocial conduct. In fact Lombroso wrote of several classes of criminal, only one of which was of the "born" variety. He began including these other classes after the first edition of *L'uomo delinquente* (Gibson & Rafter, 2006). There were "passion" criminals, who are driven by strong emotionality to crimes of violence. There were "insane" criminals, whose behavior can be traced to mental illness. Other types of criminals included the "occasional" criminals, who are composed of three sub-types: the pseudocriminal who commits crimes when forced to, such as in defense, the criminaloid who is easily tempted to do evil, and the habitual criminal who is normal but has social disadvantages that have mired him/her in lifelong criminality (Parmalee, 1911). In *Crime, its Causes and Remedies,* Lombroso discussed numerous environmental influences on crime, including weather, the media, and education. Yet, as Parmalee (1911, p. xxix) wrote, "The theory which is most closely connected with the name of Lombroso is that of the criminal anthropological type." This is still the case today, and scholars critical of the biological/psychological approach to studying criminal behavior often use Lombroso's work to highlight their concerns with the perspective, even though his ideas are now more than 150 years old (Carrier & Walby, 2014).

Charles Goring

Lombroso challenged any of his critics to take on his theory and prove him wrong. Some, including Gabriel Tarde (discussed in the next section), did (Wilson, 1954). One of Lombroso's most vociferous critics was an English medical doctor named Charles Buckman Goring (Bernard, Snipes, & Gerould, 2016), who may be credited with destroying Lombroso's theories in England and North America (Wilson, 1954). Goring wanted to put to test Lombroso's claim that criminals would exhibit various physical abnormalities. In order to investigate these claims, Goring sampled prisoners, military officers, and engineers. Additionally, he compared different categories of criminals, including burglars, thieves, and forgers. With very few exceptions Goring found no appreciable differences between criminals and non-criminals. He published his findings in 1913 in his classic *The English Convict*.

We do not want to provide a false image, however. Goring, while disagreeing with some of his ideas, was profoundly complimentary of Lombroso the man. Goring called

Lombroso "an Italian of genius, an indefatigable worker, and a man of strong personality" (1913, p. 12). He argued that Lombroso was a "humanitarian" who wanted people to be treated based on who they were and not what they did. And so Goring did respect Lombroso and took him seriously—something future criminologists would fail to do (DeLisi, 2012).

Yet as far as science goes, Goring found a "total lack of the scientific spirit in the mind and methods of Lombroso himself" (p. 12). He was not at all convinced by the theory of atavism and by the evidence Lombroso supplied. Goring wrote (p. 13):

> As evidence for this doctrine, it is supposed to have been proved that the criminal is distinguished from the law-abiding community by marked differences in physique, revealed by measurements, and by the presence of conspicuous, physical anomalies, or stigmata. And, based upon what we would call a superstitious belief that there is an intimate relation between the spiritual and physical conditions of man, it has been deduced, from the supposed presence of these anomalies, that the moral condition of the criminal is akin to the mental condition of the insane, and that, consequently, he should not be held responsible for the crimes he commits.

Goring seemed to imply that Lombroso was prejudiced in his work by his "revelation," actively rooting for findings that would support his theory. "Naturally, and almost inevitably," Goring argued, "he soon found the evidence he sought" (1913, p. 13). Goring then reviewed the physical traits that criminal anthropologists claimed were markers of criminality. In reviewing the findings, the contempt Goring had for Lombroso's methods was palpable. It led, he wrote, to a "modern criminology" that is "an organized system of self-evident confusion" (1913, p. 15).

In summarizing his findings, Goring wrote that Lombroso's theory had been disconfirmed. "The preliminary conclusion reached by our inquiry is that this anthropological monster has no existence in fact. The physical and mental constitution of both criminal and law-abiding persons, of the same age, stature, class, and intelligence, are identical. There is no such thing as a criminal anthropological type" (1913, p. 370). And so it would seem that biological theories may have been not long for the criminological world. This was not the end of the story, however.

Goring provided an interesting interpretation of his results. Despite finding little support for a "born criminal" with the stigmata that Lombroso outlined, he concluded that criminals were actually different than "normal people." There were physical and mental disparities, Goring argued. "That is to say, our evidence conclusively shows that, on the average, the criminal of English prisons is markedly differentiated by defective physique—as measured by stature and body weight; by defective mental capacity—as measured by general intelligence; and by an increased possession of wilful anti-social proclivities—as measured, apart from intelligence, by length of sentence to imprisonment" (1913, p. 370). Goring wrote that sociological theories of crime were also wrong: "relatively to its origin in the constitution of the malefactor, and especially in his mentally defective constitution, crime is only to a trifling extent (if to any) the product of social inequalities, of adverse environment, or of other manifestations of what may be comprehensively termed the force of circumstances" (1913, p. 371).

Finally, Goring argued that crime seemed to be heritable. Criminals are generally inferior (they are weaker mentally) and this inferiority can be passed down through generations. He provided a theory of hereditary inferiority and concluded the review of his findings this way (p. 372):

> We have seen that the principal constitutional determinant of crime is mental defectiveness—which, admittedly, is a heritable condition; and scarcely less than 8 per cent of the population of this country are convicted for indictable offences—which could only be possible on the assumption that crime is limited to particular stocks of the community: from these facts the conclusion seems inevitable that the genesis of crime, and the production of criminals, must be influenced by heredity. Our family histories of convicts bear testimony to this truth; and the fifth and final conclusion emerging from our biometric inquiry is as follows: that the criminal diathesis, revealed by the tendency to be convicted and imprisoned for crime, is influenced by the force of heredity in much the same way, and to much the same extent, as are physical and mental qualities and conditions in man.

It was his conclusions, along with those of Lombroso, that provided justification for eugenic policies that followed in the decades after *The English Convict.* Goring even wrote as a possible policy implication that society may profitably "regulate the reproduction of those degrees of constitutional qualities—feeble-mindedness, inebriety, epilepsy, deficient social instinct, etc.—which conduce to the committing of crimes" (1913, p. 373).

The debates between classical and positivistic researchers early in the history of criminology defined the trajectory of criminology to come. In the later part of the 1800s and into the early 1900s sociology entered the realm of criminology. Two sociological scholars, both from the "French school" of thought, introduced new ways of thinking about human behavior. Emile Durkheim, often credited as the "father of sociology," believed that the larger social structure could influence behavior, while his contemporary, Gabrielle Tarde, thought that imitation was the cause of behavior. Durkheim's view was more purely sociological while Tarde's was social psychological. It is to their contrary perspectives that we turn to next.

DURKHEIM VS. TARDE

Several years ago one of us (Posick) was working on his 30th birthday when horrific news crossed his news feed. On December 14, 2012, Adam Lanza walked into Sandy Hook elementary school in Newtown, Connecticut, and shot and killed 20 children and six adults. Before that he had shot and killed his mother. After all of this Lanza delivered the final shot to his own head—killing himself before he could be questioned or stand trial. Little is known about the motivation behind the attack, but this did not stop people from speculating.

Many argued that larger societal issues were at play in the incident; mainly that the culprit behind the attack was lax gun laws that enabled Lanza to quickly and easily obtain firearms to commit his offense. This prompted gun control advocates to argue for stricter gun laws across the United States. This coincided with the belief that a culture of violence and hypermasculinity in the United States (especially coupled with easy access to weapons) promotes the types of crime witnessed in Newton. These are the types of arguments, often promoted by sociologists, which place the blame (at least partially) for bad behavior on broad societal factors.

Others, however, had a different view on the causes of Lanza's crime. These individuals did not look to society to answer the "why" question but to Lanza himself. This echoes the trite saying "guns don't kill people, people kill people." Society, in this view, does not make anyone do anything—a person decides what to do and how to behave. Some blamed Lanza's mental stability and emotional regulation for his crimes, while others blamed his lack of morals. In fact a report was released after his death indicating that Lanza had been anorexic to the point of damaging his brain through malnutrition. Looking to the individual, as opposed to society, is a typical strategy employed by psychologists. As one can easily see, this opens up a large debate among sociologists and psychologists on the origins of behavior. Current efforts to combine insights from both perspectives, called social psychology, have made some inroads in reconciling these perspectives, but a contentious history, which we cover next, continues to make this difficult.

Emile Durkheim

At the turn of the 20th century sociological and psychological sciences were developing and dominating behavioral theorizing and research. Arguably some of the most important work that would guide research on human behavior for decades was burgeoning in France. During this time one of the "founders" of sociological sciences, Emile Durkheim, Chair of Educational Science at the University of Paris, was forging the shape of sociology to come. His focus on "social facts," which viewed environmental and social structures as independent of individual people in society, led to the perspective that human behavior is dependent on social and environmental factors. This perspective clashed with more psychological views of human action which saw behavior as dependent on internal mechanisms. For Durkheim, all human behavior could be explained by external, social, forces—even those things that seemed to be utterly personal. He illustrated this cogently with his 1897 classic *Suicide*.

Gabriel Tarde

One of the proponents of the psychological view was Gabriel Tarde, Professor and Chair of Modern Philosophy at the College of France (Vargas et al., 2008). In a creative piece by Eduardo Vargas and colleagues (2008), a recreated debate between Tarde and Durkheim from 1903 is transcribed.[2] Tarde, in this debate, seeks to make the case that sociology as a science should draw more on psychology than Durkheim allowed. He believed that sociology was going too far, too fast without acknowledging the merits of psychology (Vargas et al., 2008). The reason for human behavior is due to personal differences within the individual. Durkheim and Tarde were at odds on two main issues: 1) what should be the guiding model for social sciences (sociology or psychology); and 2) were people guided by external social factors (coercive external factors) or internal factors—particularly imitation, which Tarde called an "interpsychic" phenomena. Interestingly Tarde (1903) seemed to be an early fan of great debates, and in the preface to his magnum opus *Laws of Imitation* he encouraged sociologists to ". . . criticize my view in its entirety" (p. ix).

As to the first question, Tarde believed that Durkheim gave too much power to society and even lifted society to the level of a divinity. This was misguided because, to Tarde, society did not have the kind of influence to drive individual behavior—only people could do that—and often behavior is modeled after others' behavior. Ultimately, knowledge and culture do not pass from society to the individual but from individual to individual. Therefore society is not an overarching *suis generis* but just the collection of individual beings. This is at the heart of debates between sociological and psychological theories: does society have the power to influence individuals and provide a guiding force for the individual, or is society nothing more than a collection of individuals that only reflects the interactions between those of a particular place and time?

A useful comparison of Tarde and Durkheim's views was published by Bjø Thomassen (2012). He wrote that Tarde's major ideas regarding social behavior resulted from the insight "that particular crimes appeared to spread in waves through society as if they were fashions. It was this interest in 'waves' and patterns that led him toward the social sciences. Tarde intuited that the epidemiological aspect of criminal activity might be just one instance of a more general feature of the social world" (p. 234). Durkheim disagreed with Tarde's position regarding imitation, and, as Thomassen (2012) demonstrated, sought actively to provide negative evidence on the theory. To him, social, not psychological, forces could wholly explain human action, and society existed apart from individuals who lived within it; in other words, society is not just a conglomeration of its people but is something larger.

As to the second question, Durkheim was a staunch believer that society was the guiding force behind all behavior. His major work, *Suicide* (which used data that Tarde provided to Durkheim via his position as Chief of the Bureau of Legal Statistics, (Thomassen, 2012)), was intended to show that even one of the most intimate and idiosyncratic of actions, killing oneself, was the result of "social facts" or larger societal factors that influence behavior—particularly the extent of social integration. Through a comprehensive and international exploration of suicide, Durkheim linked social facts to the rates of suicide in different social environments, supporting his hypothesis that behavior was, indeed, related to societal "causes."

Tarde disagreed with Durkheim's claim that behavior is directed by outside social influences and instead believed that behavior was the product of imitation. Imitation was a result of the individual, internal psyche. Certainly we acquire beliefs and perspectives from outside ourselves, but this acquisition is due completely to social inter- action with each other and from imitating those who we know and trust. Society is a collective of individuals and there is no grand power of society itself.

With respect to criminal behavior, Durkheim is perhaps most famous for his views on the "normality" of crime, which he published in *The Rules of the Sociological Method*. In that book Durkheim argued that crime is not necessarily a social ill, but is indicative of healthy social functioning. His rationale for why crime is "normal" stems from two main points.

First, there are no societies in which crime is completely absent. Even in a highly regulated and isolated community such as a monastery there are acts which rise to the level of deviance. Depending on the type of community, the sorts of behaviors considered antisocial differ. In a monastery, for example, missing a worship session may be cause for scandal, whereas in a less regulated society such a misstep may not be considered as egregious. As he explained (Durkheim, 1895/1982, p. 100):

Imagine a community of saints in an exemplary and perfect monastery. In it crime as such will be unknown, but faults that appear venial to the ordinary person will arouse the same scandal as does normal crime in ordinary consciences. If therefore that community has the power to judge and punish, it will term such acts criminal and deal with them as such. It is for the same reason that the completely honourable man judges his slightest moral failings with a severity that the mass of people reserves for acts that are truly criminal.

Second, if there was no crime this would indicate a society in which the values and norms are so ingrained in people that they are inflexible and negatively constraining. This would put a damper on creativity and freedom of expression. Crime, he argued, also paves the way for "necessary changes" (p. 102) to society. Without crime, repressive social regimes and structures may not ever change because the collective conscience would be too strong. Durkheim's views on crime are linked to the functionalist school of sociology, which views all patterns and characteristics of a society as useful and contributing to social cohesion (Barkan, 2011). This changes the nature of punishment, for Durkheim, as it should not be thought of as eliminating a social ill, since crime is beneficial to society.

For Durkheim, punishment was not meant to reduce crime; that is not its function. Instead, punishment, as a reaction to social violations, is a way to reaffirm social norms and "collective sentiments" (Durkheim, 1893/1960, p. 104). Even if punishment *was* meant to reduce crime, Durkheim did not feel it did so. In *Division of Labor in Society*, originally published in 1893, Durkheim wrote (1893/1960, p. 108):

> The case is the same with punishment. Although it proceeds from a quite mechanical reaction, from movements which are passionate and in great part non-reflective, it does play a useful role. Only this role is not where we ordinarily look for it. It does not serve, or else only serves quite secondarily, in correcting the culpable or in intimidating possible followers. From this point of view, its efficacy is justly doubtful and, in any case, mediocre. Its true function is to maintain social cohesion intact, while maintaining all its vitality in the common conscience.

Tarde wrote extensively about crime and criminals. He did not only disagree with Durkheim, however. According to Margaret Wilson (1954), "His devastating attack on the Lombrosian theory undermined the influence of that School in Europe" (p. 3). To Tarde, crime, like all social behavior (even or especially suicide), is the result of imitation. All types of crime we see was invented somewhere and spread, like a contagion. "The father who is religious, violent, vindictive, and more often than not a poacher, and in this himself an imitation of his former lords, is the type after which the son is modeled . . .," Tarde wrote (1912, pp. 346–347). He wrote that there is no "natural predisposition" to crime for most criminals, whose "fate is often decided by the influence of their comrades" (p. 252). Thus, as Wilson argues, crime for Tarde is a result of social conditions and association with others (foreshadowing the work of Edwin Sutherland, discussed in the next chapter).

When it comes to punishment, Tarde differed from Durkheim. He also differed from the work of Lombroso, who felt that, for some born criminals, punishment would not "work" to deter them. For Tarde it seemed obvious that punishment can deter offenders (contrary to what Durkheim thought). He wrote (Tarde, 1912, pp. 474–475):

In the first place, however lacking in foresight criminals may be, they are no more so than are school boys. However, will anybody deny the efficaciousness of punishments in schools? I know that they may seem useless in the case of the best pupils, and without any permanent effect, if they are not repeated in the case of a few undisciplined boys; but three-fourths or four-fifths of a class will feel the effect of this brake. Do away with punishment, you will see.

Tarde believed punishment can be effective, but it must be based on evidence. He believed that criminals do know what punishments await them if caught: "the articles of the Penal Code are of very great concern to delinquents" (1912, p. 476). He provided considerable anecdotal evidence, including the decrease in poisoning deaths in the 19th century after technology advanced enough to identify poisonings when they happened. He suggested that, once liability had been determined, punishments should be decided on a case-by-case basis. He did not agree with the classical school view that punishments should be uniform across crimes. As Wilson wrote, Tarde felt "that it was unfair to give the same punishment to a country thief as to a city one. The city thief would feel much more deprived by the punishment than the country thief since he would be deprived of many more satisfying activities" (1954, p. 9). Because punishment typically involves some form of deprivation, the more pleasures a society has the more severe such deprivations are; thus, for Tarde, punishments not only should vary for different classes of people but also for different societies (Tarde, 1912). This is similar to Durkheim's argument that punishments change form from "repressive to restitutive" as societies move from mechanical to organic (Spitzer, 1975, p. 613).

POLICY IMPLICATIONS: SIDE-BY-SIDE

In the first section of this chapter we described debates between Cesare Beccaria and Cesare Lombroso. These debates involved two men, but were larger than that; they were about the essence of the classical and positivist schools of criminology. We will keep our discussion here relatively brief because we take up the differences in terms of policy between the two schools in Chapter 9. Suffice it to say here that the classical school viewed the crime and the law to be the areas on which the justice system must focus. Beccaria, for example, argued that, in order to reduce crime, punishment must follow the offense swiftly and with relative certainty. In addition, the punishment must be proportional to the crime.

Research casts a long shadow on the efficacy of the law to influence crime. The centerpiece to the deterrence perspective is that if we increase the cost of crime we can influence the offender calculus reducing crime. It sounds good, but in actuality offenders are not deterred by the increased severity (costs) of committing crime (Paternoster et al., 1983). While there is a bit more support for increasing the certainty of punishment in reducing criminal behavior, even this relationship is weak when considering individual-level offending factors (Paternoster, 1987).

In contrast, positivists viewed the criminal to be where the action was. Criminals are different, they argued, and we must find out the sources of those differences if we hope to reduce crime. Lombroso, in terms of policy, did suggest that social factors mattered; for example, social inequality produces some forms of crime. But for the atavists there was, he argued, "no social cure and must be eliminated for our own defense, sometimes by the death penalty" (Lombroso, cited in Gibson & Rafter, 2006, p. 354). He also suggested busying some criminals in occupations that would redirect their antisocial tendencies for social good. Goring did not seem to have much more faith than Lombroso that criminals could be socially engineered away. He wrote that three factors influenced crime: chance, circumstance, and heredity. To him, "legislatures" must focus on what really matters: heredity. It should be noted that Goring did not think heredity meant determinism—those inclined to criminality could be steered away with "training." This, along with isolation of the criminal and restrictive reproductive measures, represented Goring's policy suggestions.

Looking at sociological and social psychological perspectives we also find many differences in how to approach public policy. Durkheim believed that society was the driver of behavior, while Tarde places the individual in the driver's seat. This would become a disagreement between sociologists and psychologists for many years to come. Durkheim's sociological model suggests that one should look to larger societal factors for the etiology (or origins) of behavior. To him, factors that permeate through entire cultures, such as individualism, social integration, and egoism, were the ultimate causes of behavior. Yet he also felt that we should not regulate crime too much; a certain level is preferable. While Tarde agreed that crime is "natural," he also thought that our anger at the criminal is also natural and should not be ignored (Tarde, 1912, pp. 505–506). As we saw, for Tarde, punishments should fit the crime *and* the criminal to be effective.

CONCLUSION: TALE-OF-THE-TAPE

We can very easily provide a conclusion for the first debate, between Lombroso and Goring, because they were both wrong in many ways. Before providing our critique of both individuals and their perspectives, we would like to point out that both Lombroso's and Goring's approaches provided criminology with important advances. Lombroso was among the first to explore crime through a scientific approach. He relied on empiricism—hands-on examination of human bodies—to establish his conclusions. Therefore he catalyzed the first big paradigm shift by moving the study of crime to positivism. Likewise, Goring's study was the most rigorous of his time. He studied more than 1,000 people and used the most advanced statistics of the time. In fact his laboratory partner was the famous statistician Karl Pearson. This scientific approach to criminology, and any social science, is essential in our opinion.

However, we are quick to acknowledge that good science is not the only priority in theory and research. The implications of one's research are also important—particularly in light of the probability that any one research finding will be wrong. With advancements in technology, methods, and analytics it is very likely that at least some findings of today will be disproven tomorrow. So we must tread lightly. However, the only way to progress and improve society is through sound scientific discovery.

Lombroso's theory that criminals are somehow different physically and biologically from non-criminals is almost, but not entirely, disproven. Most people, especially males, engage in some delinquent activity. Does that make them different than "normals?" Not so much. In fact normal might be some engagement in crime early in the life-course. Speaking of life-course, most individuals, even those who engage in frequent, violent

TABLE 1.1 TALE-OF-THE-TAPE. BIOPSYCHOLOGICAL THEORIES VS. SOCIAL THEORIES

Theory	Biopsychological theories	Social theories
Theorists	Cesare Lombroso; Charles Goring; Gabriel Tarde	Emile Durkheim
Main arguments	Behavior is the result of inter-psychic and biological factors; criminality is due to heritable biological characteristics (Lombroso) and imitation (Tarde)	Behavior is the result of the social environment; crime is normal and is driven by macro-level factors
Period of popularity	1870s–present	1890s–present
Seminal pieces	*Criminal Man* (Lombroso); *The Laws of Imitation* (Tarde); *The English Convict* (Goring)	*The Rules of Sociological Method* (Durkheim); *Suicide* (Durkheim)
WINNER	✓	

crime early in life, stop offending or desist from crime. Are these individuals much different than the rest of us and infrequent offenders physically? Generally not.

Lombroso and Goring both believed that there was a hereditary component to crime. In this case they were partially correct, although they likely overestimated the heredity of violence and the permanency of delinquent behavior across the life-course. Today we know offending behavior does travel in families—often referred to as the "intergenerational transmission of violence" (Thornberry et al., 2003). Twin and adoption studies have provided strong support for a hereditarian perspective on violent behavior. For instance, having criminal parents (both biological and adopted) will increase the likelihood of criminal behavior. The effect has been found to be even greater for biological parents when compared to adoptive parents (supporting a biological foundation of violence). An even stronger likelihood for violence exists for children who have both criminal biological and adoptive parents (Mednick, Gabrielli, & Hutchings, 1984). Studies on twins support findings showing that criminal behavior is very similar among identical twins, less so among non-identical twins but still more similar than among distant relatives (Rhee & Waldman, 2002).

Despite these findings there is ample evidence that crime is not only hereditary but due to environmental and other biological factors not necessarily inherited (Beaver, 2008). The unique experiences that individuals go through during their lives matter and, as the work of Sampson and Laub (1993) and others show, can increase or decrease involvement in delinquency. So, yes, the traits and personal characteristics conducive to antisocial behavior can be inherited, as Lombroso and Goring thought. But that is far from the whole story. The social environment in which people live and their unique experiences can also influence their behavior. And often these two factors are intricately intertwined, as we will discuss later in the book.

When it comes to physical features, Lombroso and Goring were again not too far off, but still not quite on target. Tattoos, facial hair, and other stylistic features of a person's appearance are not linked to behavior. "Stigmata," in the sense that Lombroso envisioned the term, is fairly useless in today's criminology. However, there has been a modest amount of support that some physical abnormalities, called minor physical abnormalities (MPAs), such as low-set ears and a furrowed tongue, are associated with heightened aggression (Arseneault et al., 2000). MPAs are often markers of some biological deficiency, neurological problems, or developmental problems. Delinquent behavior of those with MPAs is particularly prevalent when parental support is low—highlighting the importance of biological and sociological interplay (Raine, 2002). Once again there is some partial support for Lombrosian thought.

While Lombroso and Goring were clearly misguided in their work, that does not mean that the winner is decidedly Beccaria (who Goring was not addressing anyway). His ideas certainly had much impact in the world, having been read by leaders in Europe and America (Bessler, 2009). But his theory that the only way to reduce crime is to change punishment structures does not appear to be supported by recent research, which has shown the efficacy of rehabilitation and treatment for offenders (Gendreau, Little, & Goggin, 1996; Sherman et al., 1998).

Another knock on Beccaria is that the rationality of offenders, the basis of his deterrence model, is not entirely clear cut. For example, de Haan and Vos (2003: p. 49) conducted interviews with street robbers and concluded that "Before, during and after an offence, perpetrators often experience contradictory feelings. In addition to relief and pride, they also experience feelings of fear, regret, shame and guilt." Similarly, Hayward (2007) suggests that while a reasoning criminal makes sense for instrumental crimes, it is much more difficult to place emotionally driven crimes within the rational choice framework. The "red-hot" husband who murders the man found in bed with his wife does not reason like the street criminal who burglarizes a neighbor's home when they are out of town. This challenges the rational choice perspective that people weigh costs and benefits and make a straightforward decision on whether or not to commit a crime.

However, in the end we award the points here to Beccaria over Lombroso and Goring, whose biological/heredity theories were not entirely misguided but were misguided enough to have caused lasting damage. We wish to reiterate that we are comparing the thoughts of Beccaria, Lombroso, and Goring and not contemporary deterrence and biosocial theories. It remains the case today that biosocial perspectives in criminology are not easily accepted by mainstream scholars, in part because of these early researchers. This is unfortunate because the new work has much to say about crime and justice and could easily (we think) be integrated with more sociological theories.

With respect to Tarde and Durkheim, the winner of this debate seems a bit clearer. Durkheim was seeking to establish sociology as a serious discipline, capable of addressing important questions without reliance on other fields. Perhaps because of this he was a bit dogmatic in his views. He did not want sociology to draw on other areas (like psychology) and felt firmly that "social facts" could only be explained by social factors. In our view, when it comes to explaining behavior, sociological perspectives are invaluable; however, they are incomplete. Psychological, economic, biological, and political perspectives are needed. This is why criminology is a multidisciplinary discipline, a topic we take up in more detail in Chapter 7. While sociology is not multidisciplinary, it does gain much from social psychological, micro-level perspectives. With respect to sociological criminology, as the next chapter will show, the person most responsible for "claiming" criminology for sociology was Edwin Sutherland. Sutherland devised one of the first sociological perspectives of antisocial behavior. As we will see, that theory, differential association theory, drew in no small part on imitation and other social psychological aspects of learning.

NOTES

1   www.debate.org/opinions/is-aristotle-the-greatest-philosopher
2   A video of the re-enacted debate can be found at www.bruno-latour.fr/node/354

Does crime originate from the person or the environment?

Sociological vs. psychological perspectives

2

CHAPTER OUTLINE

N 2012 NATIONAL PUBLIC RADIO (NPR) ran a story exploring why people commit unethical acts (Joffe-Walt & Spiegal, 2012). The story focused on a man named Toby Groves. Toby came from a nice family—parents who cared about him and provided for him, ensured he and his siblings had an excellent education—and the American Dream was on the horizon. Upon graduation Toby started a mortgage loan company, which was off to a great start. One thing that was particularly important to him was to run his company with the utmost integrity, crossing all his t's and dotting all his i's. In fact, as it turns out, his father had implored him to do everything the right way, and he had agreed.

At first things went well. Then they didn't. The company began to get into financial trouble and Toby could not make ends meet the legitimate way. So, rather than let his company fail, rather than put decent people, his friends, out of work, Toby decided to fudge things a bit. He misrepresented his business earnings to grease the wheels and that, as it happened, set him down the slippery slope of shady dealings. He was eventually sentenced to prison in 2008 for his misdealings and, in all, he was on the hook for $5.5 million.

Why did Toby engage in this fraud? Can criminology help us understand his actions? The NPR piece used Toby's story to illustrate recent psychological efforts to understand how we justify such deviance and how people often do not see fraud as hurting others. In fact Groves himself has become a researcher of behavior and has given talks on "the psychology of fraud." In the NPR article, Groves' crimes are explained away by appealing to what are called "cognitive frames." When engaging in the fraud, it is argued, Groves was not thinking about the ethics of the act, but rather was solely focused on being a good businessman. The way we interpret actions can have vast implications for whether or not they are appealing or even worthy of our consideration. So is it psychology we should turn to in order to better understand financial crimes—or crimes in general?

There is more to the story, however. It turns out that Toby had made the promise to his father that he would keep his nose clean because his brother had been jailed for fraud in 1986. In other words, Toby had a sibling who had engaged in very similar behavior. In addition, Toby's actions were aided by his co-workers at the company, who helped him paint a convincing but fraudulent picture. Not only that, but folks outside of his company were also complicit. Thus there was a rather large social and environmental element to this story. Can psychology alone help us understand why Toby and his brother engaged in similar acts, why they both ended up in front of the same judge for those acts? Would Toby have engaged in the fraud if he did not work in an environment that, in essence, condoned such behavior?

Here we have a classic debate between social vs. psychological theories of behavior. Which can shed more light on crime and delinquency? Do we learn to be deviant from our peers, as is assumed in the age-old parental fear that Johnny will run around with the wrong crowd? Or is antisocial behavior traced to personality traits and other biological processes? Interestingly, after the Durkheim/Tarde debate, explanations of criminal behavior that seemed to resonate most clearly with the academic and lay community were largely psychological in nature. The sort of psychology that was popular at the time focused on personality and brain deficits to explain bad behavior. In particular, this train of thought pointed to low intelligence as the major culprit.

Soon, however, a new, fully social perspective on crime and deviance began to take shape, one that was developed in part to counter the psychological narrative. Edwin Sutherland's differential association theory emerged over the course of several editions of his book *Principles of Criminology* (which was originally published as simply *Criminology* in 1924). Sutherland worked hard to claim criminology for sociology, which he saw as the superior discipline to understand deviance as compared to biological or psychological perspectives. His reasons were multiple, but stemmed largely from a belief that many—if not most—criminals were not "defective." There were plenty of criminals who were normal, even intelligent; those such as Toby Groves, who had a good education and upbringing.

In this chapter we begin our foray into theoretical debates in early 20th century criminology. We focus on the "great schism" characterizing the disciplinary tug of war between psychological or biological approaches and sociological stances. We discuss the formation of Sutherland's theory, his outright dismissal of non-sociological approaches to explain crime (drawing on Laub and Sampson's 1991 article and Sutherland's original works), and the stranglehold sociology held on criminology into the late 20th century. We then move on to describe more recent environmental vs. individual/psychological perspectives on crime, focusing on life-course criminology and its juxtaposition to developmental work. We conclude with an assessment of whether criminology is still "sociological" and whether that is something to be desired.

SOCIOLOGY AND CRIMINOLOGY—FROM COURTSHIP TO MARRIAGE

In the early part of the 20th century criminology was a fledgling field of study. In fact no such organized field really existed. In histories of criminology we often hear about "fathers" and those who produced important, seminal, works; we hear about Lombroso, Beccaria, Goring, and Durkheim. Criminology "textbooks" existed in the late 1800s and early 1900s, but use of the word "criminology" to describe the scientific study of crime seems only to have just emerged at this time. Accounts vary and no one seems sure when the term criminology was first used, but some point to the work of Garofalo in 1885 (Wilson, 2015). Nicole Rafter puts the official birth of American criminology at 1893, with the publication of Arthur MacDonald's *Criminology* (Rafter, 1992). However, in the early 1900s "American criminology was primitive and virtually without structure" (Gaylord & Galliher, 1988, p. 53).

If we imagine criminology to be a discipline or a field of study, one would expect that its emergence would coincide with college programs. Yet the first criminal justice school was not created until 1916 by August Vollmer at UC Berkeley (Dinkelspeil, 2010). Most of what we think of as criminology today was really "police science" in those early days. For example, the flagship US organization which represents the science of criminology as an academic field of study, the American Society of Criminology, was initially called, in 1941, the National Association of College Police Training Officials. It was formally renamed the Society for the Advancement of Criminology in 1946, with criminology "defined as the study of the causes, treatment and prevention of crime" (Morris, 1975, p. 128).

In the early 20th century, while criminology was not well structured or coherent, the dominant perspective was psychological in nature. What theories of crime existed in America and abroad during this time? Parmalee's (1918) *Criminology* is instructive here. Parmalee begins his foray into explanations of crime by discussing "equivalents of crime and punishment among animals," which suggests biological foundations (p. 7). Other chapters discuss economic factors and crime, demographic factors (urban vs. rural crime rates), political factors, and climate/weather related factors. Part Three of the book spans about 50 pages and covers biological explanations, with the majority of the section covering mental ability or intelligence. Parmalee (1918, p. 156) remarks, in Chapter 9:

> In recent years much study has been devoted to the aments, or the feebleminded, as they are ordinarily called. This study has revealed the fact that some of these feebleminded folk are morally deficient in the sense that they are intellectually incapable of grasping the meaning of moral ideas, frequently lack the self-control and will power to restrain themselves from acts which are harmful to themselves or to others, and for other reasons connected with their mental defectiveness are frequently led into criminal conduct. Furthermore, numerous criminological investigations have revealed the presence of many of these aments among criminals.

Goring's (1913) work testing (and largely discrediting) the Lombrosian theory of the born-criminal, nonetheless argued that convicts were differentiated from "normals" by their low intelligence. William Healy, in America, also emphasized psychological or mental factors in crime and delinquency (Healy, 1915), and eventually began working on measuring mental faculties of criminals with his research partner and wife, Augusta Bronner (Welsh, Zane, & Rocque, 2017). Feeblemindedness theories were relatively short-lived (Rafter, Posick, & Rocque, 2016), but the notion of criminality being caused by mental defects was largely in vogue during this time. Mental defects were viewed as a major part of multiple factors that explained crime from a deficit perspective. In other words, the major story was that crime was only something done by people who had something wrong with them. Normal people, those with social and personal advantages, would not stoop so low.

The Michael-Adler report and claims of a lack of criminological science

The science of criminology as we know it today is a relatively recent development. Prior to the mid-20th century the "soul" of criminology was still unknown or, at least, unclaimed (Laub, 2006). According to criminologist John Laub, the turning point was the publication of a 1933 book by Jerome Michael and Mortimer Adler, which spared no one in dismissing the state of knowledge about crime and justice. The Michael-Adler report, on which the book was based, was commissioned by the Bureau of Social Hygiene and was meant to survey the extent of knowledge on the causes and prevention of criminal behavior. If such knowledge was sufficiently found, a governmental institute of criminology and criminal justice might then profitably be developed. However, when the two men began their survey they "were appalled. Just appalled. These men [criminologists] were saying that they knew the causes of crime; they were making preposterous claims" (Geis, 1971, p. xi, cited in Goff & Geis, 2008, p. 351).

The 1933 book was a tome, covering more than 500 pages and discussing numerous topics from defining crime, to criminology as a science, to criminal justice practices. In Part Two the authors took criminology to task. They claimed research to date was mostly "informational," that is descriptive, and had not contributed to knowledge about how to reduce crime. "If we use 'scientific knowledge' arbitrarily to refer to knowledge which goes beyond mere description, we can conclude our analysis thus far with the statement that the work of criminologists has not resulted in scientific knowledge of the phenomena of crime" (Michael & Adler, 1933, p. 54).

To Michael and Adler "a science of criminology" (p. 72) was possible. To get there it was up to sociologists and/or psychologists. Yet, to that point, they argued that neither psychology nor sociology had taken steps to distinguish itself as a science. Thus it may be left to scholars from other fields to save criminology (it was not really clear which they preferred). But the stage seemed to be set for either psychology or criminology to respond to the book by organizing itself as an empirical science and formulating testable propositions with empirical support surrounding the nature of crime and delinquency.

As Laub (2006) as well as Goff and Geis (2008) showed, Edwin Sutherland seemed to have the most profound reaction to the Michael-Adler report. By this point he had published his book *Criminology* and was about to publish the second edition (1934). He responded (Sutherland, 1932–33/1973) strongly to what he saw as the main take-away points of the report. He argued that the field of criminology was immature, true, but it was growing and developing. He rejected the notion that criminology had no theories, just generalized data, by detailing several, including those of Charles Goring and Clifford Shaw. Sutherland was left shaking his head at these errors and "assuming that they (Michael and Adler) know very little about criminological research" (Sutherland, 1932–33/1973, p. 240). Finally, he rejected wholesale the recommendation that an institute be created with experts from other, mature, sciences. To Sutherland this was a mistake because sociologists/psychologists were just fine, and scientists from other fields should not be wading into behavioral territory. As he claimed, "When they get away from their own data, they are quite as biased and fallible as other persons. To demonstrate this, nothing more is needed than a ten-minute conversation with a physicist on a political problem" (1932–33/1973, p. 243).

Michael-Adler had stated "that the work of criminologists has not resulted in scientific knowledge of the phenomena of crime" (p. 54). What was the reason? Criminology, they argued, did not contain scientific propositions. Scientific propositions speak to empirical evidence and are able to make claims that go beyond current evidence. They can be tested. In addition, "A scientific proposition is always a proposition in science and a science never consists of a single proposition; a scientific proposition is one of a set of propositions. . . . A set of scientific propositions, to be a set, must consist of propositions which have common variables; that is, each proposition in the set must contain at least one variable which is to be found in some other proposition in the set" (p. 59).

Sutherland's reaction to the Michael-Adler report

Sutherland took the Michael-Adler report as a challenge. Readers familiar with differential association theory may be surprised to learn that Sutherland did not initially consider it a "theory" but a "point of view" since criminological knowledge was too immature to permit full-fledged "universal propositions" (Schuessler, 1956/1973, p. xvi). Yet in the critique of criminology by Michael and Adler we see an attempt to make criminology "scientific" by organizing a set of propositions in the manner Michael and Adler described. Indeed, as Laub (2006, p. 239) argued, "differential association theory was created in response to the Michael-Adler report. In arriving at the theory, Sutherland sought to identify a paradigm for the field of criminology."

Sutherland was preparing the next edition of his 1924 book *Criminology* when the Michael-Adler report (and book) was published. In the next edition, now called *Principles of Criminology*, Sutherland directly addressed some of the report's critiques. He wrote, "The argument has been made, however, that criminology cannot possibly become a science" (1934, p. 17), clearly referencing the Michael-Adler report. He especially took umbrage at the idea that universal propositions cannot be made about crime, calling it "invalid" (p. 18). Just because crime is relative (both legally and socially) does not mean propositions explaining it are not possible. The behaviors which are considered illegal have much in common with other behaviors that are not illegal, and that element is possible to explain. As he argued, "it is probable that if a type is thus defined, the characteristics will appear in behavior which is not in violation of the law. Thus the explanation which starts with illegal acts is likely to extend into the behavior which is not illegal. This will mean that the definitions, descriptions, and explanations will not lie entirely within the field of criminology" (p. 19).

The answer Sutherland eventually arrived at, through various starts and stops, was differential association theory. The 1934 edition of *Principles* did not contain any propositions of the sort Michael and Adler chided criminologists about lacking. Instead there was one paragraph in his chapter on the causes of crime that stated: "First, any person can be trained to adopt and follow any pattern of behavior which he is capable to execute.... Second, failure to follow a prescribed pattern of behavior is due to the inconsistency and lack of harmony in the influences which direct the individual. Third, the conflict of cultures is therefore the fundamental principle in the explanation of crime. Fourth, the more the cultural patterns conflict, the more unpredictable is the behavior of a particular individual" (pp. 51–52). This was not a unique description of the causes of crime, deriving, as it did, from the work of Louis Wirth (1931, see Sutherland, 1942/1973). Seven propositions of differential association theory were first put forth in the next edition (1939) of *Principles*. These were (Sutherland, 1939, pp. 4–8):

1) The processes which result in systematic criminal behavior are fundamentally the same form as the processes which result in systematic lawful behavior;
2) Systematic criminal behavior is determined in a process of association with those who commit crimes, just as systematic lawful behavior is determined in a process of association with those who are law abiding;
3) Differential association is the specific causal process in the development of systematic criminal behavior;
4) The chance that a person will participate in systematic criminal behavior is determined roughly by the frequency and consistency of his contacts with the patterns of criminal behavior;
5) Individual differences among people in respect to personal characteristics or social situations cause crime only as they affect differential association or frequency and consistency of contacts with criminal patterns;
6) Cultural conflict is the underlying cause of differential association and therefore of systematic criminal behavior; and
7) Social disorganization is the basic cause of systematic criminal behavior.

The propositions were fully fleshed out into the nine that are most well-known today in the 1947 edition of the book. In both the 1939 and 1947 editions the theory is found on the very first pages of the text under the heading "A Theory of Criminology." In that chapter Sutherland discussed what he meant by a "scientific explanation", which includes "interrelated general propositions" (p. 3). These propositions were as follows (Sutherland, 1947, pp. 6–7):

1) Criminal behavior is learned;
2) Criminal behavior is learned in interaction with other persons in a process of communication;
3) The principal part of the learning of criminal behavior occurs within intimate personal groups;
4) When criminal behavior is learned, the learning includes (a) techniques of committing the crime, which are sometimes very complicated, sometimes very simple; (b) the specific direction of motives, drives, rationalizations, and attitudes;
5) The specific direction of the motives and drives is learned from the definitions of the legal codes as favorable or unfavorable;
6) A person becomes delinquent because of an excess of definitions favorable to violation of law over definitions unfavorable to violation of law;
7) Differential associations may vary in frequency, duration, priority, and intensity;
8) The process of learning criminal behavior by association with criminal and anti-criminal patterns involves all of the mechanisms that are involved in any other learning; and
9) While criminal behavior is an expression of general needs and values, it is not explained by those general needs and values since non-criminal behavior is an expression of the same needs and values.

And so we see that Sutherland, by 1947, had taken the most damning critique of criminology found in Michael and Adler (1933), that criminology was not scientific because it had no scientific propositions, and met it head on. Criminology now had not only scientific propositions but a set of interrelated propositions that consequently established a new paradigm (Laub, 2006). The impact of this theory (and we recognize it as such) was profound. It revolutionized the field of criminology and firmly established it as a branch of sociology (Gaylord & Galliher, 1988).

Sutherland claims criminology for sociology

As part of the reaction against the Michael-Adler report, as well as the ways in which Sutherland saw science in general, he increasingly sought to sharpen the disciplinary focus of criminology. It is likely that he viewed one of the problems facing the field when Michael and Adler were tasked with evaluating it as there being too many cooks in the kitchen, too many unconnected findings from various points of view that made it difficult to see criminology as a scientific discipline that clarified, more than obfuscated, crime and justice. One can trace the narrowing of focus and deliberate claiming of criminology as part of sociology through the editions of *Principles of Criminology*.

In addition, the so-called "multi-factor" approach was prevalent, which is atheoretical in nature and simply seeks to describe the various factors that contribute to criminality, without concern for a particular academic discipline or specialty. It was this perspective that Sutherland most sought to refute, it seems, in subsequent editions of his book, despite being an early proponent (Laub & Sampson, 1991).

Sutherland was never a biologist or psychologist, and so it is not the case that his thinking changed radically over time, bending toward a sociological orientation. In fact the first edition of his criminology textbook was written for Lippincott's sociology series while he was employed in the University of Illinois Department of Sociology. This book was Sutherland's introduction to criminology, though, as it was his first publication in that field (Gaylord & Galliher, 1988; Schuessler, 1973). The 1924 edition was actually, as Laub and Sampson (1991) point out, friendly to psychology. As they state (pp. 1411–1412) "Moreover, in an intriguing section of Principles [sic] entitled 'Plan for Study of Causes of Crime,' Sutherland outlines the 'ideal' data-collection strategy in criminology. This would include 'detailed records of the development of personalities,' which 'need to be very detailed and pursued from early infancy to old age' (1924, pp. 86–87). This strategy would also extend to 'mental and educational tests,' as well as interviews with parents, teachers, and a full recording of all 'conduct disorders.'" Sutherland appeared to be an early proponent of the developmental and life-course approach that has come to characterize much of the contemporary landscape in criminology.

Others have also argued that the first edition of *Criminology* was not fully sociological in its orientation, despite it being deemed "the first *sociological*" textbook in the field (Burgess, 1925, p. 491, emphasis in the original). Geis, for example, in 1976 reflected that the book was "rather multidisciplinary, and thus contrasts with later editions which would move increasingly into consideration of more parochial matters of sociological concern, producing a somewhat lopsided emphasis in contemporary American criminology." Geis argued that, with this work, Sutherland was able to "preempt criminology for sociology" (p. 304). By 1951 Marshall Clinard, a criminologist, could say that, thanks in part to Sutherland's book, "practically all American universities have a sociology department, and criminology is a standard course attracting large numbers of students. All widely used textbooks in criminology today were written by sociologists" (p. 549). "American criminology and sociology," Clinard wrote (p. 550) "have developed together."

SUTHERLAND AND SOCIOLOGY VS. INDIVIDUAL/ PSYCHOLOGICAL THEORIES

Why did Sutherland wish to move criminology into a decidedly sociological orientation? Laub and Sampson's (1991) essay on the "Sutherland-Glueck debate" is the standard source for this apparent change in focus. They note that suddenly in the late 1930s Sutherland became very critical of Sheldon and Eleanor Glueck's work, primarily their multi-factor approach. He was "vehemently antipsychiatry" (Laub & Sampson, 1991, p. 1412) as his career progressed and was "perturbed by the Gluecks' psychologically oriented conclusion that mental and/or emotional difficulties impeded the process of reformation among former prisoners" (pp. 1413–1414). Thus it was the individual-level, psychological elements of the multi-factor approach that Sutherland came to view as inconsistent with criminology as a science and the scientific goal of producing a set of propositions to explain crime. As Gaylord and Galliher (1988) note, while in the early 1930s Sutherland accepted that multiple factors were related to crime, "he felt it intellectually unacceptable to believe that a generalized explanation of individual delinquency might forever be elusive" (p. 115). Sutherland thought it was possible to use the information known about criminal behavior and look for threads the factors had in common, and thus arrive at an internally (and disciplinarily) consistent theory.

Laub and Sampson (1991) also point to two factors that led Sutherland to reject individual-level theories. First was the method of "analytic induction." Analytic induction, as a research method, seeks to build a framework under which all empirical findings apply. If any finding does not fit the framework, the framework must be changed. This method led to "Sutherland's development of a general theory of crime causation … [and] a rejection of multiple-factor theory as, among other things, unscientific" (Laub & Sampson, 1991, p. 1418). Next, Laub and Sampson suggest that Sutherland's "sociological positivism" required him to see crime and its causes in a social light, thus rejecting biological or psychological factors. As they state: "sociological positivism as practiced by Sutherland did not attempt to establish the sociological causes of crime independent of individual-level factors in the Durkheimian tradition. Rather, crime was viewed by Sutherland as a social phenomenon that could only be explained by social (i.e., nonindividual) factors. As a result, Sutherland 'explicitly denied the claims of all other disciplines potentially interested in crime' (Gottfredson and Hirschi 1990, p. 70)" (Laub & Sampson, 1991, p. 1420).

The 1934 *Principles of Criminology* differed from the 1924 *Criminology* in numerous ways, including the apparent deletion of the section on the importance of personality and mental deficiency. In fact in Chapter 6 of *Principles* Sutherland throws considerable doubt on the idea that mental deficiency is a cause of crime. He was reacting to "feebleminded" theories of the time which argued that criminals fail to obey the law because they are not mentally capable. The idea, according to feebleminded theories, was that only someone with a mental problem would resort to law-breaking. In response Sutherland stated "that the relationship between crime and feeblemindedness is, in general, comparatively slight" (1934, p. 96). In other words, now he saw much less value in mental deficiency and intelligence testing as predictors of criminal behavior. Sutherland was equally circumspect on the ability of psychoses and psychopathic personality to explain criminal conduct.

In terms of "other abnormalities in personality," Sutherland wrote that, while psychological tests were poor, they *did* seem to indicate some relationship to crime. Yet at the same time he felt that the tests were not measuring something innate: "The traits which are characteristic of the delinquents in comparison with non-delinquents are very likely to be a product of the specific situation in which they are tested rather than generalized and permanent traits" (1934, p. 103). Thus it was really the environment, not the person, which mattered and which was driving the results of personality tests differentiating criminals from non-criminals, to Sutherland.

In the 1939 edition of *Principles* Sutherland had begun to offer his own theory explicitly, and thus had more reason to reject non-sociological explanations of crime. In the 1934 and 1939 editions he was circumspect toward multiple factor theories. But in the 1947 edition he was downright scathing. For example, in a section in Chapter 4 he placed quotations around theory when describing multiple factor theory. He argued that proponents of multiple factor theory "have insisted that crime is a product of a large number and a great variety of factors and that these factors cannot now and perhaps cannot ever be organized into general propositions which have no exceptions; that is, they insist that no scientific theory of criminal behavior is possible" (p. 56). Interestingly, as late as the 1939 edition he had said "A multiple factor theory is undoubtedly closer to the facts than the earlier theories . . ." (p. 54), yet he was not altogether happy with it.

The 1947 edition of *Principles* also amended the propositions of differential association in a key way. As Gaylord and Galliher (1988) point out, in 1939 Sutherland made room for "individual differences." The fifth proposition, recall, read "individual differences among people in respect to *personal characteristics* or social situations cause crime only as they affect differential association or frequency and consistency of contacts with criminal patterns" (1939, p. 6, emphasis added). In other words, while differential association was the direct cause, personality traits still mattered. In the 1947 version the term "individual differences" was nowhere to be found. Gaylord and Galliher (1988) argue that this was because Sutherland felt personality traits are factors "that must be explained, rather than explanations of such social phenomena as criminal behavior" (p. 147).

The 1947 edition was also much harsher than the previous versions on psychopathy and crime. In 1936 William Healy and Augusta Bronner had published a study entitled *New Light on Delinquency* which had shown that 91 percent of delinquents had "emotional disturbances," as compared to 13 percent of non-delinquents. Sutherland took issue with this finding in 1939, recommending replication. However, in 1947 he eviscerated it. He argued that the psychiatrists making the diagnoses were likely biased and suggested that the non-delinquent group was not properly examined, with only 21 percent being found "even mildly delinquent" (p. 112). This, he argued, was inconceivable, given that a survey of a criminology class (we presume his own, but he never offered a citation) revealed 98 percent were mildly delinquent. He also suggested that causality had not been determined, as delinquency could result in emotional disturbance rather than the other way around. More importantly, perhaps, was that Healy and Bronner's finding could not translate into a cause of delinquency because 13 percent of the non-delinquents were emotionally disturbed. This violated the foundation of his analytic induction method.

In this chapter (7) Sutherland rejected intelligence and psychopathy as causes of crime. They were simply not important if we wanted to understand how to reduce antisocial behavior. He concluded the chapter with a clear statement on what he thought about non-sociological theories. "The explanation of behavior, apparently, must be found in social interaction, in which both the behavior of a person and the overt or prospective behavior of other persons play their parts" (p. 117).

Sutherland's two other major works also did much to swing the tide of criminology toward sociology. In 1937 Sutherland published *The Professional Thief*, where he allowed a thief, Chic Conwell, to tell his story. The book was not so much an autobiography interrogating how Conwell had gotten into the life, but an exposé on how a professional criminal plies his trade. He emphasized the organization and skill it required to make something of yourself in this area. Thus, according to Jon Snodgrass, while the book was not about theory, it really *was* about theory. He says, "*The Professional Thief* was not an etiological work, at least not in an overt sense. But it did have strong implications for contending causal theories. Theories which maintained that criminals were abnormal, or feeble-minded, or constitutionally inferior, were confronted with the planning, adroitness, knowledge, social sophistication, political acumen, organizational ability and mental stability of professional thieves" (1973, p. 5). In other words, once again, since psychological theories could not account for criminals who were intelligent and skilled they were not valid explanations of crime. Note, this work was not friendly toward poverty or social class theories of crime either, as Conwell was supposedly, along with most professional thieves, from the well-to-do.

Finally, Sutherland's last major project, published in 1949, introduced criminology and the larger social world to the notion of "white collar crime." Sutherland began his foray into examining this type of crime in a 1939 presidential address to the American Sociological Society and his work culminated in the 1949 book *White Collar Crime*. This book examined the records of 70 large corporations in the United States, covering what had to that point been considered non-criminal violations (such as unfair infringement of patents, financial fraud, and violations of trust, violations of war regulations, and so on). Sutherland's goal was to show that these acts were in fact criminal.

In expanding the definition of what constitutes crime, Sutherland was again making an emphatic point about why sociology is the discipline which must own criminology. The corporations he was analyzing were composed of intelligent, wealthy, well-educated professionals. Thus the prevailing theories of crime were dealt, to him, a fatal blow. As he argued (1949/1961, pp. 5–6):

> The scholars who have stated general theories of criminal behavior have used statistics such as those outlined above and individual case histories from which these statistics are compiled. Since these cases are concentrated in the lower socio-economic class, the theories of criminal behavior have placed much emphasis on poverty as the cause of crime or on other social conditions and personal traits which are associated with poverty. The assumption in these theories is that criminal behavior can be explained only by these pathological factors, either social or personal. The social pathologies which have been emphasized are poverty and, related to it, poor housing, lack of organized recreations, lack of education, and disruptions in family life. The personal pathologies which have been suggested as explanations of criminal behavior were, at first, biological abnormalities; when research studies threw doubt on the validity of these biological explanations, the next explanation was intellectual inferiority, and more recently emotional instability. . . . The thesis of this book is that these social and personal pathologies are not an adequate explanation of criminal behavior.

DECLARING A VICTOR IN THE DEBATE

So we see that Sutherland, by his death in 1950, had made a strong claim that sociology was the superior perspective from which to study crime and justice. Did he succeed? Most criminologists recognize, as Laub and Sampson wrote, that Sutherland was "the dominant criminologist of the 20th century" (1991, p. 1402). They also quote Don Gibbons as stating that "Sutherland was the most important contributor to American criminology to have appeared to date" (Gibbons, 1979, p. 65). Thus it stands to reason that his ideas, namely that criminology was a sub-discipline of sociology, would ultimately win out. By 1992 criminologist Ronald Akers was able to say matter-of-factly that "Criminology is a specialized field of study in sociology." While the situation seemed to be changing, he argued that "sociological perspectives still constitute what I call the intellectual center of gravity in criminology" (p. 4). Sociology had completed its takeover of criminology, though, "By the mid-1900s," when "all criminology and delinquency courses in North American universities and colleges had come to be taught in departments of sociology and 'all widely used textbooks in criminology [in 1950] were written by sociologists' (Clinard, 1951: 549)" (Akers, 1992, p. 5).

By the late 1970s and 1980s, though, other disciplines began to take umbrage at the dominance of sociology within criminology. Hirschi and Hindelang (1977), in a well-known piece, argued that IQ was an important factor in antisocial behavior but had been mischaracterized by criminologists. Why? Because intelligence research was "threatening to the integrity of the field and to its moral commitments" (p. 572). This dismissal of intelligence by criminologists was no small feat, for, as Hirschi and Hindelang show, "At the time criminology became a subfield of sociology, marked differences in IQ between delinquents and nondelinquents were pretty much taken for granted, and a major task confronting those wishing to claim the field for the sociological perspective was to call these alleged differences into question. This task was sufficiently accomplished. IQ, it was confidently suggested, doesn't matter (see Sutherland, 1924: 108)" (p. 572). C. R. Jeffery essentially agreed, arguing that "Due to historic misfortune, sociology captured the field in the 1920s. The contributions of biology and psychology have been minimized" (Jeffery, 1979, p. 7, cited in Andrews & Wormith, 1989, p. 289).

It was the psychologists Don Andrews and J. Stephen Wormith (1989), however, who published the most devastating critique of criminology with respect to its overlooking or unfair dismissal of psychological research. They suggested that sociological criminologists had engaged in "knowledge destruction" when it came to individual differences research. They show that, for reasons other than empirical science, sociologists "promote[d] the importance of their favored variables" (p. 291) to the exclusion of individual-level ones. They argued that the evidence actually showed that personality traits and other psychological factors were important in differentiating criminals from non-criminals and that the field was worse off for having ignored them.

It seems reasonable then to suggest that Sutherland "won" the debate. By the time of his death he had succeeded in claiming criminology as sociology's own. And, in the process, he had succeeded in downplaying individual-level, psychological traits as important in explaining crime. However, the Andrews and Wormith piece was not the end of the story. Present day criminology is a much different landscape than it was 30 years ago. It is to modern developments in the disciplinary tug of war that we now turn.

MODERN DEBATES BETWEEN SOCIOLOGY AND PSYCHOLOGY

While, in 1989, Andrews and Wormith could angrily lament the dismissal of psychology in criminological work, the situation would soon change. Andrews and his collaborator James Bonta (2010) would go on to develop what they called "the psychology of criminal conduct," which emphasized personality and other psychological factors influencing crime. Just a year after the 1989 knowledge destruction piece, Andrews and his colleagues (1990) published a meta-analysis of correctional program evaluations "informed by psychology." The study demonstrated that programs adhering to certain principles were very effective in reducing crime. This work would lead to arguably the dominant perspective in North American corrections, called the "risk-need-responsivity" approach. Briefly, this approach suggests practitioners must examine risk levels of offenders, criminogenic needs, and learning styles to configure the best treatment approach.

The change in the field regarding the acceptability of psychological factors was apparent by the end of the 20th century. In the third edition of Andrews and Bonta's *Psychology of Criminal Conduct* they stated in the preface that "This third edition, however, was completed under conditions of some major changes in mainstream criminology. The psychology of criminal behavior is now readily evident in many mainstream textbooks and at conferences. For example, there is a renewed interest in individual differences and an appreciation of the influence of personal, interpersonal, and structural factors. Developmental criminology continues to grow and contribute" (2002, p. iii).

The emergence of developmental criminology, in fact, may be viewed as a key development in the shifting of criminology from a purely sociological field to one that takes seriously individual factors. Developmental criminology is an approach to studying crime over the life-course which views behavior as unfolding according to a particular script. In other words, "changes in social behavior . . . are related to age in an orderly way" (Thornberry, 1997, p. 1). Thornberry would go on to say that, unlike sociological theories, developmental theories are dynamic and account for change and continuity over time.

Developmental criminology officially entered the criminological scene with a 1990 essay by Rolf Loeber and Marc Le Blanc entitled "Toward a Developmental Criminology." In it they argued that criminology had been static, too focused on between-group differences, and too reliant on official records as the primary data source. Thus changes (or continuity) over time had been neglected. They defined developmental criminology as "the study, first, of the development and dynamics of problem behaviors and offending with age. . . . The second focus of developmental criminology is the identification of explanatory or causal factors that predate, or co-occur with, the behavioral development and have an impact on its course" (1990, p. 377).

Developmental criminology has, it is clear, taken an important position within criminology as a whole. Just eight years later Le Blanc and Loeber (1998) offered an update on their initial piece, an 85-page essay detailing concepts and evidence in support of the developmental approach. Numerous books and presidential addresses in criminology have focused on developmental research. And one of the most cited theories of the last 30 years[1], Terrie Moffitt's (1993) adolescent-limited vs. life-course persistent offending theory, is quintessentially developmental in nature. In 2012 the American Society of Criminology (ASC) established the Division of Developmental and Life-Course Criminology. A journal with the same name was initiated three years later. Clearly, then, developmental criminology has become, like the study of individual differences, mainstream in criminology.

Yet notice the name of the journal and ASC division. It includes what is known as "life-course criminology." Is this just another name for developmental criminology? In some sense, yes, in that the terms are sometimes used interchangeably (see Farrington, 2007) and both refer to a focus on crime over individuals' lives. But in a larger sense they represent two perspectives, one relying on psychological, individual-level factors, and one emphasizing macro, institutional structures. Robert Sampson and John Laub, two criminologists well known for their "age-graded theory of informal social controls," organized a special issue of the *Annals of the American Academy of Political and Social Sciences*, published in 2005, to hammer out these details. In their leading essay they drew the line in the sand, illustrating what life-course criminology was all about, how it differed from developmental criminology, and outlined what they saw as the drawbacks of the latter approach.

In particular, they (Sampson & Laub, 2005a) argued that developmental criminology was too obsessed with trajectory groups in which different people are classified as belonging to different groups ("high rate persister," "low rate desister," etc.). In addition, they took issue with the notion that different stages of the life-course require a different set of predictors to explain crime. To them, crime over the life-course could be understood using the same general set of factors—namely informal social controls. One of the biggest points of contention, specified in the special issue as well as Laub and Sampson's (2003) *Shared Beginnings, Divergent Lives*, is the developmental view that childhood factors can tell us about how an individual will turn out. In their data, which was reconstructed from the classic Glueck *Unraveling Juvenile Delinquency* (Glueck & Glueck, 1950) study, groups could not be predicted in this way.

The developmental, taxonomic theory they took aim at was Moffitt's (1993) group-based theory of offending over the life-course. Moffitt argued that the aggregate age-crime curve masked two distinct groups: 1) adolescence-limited; and 2) life-course persistent offenders. The first group is the largest, composed of the majority of people. Most of us get into some trouble at some point in our lives (usually our younger days). There are a few reasons for this—wanting to be like the cool, edgy kids, being biologically mature but not having social freedoms, and a host of other possibilities. But then we grow up, gain our independence, peers no longer matter as much to us, and we give up our deviant ways. Thus the term "adolescence-limited." But there is a small group (maybe 5 percent of us) that are not this way. The offending of this group stems from childhood neuropsychological problems and does not begin in adolescence. These individuals were always behaviorally challenged, engaged in more serious deviance throughout life, and do not stop upon reaching adulthood. These are the "life-course persistent" offenders.

The 2005 special issue included a response by Sampson and Laub to other essays in the issue. In that article the authors argued that childhood factors do not determine the life outcomes of people, as would be expected from the life-course persistent group. They state two points of contention with Moffitt's life-course persistent theory: "One, all offenders eventually desist from crime—in this sense, the age effect is 'invariant.' Second, conditioned on delinquency or crime (the sorting reality of the juvenile and criminal justice system), we cannot predict long-term trajectories of offending" (Sampson & Laub, 2005b, p. 75). They argue that finding "diverse lives" from a sample of boys who all shared disadvantages that should, theoretically, have tracked them onto a life-course persistent track suggests that developmental perspectives do not work.

In *Shared Beginnings* and their earlier book *Crime in the Making* (Sampson & Laub, 1993), Sampson and Laub discussed the differences between "sociogenic" vs. "ontogenetic" perspectives. The former views social institutions and relationships as key to explaining behavior throughout time, whereas the latter views individual-level characteristics as important in determining life trajectories. Key for the ontogenetic approach is another wildly popular theory, developed in the late 20th century. Michael Gottfredson and Travis Hirschi's self-control theory (Gottfredson & Hirschi, 1990) suggests that a childhood personality trait (self-control) in essence is all that matters when it comes to whether someone engages in a life of crime or conformity. Sampson and Laub take issue with this perspective and argue that social institutions can change or deflect a trajectory at any point.

What sums up Sampson and Laub's disagreement with the psychological, developmental view best is the idiom "the past is prologue." They point out that "Developmental accounts, especially from developmental psychology, focus on regular or lawlike individual developments over the life span. Implicit in developmental approaches are the notions of stages, progressions, growth, and evolution. The resulting emphasis is on the systematic pathways of development (change) over time, with the imagery being one of the execution of a program written at an earlier point in time" (Laub & Sampson, 2003, p. 33, citations omitted). To them the life-course view is different because, while it recognizes stability, it also sees the possibility of change. And that change does not always (or usually) come from within, but from without. Their theory is concerned with how social institutions and social bonds with others can guide the way lives turn out. In particular, they argue that even persistent offenders can give up crime and become largely prosocial if they obtain a meaningful career and/or marry a prosocial individual. These are "turning points" in the life-course.

Sampson and Laub also debated this individual/psychological vs. social perspective on life-course criminology in a 1995 set of articles with Gottfredson and Hirschi. It is interesting to note that both Gottfredson and Hirschi were professors at the University of Albany when Sampson and Laub were graduate students there, and whose ideas clearly influenced their students. Yet by the mid-1990s the students had come to disagree with their mentors. By this time Gottfredson and Hirschi's *A General Theory of Crime* (1990) had been published and had garnered a lot of attention. In it the authors not only specify what self-control is and how it is instilled (in childhood, by parents), but argue that social institutions such as schools, jobs, and marriage ultimately are a function of self-control and thus not causally related to crime after childhood.

The 1995 debate centered on the importance of social institutions and the need for longitudinal research. We will cover the arguments about longitudinal research in Chapter 4 on the criminal career vs. propensity debate. Key for the purposes of this chapter, however, are the arguments of Gottfredson and Hirschi that, to them, life-course criminology is not consistent with their views about how and why criminal behavior occurs. In addition, they argued that crime declines with age (called "desistance from crime") because of biological factors, not structural or institutional factors. With respect to institutional effects, Hirschi and Gottfredson (1995) suggested that "these apparent effects and identical findings reported in the life-course literature are a consequence of self-selection and statistical regression. Put in theoretical terms, they are a straightforward consequence of failure to take into consideration the decision-making capacities of the individuals making up our samples" (Hirschi & Gottfredson, 1995, p. 137).

In their reply, Sampson and Laub (1995) reiterated their life-course theory and the findings from their analysis of the Glueck data. They suggested that the results of their research laid waste to the claim that individual differences/propensity (the psychological approach) are the only causal factors that matter—to them, both do. In other words, of course psychological and personality characteristics affect life outcomes. But they do not explain *all* outcomes. Experiences with social institutions are important, too.

Here we see an intriguing difference between the Sutherland/psychological debate. In that instance Sutherland was attempting to claim criminology as the domain of sociology and so was forced to eventually deny the relevance of non-social factors. In the more recent debate it was certain developmental (psychological) theorists that explicitly denied any causal significance to sociological or structural variables. Gottfredson and Hirschi, in specifying their general theory, made the case that social or institutional effects were not causally related to behavior, because individual differences (personality traits) determined participation in those social institutions.

In recent years another developmental perspective on crime over the life-span has taken root. The work of Laurence Steinberg and Elizabeth Cauffman, both psychologists, has shown that antisocial behavior may peak in adolescence and decline thereafter because of neuropsychological factors (see Steinberg & Cauffman, 1996). In addition, understanding why people persist or "desist" from crime may be tied to what they call "psychosocial maturation." Steinberg (2010) proposed a "dual systems model" of behavior in adolescence, in which two parts of the brain develop at two distinct time periods. First, sensitivity to risk-taking increases early in adolescence, at a point when self-control is relatively underdeveloped. Later in adolescence and early adulthood, self-control systems kick in and antisocial behavior declines.

To help understand why individuals have different behavioral trajectories (some stop misbehaving in adolescence, some in early adulthood, some persist a bit longer), Steinberg and Cauffman (1996) proposed the concept of psychosocial maturity. Psychosocial maturity is composed of: 1) responsibility; 2) temperance (self-control); and 3) perspective or future orientation. These cognitive components can explain the decline in crime after adolescence and also differences in trajectories between individuals (Monahan et al., 2009).

Notice, in these theories, no social or structural elements are included. The reasons why people change or do not change with regard to their behavior are purely cognitive in nature. The elements of psychosocial maturation are psychological and are indexed by attitudinal survey questions. Thus the more recent psychological theories of offending seem to be quite siloed, with little attempt to integrate factors from other disciplines or fields.

POLICY IMPLICATIONS: SIDE-BY-SIDE

Psychological theory policies

What are the policy implications of the psychological and sociological theories of offending? Does it matter whether intelligence or social relationships are more important in determining one's proclivity to antisocial behavior? The early feebleminded and psychopathy theories of crime were used to nefarious ends, as has been well-documented. Eugenics, or the practice of controlling human reproduction based on (un)desirable traits, was based largely on the idea that certain people were mentally deficient and that the only way to weed out those traits was to stop those folks from having children— this was a purely genetic argument, as Sutherland pointed out in his textbook. This culminated in a 1927 US Supreme Court ruling in which an individual named Carrie Buck was ruled feebleminded and her sterilization constitutional. The famous phrase from Justice Oliver Wendell Holmes is chilling to this day:

> We have seen more than once that the public welfare may call upon the best citizens for their lives. It would be strange if it could not call upon those who already sap the strength of the State for these lesser sacrifices, often not felt to be such by those concerned, in order to prevent our being swamped with incompetence. It is better

for all the world if, instead of waiting to execute degenerate offspring for crime or to let them starve for their imbecility, society can prevent those who are manifestly unfit from continuing their kind. The principle that sustains compulsory vaccination is broad enough to cover cutting the Fallopian tubes. Three generations of imbeciles are enough.[2]

One can see in the language Holmes used that part of the rationale for sterilizing Buck was to prevent future criminal behavior. This story is tragic, but even more so for the fact that she was not mentally "defective" at all, as Adam Cohen (2016) recently discussed in his book on intelligence and the eugenics movement. The science of intelligence in the early part of the 20th century was also, as documented by Nicole Rafter, used as a rationale for many of the atrocities committed by the Nazis (Rafter, 2008; Rafter, Posick, & Rocque, 2016).

Of course, this does not necessarily mean that personality or psychological factors, should they correlate with delinquency, lead to such interventions. To the extent that cognitive development is tied to healthy social environments, then parenting, education, nutrition, and other factors in childhood should also help prevent antisocial behavior (Rocque et al., 2012). More recent developmental work shows that the policy implications of psychological theories are not nefarious at all. The risk-need-responsivity approach, for example, directs corrections practitioners on what rehabilitation programs are best suited to particular clients. The goal is treatment, not separation or punishment (see also Vaske, 2017).

What about Gottfredson and Hirschi's and Moffitt's theories? Gottfredson and Hirschi are clear about what matters (self-control) and what does not (social institutions after childhood). They are also clear on where self-control comes from: parenting. To them, parents must do three things in order to instill self-control. First, they must monitor their children. Second, they must recognize deviance when they see it. And, finally, they must correct it. Moffitt's theory views offending to be the result of two distinct groups. For the adolescent-limited group, relatively minor delinquency will dissipate of its own accord. For the life-course persistent group, however, antisocial behavior is rooted in neuropsychological deficits and is more biological in nature. Yet behavior is also explained by psychological problems and poor environmental contexts which interact to produce hardships. Thus environmental enrichment and developmental programming may be useful (see Raine et al., 2003, for some positive results of such programs). To the extent that life-course persistent offenders are not moved by structural or personal relationships, however, the options are limited.

Sociological theory policies

Sutherland, in the early stages of this theoretical explication, felt that cultural conflict was the major cause of criminal behavior. His full-blown differential association theory eventually would clarify that associations with individuals and their attitudes toward the law is the sole cause of crime. What kinds of policy implications does this theory hold? In Chapter 29 of the 1947 edition of *Principles,* Sutherland discussed crime prevention. Earlier chapters covered prisons and probation/parole, but punishment, he argued, was less effective than prevention for the simple fact that "Perhaps 10 per cent of the serious crimes result in arrests, and certainly a much smaller percentage result in official treatment" (p. 614). One program type in which Sutherland apparently found much to like was social organization efforts, or "local community organization." The Chicago Area Projects are a good example of the kind of effort Sutherland had in mind. These projects included having local community members organize group activities and recreation in an effort to help structure the lives of community members, particularly the youth.

Interestingly, however, when it came to white collar crime Sutherland seemed to suggest that punishment is what would be most effective. "The definition of specific acts as illegal is a prerequisite to white collar crime, and to that extent the political society is necessarily organized against white collar crime. The statutes, however, have little importance in the control of business behavior unless they are supported by an administration which is intent on stopping the illegal behavior" (1949/1964, p. 255). In other words, the state needs to recognize white collar crime as crime and act accordingly.

More recent sociological perspectives, focusing on the life-course, have emphasized the importance of social ties. Laub and Sampson (2003) reiterated that they view focusing on risk factors in childhood to be misguided. If social ties such as those stemming from meaningful employment and healthy, supportive marriages matter, then policies should focus on helping build bridges to those social institutions. Job training and education programs in prisons would be recommended. Punishment for the sake of punishment would not—incarceration tends to cut off social ties, Laub and Sampson showed. "What is needed," Laub and Sampson wrote, "is a mechanism or, better yet, a series of mechanisms to bring offenders back into the institutional fabric of society" (Laub & Sampson, 2003, p. 291). Laub argued in a recent piece (2016) that a life-course perspective would recognize not only the possible life damage wrought by criminal justice sanctions but also that antisocial behavior can lead to "cumulative disadvantage" in that "delinquency incrementally mortgages the future by generating negative conse- quences for the life chances of the stigmatized and institutionalized youth" (p. 632). This cumulative disadvantage culminates in what some call a "crystallization of discontent"— an uneasy state not unlike a "rock bottom" that can catalyze individual change (Paternoster & Bushway, 2009). Thus, at each stage of the life-course, efforts should be made to strengthen social ties. Perhaps the most effective policies would be thoughtful about crime prevention, stopping antisocial behavior before it begins—here we see similarity with respect to the recent and past sociological perspectives.

A relatively newish approach to reducing crime from a life-course perspective involves helping offenders with decision-making so that they actively choose to be prosocial. This incorporates the notion of "human agency" which Sampson and Laub have emphasized in their work of late. Laub (2016) draws on a concept of "nudge" to suggest that policies could be constructed to "organize the context in which people make decisions" and thus to "nudge" them toward better decision-making (p. 632). Perhaps ensuring offenders have some sort of stake in conformity, as Jackson Toby (1957) wrote more than 60 years ago, would help nudge decision-making away from the criminal toward the prosocial.

CONCLUSION: TALE-OF-THE-TAPE

The "great debate" in the 20th century (and into the 21st) regarding theory and the intellectual home of criminology (which we will discuss at length in Chapter 7) centered on whether it makes more sense to explain crime and justice from a sociological or psychological view. It is fair to say that in the early 1900s the psychological perspective was dominant. The measurement of intelligence was coming into vogue and the idea that feeblemindedness was inherited was a popular explanation of deviance—one that divested the public from any social responsibility. As Nicole Rafter wrote with us recently, "For a brief period, the feeblemindedness explanation of crime became the most broadly—and enthusiastically—endorsed explanation of lawbreaking in US history. Judges, university presidents, lawmakers, novelists (think of Lennie Small, the accidental killer in John Steinbeck's *Of Mice and Men*), ex-president Teddy Roosevelt ("we have no business to permit the perpetuation of citizens of the wrong type"), Winston Churchill, psychiatrists, prison superintendents, and the heads of institutions such as the Virginia State Colony assumed the theory's validity and helped propagate it" (Rafter, Posick & Rocque, 2016, p. 133).

Things changed gradually throughout the 20th century, and by the 1950s sociology had won the battle. Sutherland succeeded in dismissing other perspectives as unscientific and his differential association theory reigned supreme. This was a nearly total victory, as criminology in the US became synonymous with sociology. Those wishing to study crime and deviance needed to major in sociology and specialize in criminology (as one of us actually did in the early 2000s). But the Sutherland coup was perhaps less based on empirical merit than a desire by the theorist to invoke some consistency and what he saw as scientific principles to the field. As Laub and Sampson (1991) showed, Sutherland's thinking seemed to shift suddenly and he began to criticize work and ideas that he once supported. The sociological victory, however, did not last. At the end of the 20th century psychological scholars began to make their voices heard, showing that, in fact, personality and individual differences do matter in explaining antisocial behavior. By the turn of

TABLE 2.1 TALE-OF-THE-TAPE. DIFFERENTIAL ASSOCIATION THEORY VS. PSYCHOLOGICAL THEORIES

Theory	Differential association theory	Psychological theories
Theorists	Edwin Sutherland; Ross Matsueda; Ronald Akers	Cesare Lombroso; Charles Goring; Havelock Ellis; Don Andrews; James Bonta
Main arguments	Crime is learned through social interaction; crime is not the result of individual differences	Personality traits or mental deficiencies are important in explaining crime
Period of popularity	1930s–present	1870s–1930s; 1990–present
Seminal pieces	*Principles of Criminology* (Sutherland); *The Professional Thief* (Sutherland); *White Collar Crime* (Sutherland); *Deviant Behavior* (Akers); *Social Structure and Social Learning Theory* (Akers)	*Criminal Man* (Lombroso); *The English Convict* (Goring); *Psychology of Criminal Conduct* (Andrews & Bonta)
WINNER	✓	

the 21st century criminologists would be in a sort of crisis, lamenting a loss of paradigm or world view (Savelsberg & Sampson, 2002).

So who is the current winner? At present it seems that sociology is still a dominant part of criminology. Some argue that "Environmental theories that largely ignore individual differences . . . constitute the dominant paradigm of mainstream criminology today" (Cooper, Walsh & Ellis, 2010). Cooper and colleagues (2010), in a survey of American Society of Criminology members that took place in 2007, found the modal form of training was sociology (41 percent of the sample). Yet sociology's lack of total dominance is seen, in that more than half the sample was trained in criminology, criminal justice, or even psychology (6 percent of the sample). Sampson and Laub's age-graded theory of informal social controls is perhaps the most popular theory of crime over the life-course, but the scene is now filled with many competing explanations, some of which give primacy to psychological factors (such as David Farrington's [2003] integrated cognitive antisocial potential theory).

It can be said that sociology holds onto criminology in a tenuous manner. More and more the field is seemingly accepting its multidisciplinary side, and even sociological criminologists are recognizing that individual factors need to be taken seriously (Cullen, 2009). Cullen argued that while sociology would remain the dominant perspective in criminology for some years, the end was coming. Has that point arrived? Is criminology truly multidisciplinary? We do not think so . . . just yet. But it is absolutely more multidisciplinary than it was for much of the 20th century. And we can thank the "great debate" of Sutherland/sociology vs. psychology for much of that development.

The next chapter changes focus from a disciplinary debate to a more fundamental theoretical one. For much of the late 20th century to today there have been three dominant theoretical (largely sociological) perspectives. They are strain, social learning, and social control theories. The debates between social learning (or cultural deviance theories) and control theories have served to sharpen both perspectives and our own understanding of the causes of crime and what a theory must do to serve as an adequate explanation of the phenomenon. These debates are still raging today, with both camps seeking the upper hand.

NOTES

1 According to Google Scholar, the original article specifying the theory has been cited nearly 9,000 times
2 www.law.cornell.edu/supremecourt/text/274/200

PART II

Great debates in the mid-to-late 20th century

Is crime natural or do we learn it?
Control and cultural deviance theories

3

I N THE EARLY 1900s a baby boy was born to a single mother and taken to a hospital where he was then evaluated. He was a healthy boy and was particularly even-keeled at the age of only a few months. This made him a perfect candidate for . . . laboratory experiments. At around nine months the boy, now known as "Little Albert," was exposed to a barrage of tests inside the laboratory of famous psychologist John B. Watson. At 11 months Watson conducted a fear-conditioning experiment where a rat was presented to Little Albert (which he fondly reached out to touch) and, just as he touched the rat, a metal bar was struck producing a startlingly loud noise. This process was repeated with Albert several times. When the rat was later presented to Albert he would initially reach out to the rat but pull his hand back before making contact— a behavior not seen with other objects. This led Watson to claim that behavior is learned through conditioning and that people are not born with many inherent emotions or behaviors. In fact he famously stated, "Give me a dozen healthy infants, well-formed, and my own specified world to bring them up in and I'll guarantee to take any one at random and train him to become any type of specialist I might select—doctor, lawyer, artist, merchant-chief and, yes, even beggar-man and thief, regardless of his talents, penchants, tendencies, abilities, vocations, and race of his ancestors" (Watson, 1945, p. 82).

Watson's behaviorism is akin to what some call "blank slateism"—the idea that humans are born with few "original" emotions, thoughts, and behaviors (Pinker, 2002). They are simply balls of clay, waiting to be molded into some distinct form. Unique personalities, in this view, are acquired through exposure and learning. While studies such as the one with Little Albert highlight the possibility of learning some behavioral reactions, other theorists believe that much behavior, including criminal behavior, is innate. Contrast the story of Little Albert with those individuals in more recent experiments exploring behaviors and emotions that exist very early on in life, before much social learning can take place. In a recent Yale experiment, babies around 10 months of age were presented with two toys to play with and they overwhelmingly picked one over the other. Why? In a video, one of the toys was a "helper toy" that assisted another toy in walking up a hill while the other toy hindered the progression up the hill. Babies already were wanting to associate with the helper and not the hinderer.[1] A host of other experiments have shown that fairness, cooperation, and emotion contagion are evident early in life, as a product of evolution, without much social learning (see Bloom, 2013, for more instances of innate baby behavior).

These perspectives have much to do with criminology. In order to find out the origins of criminal behavior, one must ask: "why do they do it?" or, perhaps, "why don't they do it?" The first question is common among social learning theorists, while the second is common for social control theorists, given their perspectives on human nature. We begin our discussion of debates on social learning and social control theories by first reviewing the theories and the assumptions they make about human nature. Next we cover the critique hailed against social learning theories by Ruth Rosner Kornhauser in her highly influential book *Social Sources of Delinquency: An Appraisal of Analytic Methods,* published in 1978. Finally, we get to the heart of the debate, detailing the responses between the two camps and the evolution of the theories to date.

SOCIAL LEARNING VS. SOCIAL CONTROL THEORIES IN CRIMINOLOGY

In the 20th century three perspectives on crime and delinquency, what we call the "seminal trio," developed and took hold in the field. Strain and social control theories originated in the work of the sociologist Emile Durkheim, whose concept of *anomie* was influential to many theorists including present day scholars. In several of Durkheim's books, anomie was discussed and used to analyze what he called social facts. Anomie is generally thought to represent a state of "normlessness," in which society is in flux or undergoing some sort of change that renders the normal regulations that bind us together moot, though the meaning of anomie changed throughout Durkheim's career (Marks, 1974).

Strain theory, one of the first sociological theories of crime, was developed by Robert K. Merton. In his article "Social Structure and Anomie," Merton argued that antisocial behavior was concentrated in the lower classes because the United States' society was characterized by a disjuncture between its culturally proscribed goals and the means deemed acceptable to reach them (Merton, 1938). Merton was mostly referring to the so-called American Dream, which provides the benchmark by which we in the US (still) are measured. Having a nice family home, a new automobile every few years, disposable income, and plentiful time to enjoy life are things we all want. Yet not only does the culture tell us what we should strive for, but also how to get there. In other words, we are judged not just by what we have but how we obtain it. In the US and much of the western world, hard work, education, and conformity to rules and guidelines are viewed as the appropriate avenues to traverse on the way to obtain the American Dream.

Here is where the disjuncture, or anomie, comes in. For some of the population the avenues are clear and easily traveled. For others the avenues are cluttered with roadblocks. Those in the lower economic strata do not have access to high-quality education, college degrees, and high-paying jobs. Yet the cultural goals of financial success and material goods are still applied to them. In other words, the cultural goals and means are not co-aligned. When this happens, trouble (read: antisocial behavior) brews. As Merton stated, "Aberrant conduct, therefore, may be viewed as a symptom of dissociation between culturally defined aspirations and socially structured means" (1938, p. 674). In a more concise description, strain theory suggests that when people are blocked from obtaining their goals, goals they have emotionally invested in, deviant behavior often results. The most obvious crime from this perspective is breaking the rules to obtain financial reward (e.g., robbery, theft, shoplifting). Merton called this an adaptation to strain in the form of "innovation."

Strain theory suggests that human beings are programmed *not* to treat each other poorly. It is when the social structure is out of whack with the culture that antisocial behavior emerges. If society is functioning well, people will tend to be prosocial. This is an assumption of human nature, one of altruism, and is associated with the philosophy of Rousseau (along with his ideas of a "social contract" that binds people in society) who argued that people will tend to behave cooperatively in a state of nature. The evils we see—crime, war, famine—are a result of unequal social structures and arrangements that push people into bad behavior.

Social control theory also stems from the concept of anomie. But it uses anomie in a much different way than strain theory, and one which is arguably closer to what

Durkheim had in mind. Whereas strain theory suggests anomic social structures *push* people into antisocial behavior, control theory suggests that anomie *allows* antisocial behavior to come to the surface. Social integration, rules, and regulations are the lid on the proverbial can; they restrict us from acting in ways that we naturally might. In a state of anomie those controls are disrupted, which allows the deviance to spill out.

Standard textbook accounts generally put the origin of social control theory in the mid-20th century, when survey research allowed criminologists to ask about relationships juveniles had with significant others. They often found that when parental and teacher relationships with youth were strained, those youth were more likely to be delinquent (Hirschi, 1969; Nye, 1958; Toby, 1957). Their interpretation was that these relationships represented anchors to prosocial society or restraints on natural deviance. Thus relationships were "controls" on behavior that were needed in order to reduce or prevent crime.

The assumption of human nature made in social control theory is an interesting one. As Hirschi so eloquently put it, "In the end, then, control theory remains what it has always been: a theory in which deviation [crime] is not problematic. The question 'Why do they do it?' is simply not the question the theory is designed to answer. The question is, 'Why don't we all do it?' There is much evidence that we would if we dared" (Hirschi, 1969/2009, p. 34). This assumption of human nature derives from the philosopher Thomas Hobbes (1651/2006), who argued in *Leviathan* that, left to our own devices (a state of nature), life is often pretty terrible. There are no social controls, rules, or regulations, so people are free to do whatever they want, follow any instinct they may have, beat up others or even kill them if they get in the way. What stops this free-for-all, this "war of all against all," is the emergence of modern societies, in which people give up some of their freedom for a bit of security and personal peace of mind. Notice that the emergence of society here brings peace and reduces violence, whereas in the strain version it's just the opposite.

Finally, the third major criminological perspective does not come from the work of Durkheim at all, but one of his contemporaries, Gabriel Tarde. Social learning theory, which was developed as differential association theory, starts from the premise that all behavior is learned behavior. This is true for walking and it is true for criminal conduct. As Sutherland stated in his theory, crime is caused by differential associations where some of us associate with those who view the law favorably and some of us associate with those who view it unfavorably. The balance of associations determines our own attitudes and therefore our behavior with respect to crime.

Social learning theory is thus most akin to behaviorism in the vein of John Watson in terms of its assumptions of human nature. People, according to the theory, are neither prone to delinquency (as suggested by control theory) nor naturally altruistic (as assumed by strain theory). Instead, social learning theory in a sense assumes that human beings are empty vessels or blank slates and they can be pulled in whatever direction the cultural winds are blowing. In that way social learning theory represents a middle ground between social control and strain theories, but is somewhat more radical in assuming basically no intrinsic human instincts, traits, or tendencies.

In this chapter we focus on social learning and control theories to the exclusion of strain theory. We do this because, in large measure, these two theories were put head to head most forcefully in the latter part of the 20th century. Another reason, however, is that until the 1990s strain theory had been relegated to the criminological dustbin.

Hirschi's (1969) study provided conclusive evidence that strain theory had little to offer as an explanation of delinquency. Adherents to strain theory were convinced enough to abandon it (Kornhauser, 1978). Hirschi had shown little relationship between being blocked from aspirations and engaging in delinquency. His own control theory was heavily supported by his data, but at the same time he could not disprove learning theory—youth with delinquent peers were more likely to be delinquent themselves.

The heart of the chapter is a fascinating debate that took place in the 1990s between Hirschi and Gottfredson (control theorists) and Ronald Akers (a social learning theorist) as well as one a few years later between Barbara Costello (Hirschi's student) and Ross Matsueda (a social learning theorist). Both of these exchanges helped clarify positions, sharpen perspectives, and, we would argue, strengthened the theoretical expositions themselves. But who was still standing when the bell clanged? We will attempt to sort that out at the conclusion of this chapter.

RUTH ROSNER KORNHAUSER AND CULTURAL DEVIANCE THEORY

In 1978 Ruth Kornhauser, wife of the political scientist William Kornhauser, published *Social Sources of Delinquency: An Appraisal of Analytic Models*. This work, which assessed sociological theories of crime, stemmed from an unpublished paper written years earlier (we have never seen this paper despite our, and others', attempts). We will discuss that report more in subsequent sections, deriving our information about it from Hirschi's paper in response to a critique by Ronald Akers. It is important to note, though, that Kornhauser offered much praise to Hirschi in the Acknowledgments of *Social Sources*, noting that he "read the entire manuscript and discussed it with me." It should come as no surprise then that Kornhauser's text presented a pure control theory explanation of crime.

Kornhauser would argue that social disorganization theories (developed by Clifford Shaw and Henry McKay in the early 20th century) were really macro-level control theories. She showed how disorganization could be thought of as an inability of a community to realize its shared values (or, more bluntly, to control itself). The idea of social disorganization was one that highlighted the varying strength of culture. When a society was "organized," this meant its culture was strong and consistent. When it was not organized, the cultural messages the community wished to promulgate were weak.

When it comes to theories of crime, Kornhauser provided a scathing critique of social learning theories. She came to dub these theories "cultural deviance theories" as a way to note that they attributed causality to differences in substance of cultures rather than variation in the strength of primary culture. Kornhauser focused on strain, control, and learning theories in her discussion, characterizing them this way: "At the heart of various sociological approaches to delinquency are two contrasting analytic models: one locates the causes of delinquency in social disorganization, the other, in cultural deviance. Social disorganization refers to the relative lack of articulation of values within culture as well as between culture and social structure. Cultural deviance refers to conduct which reflects socialization to subcultural values and derivative norms that conflict with law" (1978, p. 21). Strain and control theories fall under the first category, social learning the second.

The problems she saw with social learning or cultural deviance approaches were numerous. First, she argued that cultural deviance theory did not separate culture from social structure and so culture became everything all at once, its importance difficult to disentangle. In addition, she argued that cultural deviance was an appropriate term to use because the theory assumes "that in this approach subcultures are deviant, individuals never" (p. 25). As we saw in Chapter 2, Sutherland's development of differential association theory was a major step in his wresting control of criminology for sociology. Part of the consequence of that move, however, was a field that—to Kornhauser—denied the reality of human nature. To her, cultural deviance theories assume people are dupes of society, entirely controlled by culture. They are incapable of deviance unless their socialization demands it.

All of this, Kornhauser argues, strains credulity. People are inclined to act in certain ways (e.g., self-interest) and there are not countless cultures each with distinct values— that would not make sense as a basis of social order. In her chapter on cultural deviance theories, Kornhauser reviews the major iterations of the theories, including any empirical support she can find (she does not find much). There's also, she says, the problem of why criminal behavior, even for those who are in the life, is so rare. If a culture demanded it, one would presume such behavior would be a lot more common. Additionally, if culture was not sharply defined, and was conflated with behavior, there was no way to use culture as an explanation of that behavior. In other words, there is no way to test the theory that cultural differences (if those differences are indicated by differences in behavior) cause differences in behavior. She sums up the evidence on the theory as follows: "The basic assumptions of cultural deviance theories are without foundation" (p. 242). "Delinquent norms, delinquent values, and delinquent subcultures have for too long dominated the thinking of criminologists; there is no evidence of their existence. This preoccupation has been rooted in the inability to distinguish among culture, social structure, and behavior and the inability to conceive of culture and social structure as variables. The belief that behavior is always rooted in slavish conformity to cultural or subcultural values, which is one of the keystones of cultural deviance theory, is utterly lacking in credibility" (p. 244).

HIRSCHI'S CONTROL THEORY

Thus the groundwork was laid for control theory to dominate the criminological scene. A decade before Kornhauser's book was published, Hirschi had provided empirical evidence that social controls, in the form of what he called social bonds, were inversely correlated with delinquency. In a watershed study Hirschi was able to specify a new theoretical approach, collect data, and analyze whether the theory had any merit. The story of Hirschi's project is told in an interview with John Laub (Laub, 2002). Interestingly, Hirschi's dissertation adviser had thought he should use the Glueck *Unraveling Juvenile Delinquency* data, but the Gluecks were unwilling to part with it. Hirschi connected with an ongoing study called the Richmond Youth Project and the director agreed to some of the additional questions Hirschi wanted to include in the survey.

What resulted was the 1969 publication of a classic in the field, *Causes of Delinquency*. In that book, Hirschi did something that was "unique ... at the time. [He] developed his theory of delinquency and then tested his own theory as well as other popular theories of delinquency using empirical data derived from self-reports from adolescents about their attitudes and behavior, the dominant research technique during the 1960s. This 'testing' approach to assessing theories of crime and delinquency became the standard in the field" (Laub, 2002, p. xxiii). Hirschi specified that social controls and socialization can be represented by the social bond an individual has to society. In particular, attachments were the emotional ties one had with others, such as parents and teachers, commitment was the level of obligation or dedication one had to conventional lines of action, involvement was the degree to which one was taking part in conventional lines of action, and belief was how much one felt the law should be obeyed and was legitimate. These were the four elements of the social bond. Hirschi operationally defined each of these bonds so that they could be measured using survey items.

Hirschi also specified what strain and social learning theory implied and how they should be measured. Eventually he tested the three theories using data from 4,077 junior and high school students in western Contra Costa County, California. He summed up his findings this way: with respect to strain theories, they "have a decided defect; they are not consistent with the data" (Hirschi, 1969/2009, p. 228). With respect to cultural deviance theories, while he did find some support, particularly with respect to "the importance of delinquent friends," "the data suggest, there are no groups of substantial proportions in American society that positively encourage crime in the sense that those belonging to the groups in question would prefer their children to follow their own rather than a conventional way of life" (p. 230). The control theory seemed to be most supported by the data.

So now there were data supporting the control explanation of crime; Kornhauser's book provided the philosophical and logical framework. Hirschi was clear that his specification in *Causes* was not the final word on the explanation of crime. In the 2001 introduction to the book Hirschi explained that Kornhauser "was not overly impressed with the exposition of control theory in *Causes of Delinquency*, but she was eventually *convinced by its data* that her favorite theory, the 'strain model' of Merton, Cohen, and Cloward and Ohlin, was wrong" (Hirschi, 1969/2009, p. xi, emphasis in the original). Kornhauser's book would shore up the theoretical weaknesses found in Hirschi's.

AKERS' SOCIAL LEARNING THEORY

At this point in the story it would appear that control theory had the upper hand empirically and in terms of logical consistency. After decades of dominance, Sutherland's differential association theory indeed had been dealt a fatal blow by both Hirschi's and Kornhauser's assaults. Yet that was not the end for the theory, as it would come to be reshaped, reformed, and reinvigorated by one of Hirschi's colleagues, Ronald Akers. In 1966 Akers and Robert Burgess published an update of differential association theory, filling in the gaps Sutherland had left (Burgess & Akers, 1966). Specifically, Akers recognized that Sutherland did not specify the mechanisms of learning that take place with behavior. He was actually quite vague on this point. Burgess and Akers therefore updated the theory, using what was known at the time with respect to behavioral principles such as classical and operant conditioning.

Akers, in his 2009 *Social Learning and Social Structure*, described how the theory came about. He and Burgess were hired at the University of Washington in 1965 as assistant professors and were office neighbors. Burgess, Akers tells us, was a psychologist who was well versed in the operant conditioning literature. They began to chat, each teaching the other something about their respective specialties, and began to see some possible benefits from examining how the principles of operant conditioning could be applied to the study of crime. They focused on Sutherland's theory with an eye toward explicating the eighth proposition, which simply stated that the "process of learning criminal behavior by association with criminal and anti-criminal patterns involves all of the mechanisms that are involved in any other learning" (Sutherland, 1947, p. 7). The paper with Burgess was published under the title "A Differential Association-Reinforcement Theory of Criminal Behavior."

Burgess and Akers' new formulation of differential association-reinforcement theory incorporated seven propositions. They combined Sutherland's first and eighth proposition into "Criminal behavior is learned according to the principles of operant conditioning," after spelling out what operant conditioning means, along with positive and negative reinforcement (p. 137). The second proposition, reformulated, was "Criminal behavior is learned both in nonsocial situations that are reinforcing or discriminative, and through that social interaction in which the behavior of other persons is reinforcing or discriminative for criminal behavior" (p. 139). This proposition amended one of Sutherland's, which had stated that learning occurs in a process of communication —Burgess and Akers added that learning can occur in nonsocial situations (such as learning to enjoy the effects of drugs) as well. The third proposition of the new formulation read "The principal part of the learning of criminal behavior occurs in those groups which comprise the individual's major source of reinforcements," in keeping with the operant conditioning approach (p. 140).

Burgess and Akers' fourth proposition read "The learning of criminal behavior, including specific techniques, attitudes, and avoidance procedures, is a function of the effective and available reinforcers, and the existing reinforcement contingencies" (p. 141). This proposition reformulated Sutherland's proposition regarding what is learned in differential association. It is a somewhat vague statement that simply suggests we learn whatever is reinforced. The fifth proposition translated Sutherland's regarding whether people learn to be delinquent or prosocial (depending on their definitions of the law as favorable or unfavorable) to "The specific class of behaviors which are learned and their frequency of occurrence are a function of the reinforcers which are effective and available, and the rules or norms by which these reinforcers are applied" (p. 142). The sixth Burgess and Akers proposition was "Criminal behavior is a function of norms which are discriminative for criminal behavior, the learning of which takes place when such behavior is more highly reinforced than noncriminal behavior" (pp. 143–144). This proposition took the place of Sutherland's, which read that one becomes a delinquent when the balance of definitions favorable to the law is outweighed by those unfavorable to it. Finally, the seventh proposition in the new theory changed the Sutherland statement on how differential associations vary to "The strength of criminal behavior is a direct function of the amount, frequency, and probability of its reinforcements" (p. 144).

Burgess would not go on to continue work in refining differential association-reinforcement theory, but Akers would. His name has become synonymous with what is now known as social learning theory in criminology. A few years after this initial article Akers published a book called *Deviant Behavior: A Social Learning Approach* (1973) which was intended to follow in the footsteps of "how Sutherland (and later Cressey) had presented and applied his theory in a textbook" (Akers, 2009, p. 15). The 2009 book *Social Learning and Social Structure: A General Theory of Crime and Deviance* (originally published in 1998) was Akers' magnum opus on social learning theory. In it he presented both the macro and micro versions of learning theories and discussed his general thinking that most other theories could be subsumed under the processes of social learning (in other words, no other theory is needed but social learning theory!).

In that book Akers reduced the theory from seven propositions to a focus on four concepts: 1) differential associations; 2) differential reinforcement; 3) definitions; and 4) imitation. His statement of the theory read "The basic assumption in social learning theory is that the same learning process, operating in a context of social structure, interaction, and situation, produces both conforming and deviant behavior" (p. 50). Akers, incorporating the four concepts, then described how social learning theory explains criminal behavior (Akers, 2009, p. 50):

> The probability that persons will engage in criminal and deviant behavior is increased and the probability of their conforming to the norm is decreased when they differentially associate with others who commit criminal behavior and espouse definitions favorable to it, are relatively more exposed in-person or symbolically to salient criminal/deviant models, define it as desirable or justified in a situation discriminative for the behavior, and have received in the past and anticipate in the current or future situation relatively greater reward than punishment for the behavior.

Finally, in showing how social learning theory explains both individual and macro patterns in criminal behavior, Akers specified his social structure and social learning theory. This full model was composed of four components. First, differential social organization refers to variations across place in terms of culture, institutions, and demographic factors. Second is differential location in the social structure, which refers to individual factors that influence how one experiences the world, such as age, race, gender. Third is theoretically defined structural variables, such as anomie, patriarchy, and group conflict. And, fourth, differential social location refers to one's location in primary, secondary, and reference groups. These four components, Akers argues, show how the theory can explain macro and micro criminal behavior using the same theoretical framework. Akers demonstrated that data are generally consistent with his model and thus that the theory is useful in explaining crime and delinquency.

THE DEBATE: SOCIAL BONDING THEORY VS. CULTURAL DEVIANCE THEORY

Before we dive into the bonding/cultural deviance debate specifically, we want to point out an exchange between control and learning theorists in the 1980s. As we will discuss in the following chapter, Travis Hirschi and Michael Gottfredson published in 1983 a controversial and now classic article on age and crime. In it they argued that age was related to crime in a curvilinear fashion everywhere and across history. To them that meant that no criminological theory could explain it. John Baldwin, in a response to that article, suggested that "thrill and adventure seeking" (TAS) could account for the age crime relationship. This variable reflected a social learning mechanism that drew on reinforcement. Baldwin argues that TAS rises and peaks in adolescence and then declines. Crime is a part of what is rewarding when TAS is high. Not surprisingly, Hirschi and Gottfredson (1985) were not convinced. They argued that there was no evidence to support a link between TAS and crime, and in effect Baldwin was using TAS to refer to criminal behavior—a circular type of reasoning referred to as tautology. In a preview of their self-control theory they ended the article by suggesting that their age crime arguments indicate "the possible isolation of a factor with what used to be called 'inherent pathogenic qualities.' Sociology abandoned the search for such factors about the time it decided that it had theories to explain just about anything. Our article in effect asks for a reconsideration of this decision" (Hirschi & Gottfredson, 1985, pp. 1332–1333).

Let's begin the social bonding/cultural deviance debate with a bit of discussion on the names of these two theories. It is interesting to note that both "sides" have taken to naming the other theory with a slightly pejorative label, one that the other side does not appreciate. For example, Akers has called Hirschi's version of control theory "social bonding theory." As Laub points out in his interview with Hirschi, social bonding theory is "a term Hirschi is not inclined to accept" (Laub, 2002, p. xxiii). Hirschi, in his 1996 article critiquing social learning theory, argued that the social bonding term was a "gross and repeated mislabeling of control theory" (p. 250).

For his own part, though, Hirschi recognized that Akers did not approve of the cultural deviance label he and Kornhauser had applied to his theory, but said "Worse, I must admit, I like the cultural deviance label. It fills me with the warm glow of understanding and rewards me with successful prediction" (p. 250). In disapproving of that label, Akers argues that it relies on "gross misinterpretations" of the theory (Akers, 2009, p. 92). Another major social learning theorist, Ross Matsueda, also disapproves of the label. He wrote that "Unfortunately, by forcing differential association theory into an oversimplified depiction of cultural deviance theories, she [Kornhauser] misconstrues Sutherland's enterprise and reduces his theory to a caricature" (Matsueda, 1988, p. 290). The gloves, in metaphorical terms, were off.

Matsueda's defense of differential association theory

The terms matter more than as ways of poking fun at rival theories. They say something about how the theories themselves, and their proponents, mischaracterize the fundamental properties of the explanations. We begin in this section with Matsueda's (1988) response to Kornhauser's (1978) critique of social learning theory. Matsueda helpfully lays out what he sees as the main points of Kornhauser's argument opposing social learning theory: first, according to the theory, humans have no inherent human nature; second, consensus in society does not exist; third, total consensus is necessary for social order; fourth, behavior is relative in terms of what is deemed deviant or prosocial; fifth, criminal and prosocial cultures are equitable in terms of influence; and, sixth, behavior reflects cultural values, so there is no deviant behavior, only deviant cultures (Matsueda, 1988, p. 290).

In a comprehensive manner, Matsueda addresses the six assumptions, arguing that they "exaggerate" Sutherland's theory. He suggests that nowhere did Sutherland say humans have no nature, that societies are full of conflict. One of the more interesting critiques leveled by Kornhauser was that social learning theory assumed culture was not variable—but Matsueda points out that in Sutherland's propositions he specifically said differential associations vary in frequency, duration, priority, and intensity. Matsueda also argued that Kornhauser overlooked Sutherland's "logical abstraction, and differentiation of levels of explanation" (1988, p. 292). He says that (p. 292):

Kornhauser confuses the statement of an abstract generalization with the statement of concrete conditions that can be explained by the generalization. Thus, while not formally stated in the abstract generalization, Sutherland clearly intended that the learning of definitions of crime is not the result of aleatory processes, but is structured by the concrete elements of social organization that determine communication patterns. . . . That is, the concrete conditions vary in time and space, but the abstract mechanisms remain invariant.

Sutherland, according to Matsueda, did differentiate between social organization and the individual, micro learning processes. When Kornhauser suggests that cultural deviance theories do not distinguish between structure and culture she misinterprets the theory.

In the end, Matsueda argued that it was control theories that have misguided assumptions of human nature. They "assume that the procriminal beliefs, motives, and interests of criminals do not vary appreciably (if they exist at all) and do not have any causal impact on criminal behavior. All that varies are commitments and beliefs in conventional behavior" (p. 293). He ends by suggesting that control theories assume a social world that is only one of many allowed by differential association/social learning theory. In other words, they are not as incompatible as control theorists say. And while Kornhauser argued that the evidence of empirical tests supported control theories, Matsueda says new analyses support social learning.

Akers vs. Hirschi (1996)

Akers, in 1996, also responded to Kornhauser and the "cultural deviance" critique (a label, we note, Hirschi also used in his 1969 *Causes of Delinquency*). The Akers essay, a version of which is reprinted in his 2009 book, is very clear and much easier to follow than Matsueda's. Akers points out that, to Kornhauser, the assumptions of differential association theory make it inapplicable to individual behavior. It can only explain group or cultural differences in behavior. The theory also assumes that people blindly follow their culture, such that if they belong to one in which crime is proscribed, they must obey.

Akers responded by showing that differential association theory was a theory of individual behavior, not group behavior. He says that only in "extreme" cases are people perfectly socialized by their culture, according to the theory. Akers suggested that Hirschi and Kornhauser, in their critiques, did not pay attention to Sutherland's actual work. Kornhauser, he said, "includes no specific discussion or analysis of the nine propositions in differential association theory to support her description of it as the model of cultural deviance theory" (Akers, 1996, p. 233). Interestingly he also accused Kornhauser of selectively quoting Sutherland to make her point. For example, in discussing "criminal tribes of India," Sutherland had written that this group represents an "extreme form" of the theory. Kornhauser left that part out.

In his essay Akers admitted that some of the misinterpretation of differential association/social learning theory stems from Sutherland's lack of clarity on the meaning of "definitions." Are they attitudes? Motivations and drives? Akers, focusing on Sutherland's fifth proposition, suggested motives and drives are caused by definitions, but said this is not an easy line of logic to follow. But it is a stretch, he wrote, to assume that definitions are strongly held beliefs that *require* particular behavior. In any case, to

Akers, this is all moot since his revision of differential association theory takes care of all this lack of clarity.

Akers argued that "Kornhauser's reasoning is circular. She begins by imputing to cultural deviance theory the assumption that cultural definitions are the sole cause of criminal behavior. Then she rejects any learning theory concept or proposition that would explicitly contradict the assumption precisely because it does not fit the imputed assumption with which she began" (p. 241). Thus cultural deviance is a term that mischaracterizes both differential association and social learning theory. Interestingly Akers brings in Hirschi, who had used the cultural deviance label in his 1969 *Causes* and in later work on self-control (Gottfredson & Hirschi, 1990).

Fortunately for those of us who enjoy debates, Hirschi was given a chance to respond to Akers' essay. While his response was much shorter, he was able to make several strong points to refute Akers' argument that cultural deviance was a mischaracterization of differential association/social learning theory. He was also able to fill in readers about a mysterious unpublished paper by Kornhauser which both Matsueda and Akers had referenced. Akers had said that Kornhauser's unpublished 1963 paper was the beginning of the cultural deviance name; Matsueda (1988, p. 289) also had noted that "Kornhauser's (1963) earlier version of [her book] served as a theoretical framework for Travis Hirschi's (1969) key empirical study." Hirschi (1996) took his role as defender of Kornhauser's arguments seriously (she had died a year before the exchange was published). Hirschi (1996, p. 250) took a shot at Akers' and Matsueda's "guesses" about the paper, indicating they had not read it but felt comfortable enough to make arguments about it. In a footnote on page 250 he stated

> Neither Akers nor Matsueda has read Kornhauser's 1963 report. Both depend on references to it in Hirschi (1969). Apparently my debt to this report was properly acknowledged, at least for Akers's purposes. He has me "reiterating" Kornhauser's statements nine years before her book was published. Matsueda (1988:289) goes beyond my acknowledged debts, asserting that Kornhauser's unpublished work "served as a theoretical framework" for *Causes* of *Delinquency*. Kornhauser had read *Causes* and knew better, as she acknowledged (1984:viii).

After correcting the record on Kornhauser's unpublished report and her support of strain theory early on (before changing sides to control theory in the face of survey research), Hirschi spelled out why it was so important to examine the "logical presuppositions" of theories (1996, p. 251). Akers, in his essay, had argued that cultural deviance is a misnomer and mischaracterizes the theory—we should look to what the theorists wrote to get a sense of what they meant. To Hirschi this was a cop-out: "Akers, in contrast, would require that analysts restrict their attention to assumptions stated as such by the theorist and included as constituent, explicit elements of the theory. Which of these views is more likely to advance theoretical understanding of crime?" (1996, p. 252).

Hirschi also objected to Akers' argument that Kornhauser mischaracterized Sutherland's ideas. Akers had stated that Sutherland's examples (e.g., criminal tribes in India) were used to illustrate extremes and did not apply in every case. But Hirschi points out that Sutherland was an empirical determinist, meaning that he advocated theories that, in fact, did apply in every case (recall the discussion in the last chapter on Sutherland's method of science). Another mischaracterization of Kornhauser, to Hirschi, is the suggestion that she said differential association theory is only a theory of group differences. "Unfortunately, I cannot find it [that argument] in Kornhauser" (Hirschi, 1996, p. 253).

Hirschi also responded to Akers' charges that Kornhauser deliberately left out key phrases when quoting Sutherland by showing that Akers himself did not include all of Kornhauser's words in his quotes. He then said, "At the same time, in my view, *there is nothing of value in the quotation provided by Akers that is not found in Kornhauser's reduced version*" (p. 253, emphasis in the original). Hirschi argued that Kornhauser should not be forced to use the entire quote in illustrating a point. It is hard to see how the phrases she left out change the meaning of Sutherland's arguments, despite Akers (without much explanation) claiming such.

Finally, Hirschi argued that Akers' fall-back position, that definitions favorable to crime merely "allow" it, not require it, is not consistent with Sutherland's theory itself. This statement will be expanded upon below. With respect to why Kornhauser ignored Akers' reformation of differential association theory, Hirschi suggested that Kornhauser was trying to evaluate the intellectual sources of the idea. He wrapped up his essay with the following points: "On one point, the record is clear. Kornhauser did not like the assumptions and cultural deviance theories. She considered them contrary to logic and evidence. And she said so" (pp. 254–255). Culture, to Kornhauser, must "be compatible" with human nature, which, recall, cultural deviance theorists assume to be pliable (p. 255). Human beings cannot, to control theorists, simply be whatever model is put before them.

In sum, the Hirschi/Akers exchange was a moment of theoretical clarity for criminology. Neither side resorted to name-calling or nasty retorts. In fact Hirschi mentioned his longstanding friendship with Akers in a footnote. Both sides argued about ideas and assumptions of particular theories of crime. But the story was not finished in 1996, however, as there was one more element to be added to the debate. In his essay Hirschi (1996) referenced an unpublished paper by Barbara Costello on the cultural deviance critique. That paper was eventually published in 1997 in *Theoretical Criminology*. It is a defense of cultural deviance theory as a label and interpretation and a reaction to Matsueda's work. The paper is also, more importantly, about social control theory (which Hirschi did not discuss in his essay).

Costello (1997)

Prior to her essay on cultural deviance theories, Barbara Costello, now at the University of Rhode Island, had published some empirical papers on control vs. differential association theory. In 1982 Matsueda had gotten hold of the data Hirschi used in *Causes* and, using a causal modeling method (e.g., structural equation modeling), found that definitions mediated the effect of social bonds on delinquency, implying that differential association theory, not control theory, was superior (Matsueda, 1982). In 1999 Costello and her colleague, Paul Vowell, analyzed the same data again. This time support was found for control theory! They argued that Matsueda's model was not correctly specified, meaning he left out important variables. It's important to note, though, that friends' delinquency was still an important factor in the model they tested (Costello & Vowell, 1999).

So much for empirical answers. Costello's (1997) essay took on both Sutherland's and Akers' theories, unlike the previous exchange. In addition, she contributed several more points to Kornhauser's that added a new layer to the debate. Hirschi viewed these arguments as particularly sharp, stating that "I cannot hope to improve on Costello's (1995) excellent recent paper on this topic" (1996, p. 249). Specifically, Costello's essay hit cultural deviance theories on the points of: a) not defining deviant norms; b) not explaining how deviant cultures form; c) not describing how norms can be identified separately from behavior; and d) not explaining how deviant norms are learned. Costello pulled no punches in the piece, arguing that cultural deviance theories have weak empirical support and logical inadequacies that should have led to the demise of the perspective long ago.

With respect to the first criticism, that cultural deviance theories were unclear on the "content" of deviant norms, Costello was referring to "whether deviant norms *require,* or *encourage,* or simply *allow* deviant behavior" (p. 406, emphasis in the original). The key to this criticism is that what deviant norms do separates cultural deviance from control theories. If definitions require or encourage delinquency, the theory is distinct—but if they only "allow" it, then this is no different than the control notion that in certain situations norms are weak and delinquency is able to bubble up to the surface (see Warner, 2003, for another treatment of the role of weakened norms and the effect of this weakening on the ability to establish informal control). On the other hand, if definitions or norms require delinquency, then the theory is hard to justify. An interesting point made by Costello is that it is difficult to determine just how a norm that "allows" behavior would be taught, or what the process would look like. Further, if behavior is simply allowed, why does it happen at all? Costello says control theories provide the answer: human nature. Cultural deviance theories do not have an answer.

With respect to the second point, that the origin of deviant subcultures is not well understood in cultural deviance theories, Costello reviewed two popular answers. First, she says cultural deviance theorists say that strain can lead to oppositional subcultures. Second, cultural deviance theorists may assert that individualistic norms and loosening of social controls may lead to the subcultures. For Costello there are problems with both answers. If strain causes deviant behavior, why are deviant norms necessary in the equation? With respect to the individualistic argument, Costello said this idea has no evidence and that it makes no logical sense to suggest that society must teach people to act in their self-interest.

Finally, Costello argued that cultural deviance theories suffer from being unable to separate norms from behavior and not explaining how norms are learned. In many of the statements of the theories, she identifies scholars demonstrating evidence of subcultures by describing differences in crime rates (which is circular, since subcultures are supposed to *cause* differences in crime rates). The last point is one that comes down to human nature assumptions. How do people learn deviant norms? If they are open to them does that mean individuals are social dupes who go along slavishly with their culture? She takes on Matsueda's (1988) argument (above) that socialization can vary in differential association theory by arguing that such an idea is not found in Sutherland's text. The theories assume that, if a person is exposed to deviant subcultures to a reasonable degree, they *will* become deviant.

Costello, in the essay, also addressed a point Matsueda (1988) had made, that control theories assume everyone is similarly motivated to crime, and that beliefs about how desirable criminal behavior is do not vary. Her response was that control theory is a micro-level theory and so social order questions are not fair game. However, as we saw, Kornhauser was able to show that social disorganization theory is a version of macro-level control theory. Thus control theory, in our view, is not simply a micro-level perspective.

Ok, if cultural deviance theories are so logically flawed, how can we explain why most delinquents have delinquent friends and that delinquency takes place often in the presence of peers? Indeed, this was a stubborn finding that led Hirschi to suggest that his control theory was not completely supported by his data. Costello suggested that delinquency happens in groups, but groups do not cause behavior—the causal ordering is wrong in cultural deviance theories. People predisposed to similar behavior often find themselves drawn to each other. This is the "birds of a feather flock together" argument (the technical term is homophily). In answer to whether the group nature of delinquency is indicative of causality, Costello says (1997, p. 422):

> Sociologists studying delinquent groups have also overlooked the fact that just as most delinquency occurs in groups, so do most other teen leisure time activities. It is rare for a teenager to go to a movie alone, for example, and I suspect that the number of movies one's friends attend is a good predictor of the number of movies the individual attends. It is unlikely that people teach each other to value movie attendance, and much more likely that the 'group influence' in such cases involves no more than the invitation or suggestion that the individual participate in the activity.

In the end, Costello argued, cultural deviance theories make strong claims that are not logically or empirically consistent. And "Attempts to moderate these claims result in the theory becoming indistinguishable from control theory" (p. 423). Thus control theory, by her reckoning, is the winner.

Matsueda's (1997) response

The title of Matsueda's response to Costello is telling. It is "'Cultural deviance theory': The remarkable persistence of a flawed term." Thus we get a sense that his opposition to the points she made are again focused on how cultural deviance as a label misinterprets differential association/social learning theories. He made an interesting point that "because [in 1988] I had spent much time trying to understand the logic behind differential association theory . . . I felt I was in a position to point out Kornhauser's mischaracterization of differential association and seek to correct it" (p. 430). The same applies to Costello's essay. In effect Matsueda was saying that, since he has spent time studying differential association theory, his interpretation, not Kornhauser's and Costello's, is essentially correct. To be fair, Costello and Kornhauser would likely argue the inverse.

In her essay Costello had written that she deliberately used extensive quotes from Sutherland's work to insulate her from accusations she had misinterpreted the theorist. Matsueda used that tactic against her. He said that she (and Kornhauser) do not understand the difference between abstract general concepts and concrete exemplars used by Sutherland. His exemplars were illustrations, but Kornhauser and Costello used them to infer generalized laws in differential association theory. He wrote, "Sutherland specified that *sometimes* definitions favorable to crime make up an important part of subcultures of criminals; Kornhauser interprets this to mean that *all* such definitions are subcultural" (p. 431, emphasis in the original). Sometimes definitions are norms; however, "most definitions favorable to crime consist of rationalizations that justify crime in circumscribed situations" (p. 433). In other words, as a way to facilitate critique of the theory he says that Kornhauser and Costello set up a straw man of differential association theory, one that little resembles the actual perspective.

With respect to the learning of deviant norms, Matsueda argued that Costello had misstated differential association theory. Instead of people being indoctrinated into cultures that teach criminal acts, what the theory is really saying is that people may learn *rationalizations* to get around the law (which is generally valued) and situations in which definitions contra crime may be ignored. In other words, it is not correct to assume that differential association theory is primarily a theory that views people as being socialized *into* crime. He turns Costello's argument, that softening of differential association theory leads directly to a version of control theory, on its head and says "If control theorists have arrived at the same conclusion as Sutherland, then *they* have failed to specify a theoretical position" (p. 438, emphasis in the original).

What about assumptions? Control theories assume that crime is natural and explained by failures in socialization. Control theorists argue that cultural deviance theories require a world in which socialization is perfect and only the content of the socialization varies. No one can be deviant, only cultures. Matsueda said this is a mischaracterization of Sutherland, who argued that both socialization may not be complete and also that motivation to crime can vary across people. How does differential association theory explain initiation? Through reinforcements, which provide definitions. "Control theories merely assume away the question. . . . All things being equal, this is the least satisfactory solution to the problem of initiation" (Matsueda, 1998, p. 439).

Recall Costello's discussion of the origins of subcultures of deviance. She argued that Sutherland's reliance on strain and individualism was not adequate. Matsueda responded to each of these in turn—he said that Costello's argument, that a strain explanation of the origin of delinquent subcultures means learning is superfluous, is only sensical from a control perspective since those theories do not need to explain motivation. Strain can explain why new "innovations" to reaching goals are developed, and then learning can explain how they are spread throughout the culture. Matsueda also disputed Costello's statement that Sutherland assumed cultures teach individualism at the expense of society. Individuals, he said, may teach other individuals, and thus the notion makes sense.

Finally, Matsueda disagreed with Costello's assertion that differential association theory cannot explain the group nature of delinquency. He argued her alternate explanations likely have some validity, but they do not explain the entire relationship between peers and crime. Note, however, he started this section (on page 443) by discussing the "effects of delinquent peers on delinquency." Therefore he was assuming there *is* an effect, while control theories assume there is a spurious relationship.

In sum, the debates between control perspectives and learning perspectives in criminology have been ongoing for nearly a century. Both sides have taken strong stands, labeling the competing theory with pejorative terms seen as offensive by proponents. Both sides have asserted that the underlying assumptions of the competing theories are incorrect. Interestingly both theories have undergone revisions through the years, from differential association to social learning and social control to self-control theories. And the debates continue.

POLICY IMPLICATIONS: SIDE-BY-SIDE

Learning and control theories have been presented, generally, as diametrically opposed perspectives on criminal behavior. They have distinct assumptions of human nature—one side views humans as particularly plastic, another views them as wired for antisociality. However, the theories have some similarities, as reviewed above, in terms of beliefs toward the law. So what would the policy implications of the two theories be? Are they vastly different?

From the assumptions of human nature that we (and others) have drawn from differential association/social learning theories, we can parse out what is needed to prevent or reduce crime from what causes it. These theories suggest something must happen to people in order for them to act deviantly—they must learn it or be reinforced for it. Thus, left to their own devices, it is assumed humans would not be antisocial. It is not the person, then, who must be targeted but those around him/her who would teach them to be deviant.

Social learning theories suggest that the primary cause of delinquency and crime is interactions with others who hold deviant attitudes, or reinforcement for deviant behavior. With respect to the first factor, differential association/social learning theories would promote two strategies. First, isolation of individuals from those with definitions favorable to the violation of the law. This is consistent with a traditional parenting edict in which parents try to ensure their child does not "run around" with the wrong crowd. In criminal justice spheres it may be realized in the risk-need-responsivity approach in which offenders are classified according to their level of risk of reoffending and criminogenic needs (Andrews & Bonta, 2010). Offenders should not be mixed with respect to risk levels, however, because of the chances that a low-risk offender would be influenced by a higher-risk one.

The work of Gerald Patterson in the Oregon Social Learning Center is instructive. The center has been operating since 1983 with the goal of studying the development of antisocial behavior. Patterson and his colleagues felt strongly that parents were the key site of intervention for at-risk children (www.oslc.org/about/history/). Parent training programs have been successful in preventing antisocial behavior in children (Farrington & Welsh, 2007).

Social learning theory has been at the heart of other prevention programs. Nicholson and Higgins (2017) review several programs that have shown reductions in crime and have followed social learning principles. For example, one of the more successful programs for offender rehabilitation involves what is called "cognitive behavioral therapy (CBT)." CBT is focused on changing erroneous thinking patterns and helping individuals problem-solve so that they recognize the antecedents of antisocial behavior and are able to use alternative approaches. Meta-analyses have indicated that CBT reduces recidivism of released offenders (Landenberger & Lipsey, 2005).

The assumptions of control theories with respect to human nature are different than social learning theories. Left to their own devices, people *would* be deviant. In other words, it is the person who must be targeted early and controlled in order to prevent crime from happening. The rest of society, the individuals' friends and family can be left alone, except to the extent that they must be taught to socialize in a prosocial manner.

Interestingly control theorists have relied on some of the same programs to illustrate support for their perspective as have social learning theorists. Recall, for example, that self-control theory suggests that parents must instill self-restraint in children or all is lost. Parenting programs, it turns out, may be useful from a control *and* learning perspective. Gottfredson and Hirschi (1990), for example, cited the work of Gerald Patterson in discussing the origins of self-control. To them the most effective forms of treatment are those that deal with children and families. Even more interestingly, in a 1977 essay Hirschi referred to "Learning theories of the control variety" which focus on the teaching of "law-abiding conduct" (p. 330). Thus we learn prosocial values, and so control theory from a prevention standpoint may not diverge as much from learning theories as initially presented.

However, with respect to offender rehabilitation we see a divergence between control and social learning theories. In the control theory view, by the time individuals have reached adulthood and involvement in the criminal justice system, efforts to rehabilitate them will likely fail. From this perspective control theorists do not see much value in programs aimed at improving correctional treatment. They also do not see much value in programs aimed at improving police strategies or even programs designed to selectively incapacitate offenders.

Control theories, whether self-control or age-graded theories (Sampson & Laub, 1993), argue that social institutions are the major forces of restraint against antisocial behavior. That is, social institutions, such as education, family, work, religion, and so on, must be sufficiently strong to rein in our natural impulses. Thus policy implications of control theories focus on these institutions, on strengthening them or at least not weakening them, by cutting off offenders from conventional society through incapacitation for unnecessarily long periods of time (readers are encouraged to dig into the perspective brought forth by Messner & Rosenfeld, 2013, which also discusses policies to reduce the chance that important social institutions are not weakened, leading to crime).

CONCLUSION: TALE-OF-THE-TAPE

In this chapter we have traced the evolution of two of the most popular theoretical perspectives in criminology, social learning and control theories. We have shown how control theories arose almost from the beginning in opposition to social learning perspectives. When it comes down to it, the major point of contention is the image of humans that each theory portrays. Control theories see humans as naturally self-interested, as caring about self-preservation above all else. They look at toddlers who instinctively hit others, who do not want to share their spoils, who demand attention, as representing raw man.

Learning theories, on the other hand, view people as the product of their environment. There is no fundamental human nature (in the sense that we know what people would be like or how they would act in the absence of society). If people are exposed to those who are law-abiding more than they are exposed to those who are not, they will be prosocial and vice-versa. While learning theory advocates have disputed this claim, we think it is relatively non-controversial to suggest that social learning theory does not assume people are naturally good or bad.

Unfortunately for the purposes of debate, the issue of intrinsic human nature is not one that is easily settled. We cannot know what people would be like outside of society because society exists everywhere. Some work (for example, see Pinker, 2002) has argued that people do have an intrinsic human nature, and it is rooted in our evolutionary

TABLE 3.1 TALE-OF-THE-TAPE. CONTROL THEORIES VS. LEARNING THEORIES

Theory	Control theories	Learning theories
Theorists	Travis Hirschi; Michael Gottfredson; Ruth Kornhauser; Barbara Costello	Edwin Sutherland; Ronald Akers; Ross Matsueda
Main arguments	Crime is natural, people will engage in it unless they are restrained by society or social forces	Crime is learned in a process of social interaction; crime is not natural or innate
Period of popularity	1950s–present	1930s–present
Seminal pieces	*Causes of Delinquency* (Hirschi); *A General Theory of Crime* (Gottfredson & Hirschi); *Social Sources of Delinquency* (Kornhauser)	*Principles of Criminology* (Sutherland); *Deviant Behavior* (Akers); *Social Structure and Social Learning* (Akers)
WINNER	✓	

past. Certain work has shown that play preferences of male and female children diverge before much socialization has taken place (Todd et al., 2016). There is also evidence of genetic and neurological effects on antisocial behavior (see Raine, 2013). Yet much of this work, couched within the biosocial criminology scholarship, in essence looks to identify what it is about criminals that makes them different. Very little of this work seeks to identify what restrains people from crime, implying that antisocial behavior is not natural but a result of a defect. This position, and much of this work, is more consistent with the strain assumptions of human nature, and not control or differential association theories.

The empirical score is a bit more of an objective metric. We can look to some of the meta-analyses, which are studies of studies, seeking to come up with an overall average effect of particular variables on outcomes such as delinquency. Fortunately for us, criminologists Travis Pratt and Frank Cullen have provided a meta-analysis of both control theory and differential association/social learning theory. First, in 2000, Pratt and Cullen examined how well self-control predicted crime and delinquency across a variety of studies. They found that the weighted mean effect size for attitudinal measures of self-control was .223, and .288 for behavioral measures. Interestingly they compared self-control measures to social learning measures of definitions and differential association. The weighted mean effect size for those were .184 and .239 respectively. Thus this study slightly gives the edge to self-control theory, as it had the highest effect size (.288). In addition, the interaction between self-control and opportunity had a mean weighted effect size of over .50, which is much higher than any of the social learning theory measures (Pratt & Cullen, 2010).

In 2010 Pratt and Cullen (along with several colleagues) examined social learning theory. Here they showed only mean effect sizes, but for all four components of social learning theory. For differential association (which included others' attitudes and behaviors) the average effect size was .225. For definitions the mean effect size was .218. For differential reinforcement the mean effect size was .097, and for modeling/imitation it was .103. Thus, in this updated meta-analysis, arguably social learning theory fared even worse than self-control theory. One last meta-analysis, however, found that self-control was a relatively weak predictor of victimization (part of the theory), with a mean effect size of .154 (Pratt et al., 2014).

In terms of effect sizes, then, while both theories seem to be significantly related to crime and deviance in a statistical sense, they are not overwhelmingly so. The meta-analyses seem to give a bit of support to control theory here (though we only have results for the self-control version). In the grand scheme of things, however, neither theory seems to be as general or powerful as their proponents hope.

There is one more measure of how well theories do in explaining crime, and that is to use the percentage of variance explained. In multivariate regression analyses this figure is denoted by R^2, which tells us how much of the variation in delinquency across the sample is "explained" by the variables in the regression model. So which theory does better here? Criminologists David Weisburd and Alex Piquero (2008) looked at R^2 for criminological theories in the context of studies published in the journal *Criminology* from 1968 to 2005 (N=169). Interestingly differential association theory had an average R^2 of .428, meaning the models testing the theory explained nearly 43 percent of the variance in crime and delinquency. Social control theory was a bit lower, at .379, and self-control theory rang in at .275. One test of self-control theory was also found to have the lowest overall R^2 with a value of just .001, meaning that study found self-control only accounted for about .1 percent of the variance in antisocial behavior. A very poor showing.

And so we are left with a pretty mixed bag. In terms of effect sizes, self-control wins. In terms of variance explained, differential association theory wins. Where are we now? After some consideration we believe the edge is given to control theory, on the basis of the meta-analyses. First, the meta-analyses cover more than one criminology journal and more studies overall. For example, the Weisburd and Piquero (2008) analysis only included seven studies of differential association theory. The Pratt et al. (2010) meta-analysis included 133 studies of social learning theory. Second, there have been multiple meta-analyses on which to base our judgement. There has—to our knowledge—only been one study assessing variance explained.

There is one last empirical issue we can focus on to test the two theories. Our belief is that the only *true* way to examine causes is in a randomized experiment. A true cause is one that directly influences the outcome, accounting for possible confounding influences. Social learning theory has been subjected to an experiment and this was done in a rather ingenious way. Paternoster and his colleagues (2013) conducted a laboratory experiment in which two groups of students were told they were engaging in a test of memory/recall. The ingenious part of the study was that the experimenter "inadvertently" showed the subjects links listing all the words they were supposed to recall, thus offering them the chance to cheat. The experimenter left the room to check on fixing this "error." In one condition there was a confederate who told the group he was going to use the link to earn more money and justified it. In the other group there was no confederate. So what happened? In the confederate, or "social learning," group 38 percent of the subjects cheated by looking at the links. In the other group? None did. Pretty impressive results for the causal effect of peers. Is there any experimental evidence for control theory? We think that a meta-analysis of self-control programs applies well here. Criminologist Alex

Piquero and his colleagues (2010) examined whether programs in childhood had the ability to raise self-control and whether those programs reduced crime/delinquency. The answer, they found, was yes to both. Thus experimental work supports both theories.

In terms of overall logic and consistency, we find more value in the control theory arguments than the differential association/social learning theory ones. We find ourselves agreeing with Costello that the origin of deviant norms and subcultures is problematic in differential association theory, and merely "allowing" or "justifying" delinquency seems to be more of a control perspective. If definitions justify delinquency, as Matsueda has asserted, one still wonders why a person would engage in it? Many of us, we believe, could engage in bad behavior when no one is looking, could sneak money here and there, maybe look at a colleague's email she left open, but usually we don't. Why? Even if it is because our "definitions" don't allow it, we think those beliefs are more of a restraint than a positive force for behavior, and that story is more consistent with control theory.

We reached out to Costello for a more updated view of the debate (Matsueda did not respond to our invitation). She argued that the term "cultural deviance" still applies to social learning theories.[2] She says "I was never convinced that I had somehow misinterpreted Sutherland's theory, primarily due to the dozens of times in *Principles of Criminology* that he says the same thing, in really straightforward language." In short, differential association and social learning theory "are both cultural theories in the traditional usage of the term in criminology—group values cause behavior. If values cause deviance, the term cultural deviance seems very appropriate."

Are there parts of the arguments she made that she would change? One is the role of peer pressure:

> On both logical and empirical grounds, it seems to me that peer pressure is not consistent with cultural deviance or social learning approaches. Coercing someone to commit crime implies that they do not want to do it. If they do not want to do it, it's more difficult to argue that the behavior is consistent with their norms and values. My book with Trina Hope presents numerous examples of coercive peer influence that seem inconsistent with social learning processes (Costello & Hope, 2016). For example, one of our respondents was pressured into making an illegal U-turn by his friends in the car yelling at him, saying "You're such a pussy! You don't have any balls! Grow up and just turn here!" (Costello & Hope, 2016, p. 29). This seems like a clear example of peer influence that bears no resemblance to the learning processes discussed by either Sutherland or Akers, and it was fairly common in our study.

Costello believes, as expected, that control theory has won out when it comes to empirical support. She argues that peer effects can be interpreted within a control theory framework and that "where Sutherland went wrong in trying to explain the peer-delinquency relationship was by looking for a complicated explanation for a very simple phenomenon. Toddlers get angry and hit their mothers. They can't get what they want so they have a tantrum. . . . None of these actions requires learned norms, values, or justifications to explain them." While social science has evolved in terms of its thinking about culture, this does not change the conclusion that a control perspective is more likely to bear fruit in explaining and controlling crime.

In the end both theories have made their mark on criminology and are likely not going anywhere. They both seem to help us understand pieces of the crime puzzle, but it seems fair to say that neither tells the total story. Rather than lament this situation, we think it means there are exciting times ahead for criminology in terms of discovering new insights, developing new theories, and refining old ones such as control and differential association/social learning theories.

NOTES

1   https://campuspress.yale.edu/infantlab/our-studies/
2   Email conversation, August 18, 2017.

Do we need to follow people over time?

Criminal careers vs. criminal propensity theories

4

T HERE ARE INNUMERABLE idioms for it. We have heard them all: "what's past is prologue," "the more things change, the more they stay the same," "once a cheater, always a cheater," "the child is the father of the man." These sayings are all alluding to the same sort of thing: once we find out about certain aspects of life, especially people, we know what to expect in the future. In other words, people are what we think they are—they don't change.

How does this apply to criminology in general and great debates in particular? It turns out, quite a lot. When studying crime and deviance, if people are who we think they are, if being "bad" in childhood means being "bad" throughout the life-course, this simplifies things for researchers. For example, we don't have to figure out how to make people turn a new leaf. We don't have to study childhood and adolescence and adulthood because a focus on one point in the life-course will do and is just as good as any other point in time. Draw up a survey for high school youth, figure out what differentiates the bad from the good, and you'll have all the information needed to protect society.

But what if the world is more complicated than that? Aren't there alternative sayings, ones that in essence signify the exact opposite of those above? "Change is inevitable, change is constant," "you cannot step in the same river twice," "things do not change, we change." These words of wisdom tell us that nothing ever stays the same; that the way we were as children may actually tell us little about the way we will be as adults. If *this* is the case, the job for criminologists becomes much more difficult. Those who are antisocial early in life may not be those who are antisocial later in life. In addition, the causes of bad behavior, or why some people stop their bad behavior, may not be the same across the life-span.

Clearly, which way the wind blows in this particular debate has massive implications for criminological theory, research, and policy. Luckily for us a debate covering these issues (in a much less simplified form) took place in criminology during the 1980s. This debate has been deemed by some as the "great debate" (Bernard et al., 2016) because it bore on the direction of criminology for the decades that followed. The debate involved some of the field's most well-known and influential scholars during the period: Michael Gottfredson and Travis Hirschi teamed up to criticize the criminal career researchers, who included Al Blumstein, Jacqueline Cohen, David Farrington, and Christy Visher, among others. This debate has often been referred to as the "criminal career" debate because it includes scholars who argue that it is useful to see the longitudinal patterning of offending over an individual's life as comprising different components, each with possibly different causal pathways and explanatory factors. Thus, they argue, we must examine the entire "career" of an offender, from when he/she starts to when he/she stops (or pauses) offending and everything in-between. On the other side of the debate are theorists who view crime as a simpler phenomenon, caused—in general—by the same trait at each stage of the life-course. By that token, longitudinal data are not necessary because the factors that matter do not change over time.

In this chapter we review the criminal career debate, taking it up to the present. While the main players debated each other mainly from the mid-1980s to the end of that decade, the debate spurred new advancements and work that continues today (Rocque et al., 2015). We start, though, at the beginning, which is generally traced to the classic Birth Cohort studies by Marvin Wolfgang and colleagues. We then get into the heart of the debate, which was largely confined to a series of exchanges in the pages of *Criminology,* and end with a discussion of work that has continued to the present, showing how it is related to the debate that took place more than 30 years ago.

THE CRIMINAL CAREER CONCEPT IN CRIMINOLOGY

Is crime a "career?" Some early scholarship in criminology seemed to indicate that this was the case. Goring (1913) discussed the careers of criminals, though seemingly using the term to simply describe the period in which a person remains engaged in crime. In the first part of the 20th century this was a very common descriptor (for example, see Glueck & Glueck, 1930; Shaw, 1931). Others used the term "career criminal" to label a person who was chronically engaged in crime, who seemed to take it as his/her vocation to sustain their livelihood. For example, Hulbert (1939, p. 11) defined a career criminal as one who "makes his living in criminalism." In other words, these were not just temporary or sporadic offenders. There are several classic examples of scholarship focused on crime as a career. As discussed in Chapter 2, one of Edwin Sutherland's primary contributions was a book co-authored with a career criminal, a professional thief he named Chic Conwell. In that book Conwell described the tactics and skills needed to be a high-level criminal, one who does, in fact, pursue crime for a living.

The idea of a criminal career is somewhat consistent with the social learning approach, described in the previous chapter. After all, with an occupation there is job training, a period of acclimation, and eventual mastering of a field. Perhaps this is part of the reason control theorists such as Gottfredson and Hirschi despised the notion so much. As they stated in a 1986 paper that we will cover in more depth later, "most offenses do not require any particular skill (doors are simply smashed open), knowledge (little training is required to snatch a purse), or even expectation of great gain ('hand over all your big bills,' the career criminal says to the cabbie); there is no evidence of escalation of any sort as the offender moves from adolescence to adulthood; and the crimes that occur most often are the crimes most frequently committed by 'career' criminals" (Gottfredson & Hirschi, 1986, p. 218). In other words, to think of crime as a job or occupation is silly. Anyone can do it and those who do typically do not stick with it for long. In fact those most predisposed to antisocial behavior, to Hirschi and Gottfredson, are those most ill-equipped to handle the responsibility of an occupation. Hirschi has been consistent on this score, noting in his 1969 *Causes of Delinquency* that career-like thinking when applied to crime is "meaningless" (Hirschi, 1969/2009, p. 50). It's important to note, though, that the criminal career paradigm which emerged in the 1980s does not use the term in the sense of an occupation, but rather to denote the "longitudinal sequence of offending" across the life-course (Blumstein et al., 1986, p. 12).

CHRONIC CRIMINALS AND CRIMINAL CAREERS: SOME BACKGROUND

Researchers have noted that dimensions of the criminal career (such as onset, frequency, and termination) were examined by criminologists in the early 20th century, including the Gluecks in their longitudinal studies in Boston (Piquero, Farrington, & Blumstein, 2003). However, a couple of studies in the 1970s helped kick off the criminal career debate. First was the *Delinquency in a Birth Cohort,* conducted by Marvin Wolfgang and colleagues (Wolfgang, Figlio, & Sellin, 1972/1987). Gottfredson and Hirschi (1986) argued that "enthusiasm for the idea [of career criminals] . . . can be traced to the rediscovery of the chronic offender by Wolfgang, Figlio, and Sellin (1972)" (p. 215). The *Birth Cohort* researchers collected information on all males who lived in Philadelphia between the ages of 10 and 18, born in 1945, and followed them up to age 18. In this way they were able to gain a more comprehensive understanding of how frequent crime was in the general population, rather than focusing on official records or individuals already enmeshed in the justice system.

In their analyses Wolfgang and colleagues examined the arrest records of the birth cohort, some 9,945 individuals, finding varying patterns of offending throughout time. They showed, for example, that crime peaked at age 16 and that a large proportion of the offenders, 46.4 percent, only committed one crime, then desisted. In fact the *Birth Cohort* researchers were among the first scholars in criminology to use the term "desistance" to describe the cessation of offending over the life-course (Rocque, 2017). The study also examined age at first offense, specialization, and repeat recidivism. The golden ticket finding from this research, however, was the discovery that a small group of the sample represented half of all the offenses recorded. More specifically, 627 individuals (or 6.3 percent) who had committed five or more crimes were responsible for 52 percent of all offending in the sample. This finding sparked the interest of scholars who recognized the significance of a small group of chronic offenders—if they could be prospectively identified, a large amount of crime could be avoided so it seemed.

It was not long after the publication of Wolfgang and company's *Birth Cohort* study that a couple of engineers, Benjamin Avi-Itzhak and Reuel Shinnar, published a paper in the first volume of the *Journal of Criminal Justice.* This piece outlined a new statistical approach for examining what they called "criminal systems." Avi-Itzhak and Shinnar (1973) introduced numerous statistical terms to describe parts of a criminal career and to model criminal careers as a Poisson process (a process that declines in prevalence over time). As far as we know they introduced the use of the symbol λ (or lambda) to refer to rate of offending for individual offenders. While their goal was to estimate crime trends, using the number of offenses per offender and the probability of conviction and subsequent incarceration, their contribution to the criminal career work would be seen in the next decade.

Shlomo and Reuel Shinnar (1975) followed up on this work in a *Law and Society* article. They used the same "crime systems" approach to examine how well the criminal justice system responds to crime. The authors were able to develop an equation for the "effectiveness of the criminal justice system." The important part of the model was that it broke down crime information into several components, including the number of active offenders, the length of the criminal career, the rate of offending (modeled statistically), and the probability of imprisonment. Interestingly, in the acknowledgments section of this paper, the authors thanked Al Blumstein, who would come to dominate the criminal career approach in the 1980s.

Blumstein, an engineer and operations researcher by training, began to focus on the criminal justice system in the 1960s. As recounted by Brame (2016), it was his research on "models of criminal justice" that "laid one of the analytical foundations of the criminal career paradigm: the idea that the causes of whether one participates in crime may be very different from the causes of the frequency or intensity of one's criminal activity." Blumstein also credited the work of Wolfgang in his *Birth Cohort* studies with stimulating his interest in career criminals or chronic criminals (Brame, 2016).

One of the first criminal career studies Blumstein engaged in was published in 1979 with his collaborator, Jacqueline Cohen. Their goal was to help researchers study rates of offending for individual offenders over their active career, arguing this was an overlooked area of research. Among their motivations was the interpretation of the well-known age-crime curve, in which criminal behavior peaks in late adolescence. Blumstein and Cohen argued that research to that point had mostly made use of aggregate data, making it difficult to know if the decline in rates that coincide with age was due to fewer crimes in older age or fewer criminals. This was important because the former suggests that people slow down and burn out while the latter suggests people drop out of active participation and those who remain active are still going strong, committing the same amount of crimes with age. In a data-laden analysis (21 tables in a 26-page paper), Blumstein and Cohen found that trajectories of arrest over the life-span varied by offense, and for some offenses (burglary, narcotics, other) arrests increased with age (see also Farrington, Ttofi, & Crago, 2017). They concluded that, for active offenders, lambda did not decrease over time as was previously thought.

A year later Blumstein and Moitra (1980) spoke directly to the career criminal issue raised by Wolfgang et al.'s finding. They wanted to know whether it was possible to prospectively identify chronic offenders, that is find out who would become career criminals before they had actually become chronic offenders. After all, if policy is to be able to use the chronic offender information to protect society, identifying them after the fact does little good. Blumstein and Moitra used arrest histories from Wolfgang and colleagues' (1972) study and examined whether the number of prior arrests could predict the probability of repeat offending. They found that by the third arrest, recidivism probabilities did not increase. They argued that "the number of arrests accumulated in a criminal career ... is a random variable" and that the "distribution is 'memoryless' in that the probability of accumulating any number of additional arrests is independent of the number already recorded" (Blumstein & Moitra, 1980, p. 324). Fascinatingly, Blumstein, perhaps the name *most* associated with the criminal career paradigm, thus argued that his findings "warrant some skepticism regarding whether the 'career-criminal' programs will serve as the crime-control panacea many hope them to be" (Blumstein & Moitra, 1980, p. 329).

Another set of analyses, published in 1982 by Blumstein, Cohen, and Hsieh, provided more estimates of the length of criminal careers. Here they defined what they meant by criminal careers, stating that it "is intended only as a means of structuring the longitudinal sequence of criminal events associated with an individual in a systematic way" (p. 5). They broke the criminal career down into several parts, including length, intensity, and specialization. Blumstein and colleagues produced some interesting findings, including that average criminal careers are not relatively long, averaging 3.3 years in duration. Much as the Gluecks had shown 50 years earlier, Blumstein and his co-authors found that the earlier the start of the career the longer it was. An important suggestion in the conclusion was offered to policymakers regarding the identification of persistent offenders for selective incapacitation. They said that the "concern about the older age of these target populations because of the presumed greater likelihood that these older offenders will be dropping out of criminal careers shortly anyway ... is misplaced. Indeed, for property crimes, including the frequent target offenses of robbery and burglary, active offenders in their thirties or forties do represent prime targets for sanctioning" (p. 71, emphasis in the original). In some ways this was a reversal of Blumstein's earlier argument that targeting certain offenders was a waste of time.

By 1980 the literature on criminal careers was established enough for Joan Petersilia to craft a 60-page essay in *Crime and Justice* reviewing it. Petersilia herself had been engaged in Rand studies on "habitual offenders" (Petersilia, Greenwood, & Lavin, 1978). Interestingly though, Petersilia had to rely on a large amount of unpublished work for her review. She argued that criminal career research was focused on persistent crime and had as its goal the examination of "how such careers are initiated, how they progress, and why they are discontinued" (p. 322). Petersilia reviewed major studies, methods, data, and results found in the studies, including prevalence of offenders, of criminal careers, volume of crime attributable to those careers, and length of career. She summarized her review with these key findings (pp. 368–370):

- Only 15 percent of the population will be arrested. Of these, 50 percent will be arrested again. Five percent of the population will begin a criminal career.
- Criminal careers have early starts, usually in the person's teenage years.
- There is no specialization—offenders commit all manner of crimes.
- Some criminal careers are marked by high crime rates, others low ones. The variation is around age, prior record, and crime type.
- Overall, the probability of being arrested given a crime is .10, but rises with age (while crime declines with age).
- The CJS (Criminal Justice System) does not have a marked impact on criminal careers.

Petersilia also echoed Blumstein's warning that chronic offenders were difficult to identify prospectively and thus any policy of selective incapacitation would be premature.

SHOTS FIRED: HIRSCHI AND GOTTFREDSON CAST DOUBT ON THE IMPORTANCE OF CRIMINAL CAREER RESEARCH

Through the 1970s and into the 1980s it seemed that criminal career research was destined to become criminology's new paradigm. It made sense from an empirical and policy viewpoint and could help save the field from the stagnation that characterized its knowledge about and impact on behavioral reform. After Martinson's (1974) devastating report on the state of offender rehabilitation science, this knowledge was needed. Yet early in the 1980s two scholars began to question this new paradigm, wondering what, exactly, the fuss was all about. While their complaints were many, Gottfredson and Hirschi were particularly disturbed by the atheoretical nature of the criminal career work. It was almost as if knowledge of how criminals actually operate and who they actually are was completely absent in this research.

In 1983 the first shots were fired in the "great debate." The 1983 Hirschi and Gottfredson paper on age and crime is now a classic in criminology for what it highlighted about the age-crime curve. But in that piece the authors also took some digs at the criminal career work that was all the rage at the time. The paper was originally being written with Hirschi's collaborator, Michael Hindelang, who fell sick and died before the paper could be finished (Laub, 2002). Hirschi explained that, after seeing age-crime curves from various time periods and data sources, he was no longer satisfied with his social control theory as a way to explain desistance. Why? Because desistance was not variable—it was constant. Thus Hirschi and Gottfredson's (1983) conclusion that no theory could explain it. In addition, the idea that we should spend time and resources identifying the lengths of careers and finding persistent offenders seemed silly—we can see that everyone eventually desists, they said.

Part of the appeal of the 1983 paper lies in its reliance on logic as well as empirical data. It also included the catchy phrases that Hirschi and Gottfredson have become known for. As one example, on the first page of the paper they claim that the age-crime curve "represents one of the brute facts of criminology" (p. 552). After presenting the claims that they were attempting to demonstrate, they wrote "We recognize the difficulty in establishing some of our theses, especially those that deny either the significance of variability not yet investigated or the power of investigations not yet advanced" (p. 554). In a footnote on page 554 they "grant that in many cases they [arguments] go beyond it [the evidence]. If we are wrong, it should not be too hard to show that we are wrong."

Hirschi and Gottfredson note that the age and crime relationship is part of the justification for the new focus on criminal careers and career criminals. They point out that some researchers (for example, see Blumstein) argue that the age-crime curve masks multiple trajectories, rather than painting a broad picture of how crime unfolds for most offenders. They examine the utility of the career criminal approach by assessing age of onset and age of desistance, finding that neither is an especially illuminating concept and neither tells us anything that we did not already know from cross-sectional research. The idea that longitudinal research is necessary to follow careers over time, to figure out who are persistent offenders and why, was a claim made by criminal career researchers. Hirschi and Gottfredson say this is a mistake. We have learned nothing more from such studies than what we already knew.

It is interesting to note that at the end of the essay, when Hirschi and Gottfredson forcibly make the point that "For predicting subsequent involvement [in delinquency], to know that a child of 10 has committed a delinquent act is no more useful than to know that a child of 15 has done so" (Hirschi & Gottfredson, 1983, p. 581), they indicate in a footnote that Blumstein had consulted with them on the piece. They say that their arguments in the paper imply that it is not necessary to identify early-onset delinquents for intervention. Again, age of onset does not tell us anything other than that the person was engaged in delinquency. What, they ask, does it mean to say that age of onset predicts later offending?

It probably means that looking back over the careers of offenders, one finds that those who have committed many offenses over a long period of time have also committed offenses when they were quite young. If so, it is (1) not clear how things could be otherwise and (2) not clear why longitudinal studies are required to look back at the records of offenders. Coupling onset and career notions with longitudinal research clearly suggests the possibility of identifying career offenders at the onset of their careers. As far as we can determine, no longitudinal study to date has identified, or even attempted to identify, the onset of a career in crime at the time of onset (Hirschi & Gottfredson, 1983, p. 581).

THE CRIMINAL CAREER TAKES OFF: THE NAS REPORT

A few pieces were published around the time of the age and crime paper on the criminal career side. Cohen (1983) published a *Crime and Justice* review essay examining the potential of incarceration to reduce crime. She argued that incarceration, as currently utilized, had only minor effects on crime, which echoes current research (see Clear & Frost, 2015). Rather than simply locking up more people, some suggested that targeted or selective incapacitation would work—by identifying those chronic offenders responsible for a large amount of crime. Cohen wrote that there were issues (ethical and empirical) with identifying people early in life who may become chronic or career criminals. But there were ways of doing so that might work. Her method was to use criminal career trajectories (after they began) to identify career criminals. This approach would avoid using individual-level predictors (such as race, previous convictions) that are questionable ethically and empirically. In other words, researchers should examine multiple components of the criminal career and use that information for crime control.

Criminologist David Farrington (1986) also participated in the criminal career research emerging in the 1980s. In an essay published in *Crime and Justice*, Farrington rejected the conclusions of Hirschi and Gottfredson that the age-crime curve was the same for everyone—he argued that participation, not frequency, is what declines with age. He also made the case that, in order to truly understand the relationship between age and crime, we need longitudinal studies. He began the conclusion of his essay as a direct refutation of Hirschi and Gottfredson (1983): "The age-crime curve is not invariant" (Farrington, 1986, p. 235). As a contribution to the criminal career literature, Farrington reviewed the research on criminal career components (or dimensions) such as age of onset, incidence, and prevalence. The publication which most comprehensively made the case for the value of these components was the *Criminal Careers and "Career Criminals"* report, submitted to the National Academy of Sciences (NAS) in 1986.

The *Criminal Careers and "Career Criminals"* report was authored by Al Blumstein, Jacqueline Cohen, Jeffrey Roth, and Christy Visher. The report was written in two volumes, with the first nearly 500 pages in length. Volume II was also hefty, coming in at more than 400 pages. The report was an empirical masterpiece, providing calculations for various components of the criminal career, demonstrating the value of divvying up the criminal career into such dimensions as (Blumstein et al., 1986, p. 1):

1. *Participation*—the distinction between those who engage in crime and those who do not;
2. *Frequency*—the rate of criminal activity of those who are active;
3. *Seriousness* of offenses committed;
4. *Career length*—the length of time an offender is active.

The report also provided estimates of these dimensions: 25–45 percent of urban males are arrested by age 18, 12–18 percent for a serious offense (murder, rape, robbery, aggravated assault, burglary, larceny, and motor vehicle theft). Lambda (λ), or frequency, varies but the report estimated 2–4 violent crimes and 5–10 property crimes per year for active criminals. They noted, though, that "Most significantly, λ varies considerably across offenders so that the distribution of λ is highly skewed: the median offender commits only a handful of crimes per year, while a small percentage of offenders commit more than 100 crimes per year. This finding is obviously especially important in developing policies to reduce crime, by concentrating on high-rate offenders, or 'career criminals'" (1986, p. 4).

Similarly, length of career varies, with the average being around five years. For those still active in their 30s, they can be expected to remain so for another 10 years. The examination of career length shed light on age of onset (beginning of career) and desistance or termination (end of career), which both became foci of research in their own right.

The report's authors called for more, rigorous, research on the dimensions of the criminal career and on the effects of policy intended to reduce crime. They especially pointed out the need for longitudinal research—the method that Hirschi and Gottfredson had, three years earlier, deemed a waste of time. They argued that each of the dimensions should be examined individually and factors that predict them should be studied comprehensively. This raised the possibility that a risk factor may explain onset but not duration, for example. In other words, a general theory of crime in which one factor may explain all crime and deviance (as Gottfredson and Hirschi were developing) was inconsistent with the idea of criminal careers.

One interesting aspect of the report was a section in Chapter 1 entitled "Basic Definitions and Symbols." The section laid out the dimensions and provided symbols to denote each one. Here we see the use of lambda as λ, which Avi-Itzhak and Shinnar (1973) had introduced. Other symbols introduced were C for overall crime rates; d participation, or the percentage of a population engaged in criminal offending; q probability of an arrest after a crime; T total crime career length; δ proportion of a population terminating their career during a specified time period; μ arrests per year per active offenders; and B percentage of population ever arrested. They also, helpfully, prepared a figure to summarize the criminal career, using this symbology, an adapted version of which is shown below:

TABLE 4.1 SYMBOLS OF THE CRIMINAL CAREER

Symbol/ Dimension	Definition/Meaning
C	Crimes per population/year
λ	Crime frequency per criminal/year
d	Crime prevalence/year
D	Crime prevalence ever
q	Arrest probability given a crime
T	Criminal career length
T_R	Time remaining in criminal career
δ	Proportion of criminal group who stop offending during time x
A	Arrests per population/year
μ	Arrests per offender/year
b	Proportion of offenders "busted"/year
B	Proportion of population ever arrested

Adapted from Blumstein et al., 1986

The criminal career report provided many "interesting puzzles" for future researchers to address (Sullivan & Piquero, 2016, p. 422). The report clearly specified a research agenda that was to focus on understanding the dimensions of the criminal career, predicting each of them and adding knowledge about how best to craft policies to disrupt long and serious careers. The criminal career notion spurred advances in theory, such as Moffitt's taxonomy, and methodology, including Nagin's (2005) semi-parametric trajectory technique, meant to uncover different patterns underlying the age-crime curve (Sullivan & Piquero, 2016).

WHAT'S THE TRUE VALUE OF LAMBDA AND LONGITUDINAL RESEARCH? ZERO

Once again, not everyone in criminology seemed thrilled by the criminal career report and the seeming turn in the field toward its core concepts. In another classic piece in the "great debate," Gottfredson and Hirschi immediately took aim at the criminal career report. The title of the article was revealing: "The True Value of Lambda Would Appear to be Zero: An Essay on Career Criminals, Criminal Careers, Selective Incapacitation, Cohort Studies, and Related Topics." This paper would be one of the most far-ranging critiques of the criminal career paradigm to date. Ironically, Gottfredson and Hirschi begin the essay lamenting the state of affairs in criminology whereby criminal career research had taken a stranglehold on federal funding agencies. Yet, in a footnote on the first page, they indicate that their essay was funded by a federal agency, the National Science Foundation.

The stated purpose of the paper was "to introduce some small degree of tension into this otherwise complacent system [the criminal career paradigm]. It criticizes the career criminal and derivative concepts, evaluates the research on which they are based, and examines the policy (selective incapacitation) stemming from them" (Gottfredson & Hirschi, 1986, p. 214). First they take aim at the career or chronic criminal notion. They argue that it: a) is not a new idea; b) is poorly defined; and c) is difficult to identify. They then show that selective incapacitation, the policy most linked to the research on chronic criminals, is short-sighted and doomed to failure.

In probably the most damning of critiques, Gottfredson and Hirschi demonstrate that selective incapacitation (the "identification of a small group of high-rate offenders early in their criminal careers in order to isolate them in such a way that they cannot pursue their criminal inclinations" (p. 216)) is not realistic. For example, one way to identify chronic criminals is by using prior records as a guide. Yet, they say, the criminal justice system already does this. So what else can be used as an identifier for this group? It is unclear. Why? Because the research stimulating interest in the career criminal was based on criminal justice records in the first place. Then these individuals prompted a search for similar individuals using different metrics. This cannot be done, they say. Thus we are left with the following: the only way to identify career criminals is to find them after they have led a life of chronic, serious crime; that is, after the fact. What good can such an exercise do from a policy standpoint? The damage has been done.

Next, Gottfredson and Hirschi show that the very idea of the career or chronic criminal is misleading because it assumes that there are offenders who simply keep on keeping on, who do not slow down with age. In fact this was the very conclusion of Farrington (1986) and Blumstein and Cohen (1979). The aggregate age-crime curve, the criminal career scholars noted, illustrated a decline in prevalence with age, not frequency. Gottfredson and Hirschi double down on their 1983 paper, arguing that all offenders, everywhere, eventually decrease their offending until they desist. There is no meaningful variation across groups, places, or time. They review data from longitudinal studies (such as those published by the Gluecks) to show that crime always declines with age.

Because, Gottfredson and Hirschi claim, the Blumstein and Cohen (1979) analyses are so divergent from established findings in criminology (that crime declines with age), they deserved special attention. First they critique Blumstein and Cohen's argument that the age effect seen in aggregate statistics is a cohort effect—that is, more recent cohorts have higher crime rates, so the decline with age that is seen is really an increase in younger groups. Gottfredson and Hirschi show that the age effect has been prevalent in all epochs and would thus require that crime rates have always increased over time, which is not supported by the data.

Gottfredson and Hirschi then utilize a baseball analogy to show why crime declines with age. They say that statistics showing a criminal has a higher rate of crime at age 30 than another at age 20 is not evidence of constant crime rates. This is, they say, like assuming superstar ball players don't decline with age just because they are better than most people at age 30. "But this is only because the performance of the superstar at advanced ages is well above that of ordinary young major league players. Mickey Mantle at 38 was better than Gene Michael at 28. Mickey Mantle at 38 was not, however, as good as Mickey Mantle at 28" (Gottfredson & Hirschi, 1986, p. 223).

As for Blumstein and Cohen's (1979) finding that crime did not decline over time in their sample, Gottfredson and Hirschi point out that they selected their sample on the basis that offenders had to have been active. Thus that they did not decline may not be very interesting. "It is neither very surprising nor very useful to learn that persons selected on the basis of predetermined characteristics actually possess those characteristics" (Gottfredson & Hirschi, 1986, p. 226).

What about the claim that lambda has zero value? To reach that conclusion they analyze data from Farrington's Cambridge Study in Delinquent Development and find that, over a period of time, lambda is constant at 1.294. Thus it is meaningless because it does not differentiate high or chronic criminals from ordinary ones. In a footnote they take the definition of lambda to task more completely—they say, for example, that what it implies is that we want to know how much variation there is in offending *among offenders* (its measurement, after all, uses the number of offenders as the denominator and the number of offenses as the numerator). But we really should be looking at what differentiates offenders from non-offenders. "The vacuity of this kind of thinking about crime cannot be overstated. No other area of scientific inquiry would accept the logic of this approach. . . . What, it would ask, distinguishes blacks who have had at least one heart attack from whites who have had at least one heart attack (Rather than, what are the causes of heart attacks—and do they differ between blacks and whites?)" (Gottfredson & Hirschi, 1986, pp. 229–230, footnote 4).

Gottfredson and Hirschi ended the piece with an appeal to the theory they were developing, based on a control perspective. They argued that crime propensity is natural and evident in most people. They stated that crime is unskilled, produces short-term benefits, and has long-term negative consequences. The typical offender, then, would not be one who would enjoy or be able to hold a job, much less a career (even of the criminal sort).

A year later Gottfredson and Hirschi (1987) wrote an essay on the usefulness of longitudinal research. Again, drawing on the age and crime paper, they suggested that longitudinal research was unnecessary, a waste of time and resources, and leads to erroneous conclusions about crime. After reviewing some early longitudinal work by the Gluecks, Gottfredson and Hirschi go on to argue that: a) longitudinal methods are not superior to cross-sectional ones; and b) the findings do not justify such designs.

With respect to the methodological superiority claimed by advocates of the longitudinal design, Gottfredson and Hirschi first note that there are also drawbacks here. These include substantial costs and testing effects (meaning that subjects' responses are associated with merely being in a study and change as a result). For prospective studies, the seeming strength that independent variables are collected before the outcome is known is not superior, they say, to simply stratifying a cross-sectional sample on known correlates of the outcome. Some argue that longitudinal research designs make causal ordering clear—but to Gottfredson and Hirschi this is not problematic in cross-sectional designs. Why? It is usually not a mystery *when* crime or an arrest occurred. We can therefore establish temporal ordering without prospective data collection.

Complex types of longitudinal research methods attempt to disentangle the effects of age, period, and cohorts. Collecting data on groups of people who experience something in common (such as birth year) creates a cohort study. A researcher can collect data on multiple cohorts over multiple time periods to separate these effects. Gottfredson and Hirschi dispense with this observation rather succinctly: "Since crime cannot cause age, period, or cohort, a longitudinal study is not required to answer the causal order question" (p. 588). The obsession with these effects (which may be real, but of little practical use), they say, takes our attention away from more important questions and concerns.

With respect to identifying and testing correlates of crime and criminal justice policies, again Gottfredson and Hirschi claim that longitudinal studies do not show anything that cross-sectional ones have not already. So when longitudinal studies identify sex, delinquent peers, and so on as important correlates, Gottfredson and Hirschi show that these same factors have been identified in cross-sectional research. They are also quick to separate longitudinal from experimental research. The former is not justified to them, the latter is. In fact, in reviewing research from Farrington's Cambridge Study in Delinquent Development, Gottfredson and Hirschi note that some of his findings differ from that of experiments. This, they say, should give us pause. Should we include experiments in longitudinal designs? No, say Gottfredson and Hirschi; experiments tell us what we want to know just fine without the added cost.

Gottfredson and Hirschi also take on the importance of longitudinal research for the examination of criminal career dimensions. Not surprisingly, since they find these dimensions to be without value, longitudinal research adds nothing. The dimensions of prevalence, incidence, and lambda "can be computed from cross-sectional and longitudinal designs" (p. 606). Part of their hostility to the use of longitudinal designs to study these dimensions is that they view the causes of crime (and all its attendant dimensions) to be the same.

In this piece Gottfredson and Hirschi spell out their budding theory more clearly. When it comes down to it, their differences of opinion with the criminal career scholars was about theory (Bernard et al., 2016). They were coming to view crime as the result of "relatively stable characteristics of people and the predictable situations and opportunities they experience" (Bernard et al., 2016, p. 608). If that is the true cause of crime, then following people over their life course makes no sense. You'll not learn anything new with that approach. Gottfredson and Hirschi made clear the stakes of the debate. If you favor criminal careers, you reject individual-level stable-trait theories.

THE EXCHANGES

In 1988 the journal *Criminology* hosted an exchange between the criminal propensity and criminal career researchers. First was a piece written by Blumstein, Cohen, and Farrington which attempted to respond to Gottfredson and Hirschi's true value of lambda article written earlier. In that piece they say that Gottfredson and Hirschi confused criminal career and career criminal—the former is a focus on the active period of offending for a criminal and the latter on a subgroup of especially chronic offenders. They clarified that "The concept of a *criminal career* refers to the longitudinal sequence of offenses committed by an offender who has a detectable rate of offending during the same period" (Blumstein et al., 1988, p. 2, emphasis in the original). There is nothing especially controversial about that and it does not imply an occupation-like career. More importantly, arguments like those made by Gottfredson and Hirschi, that most ordinary criminals do not have skill and do not specialize, say nothing about the value of the criminal career perspective—in fact such statements, were they valid, could only be declared as such by examining the criminal career! Blumstein and his collaborators also said that "The construct of the criminal career is not a theory of crime" (p. 4). In that way, the title of this chapter is slightly misleading as the criminal career framework was only meant to be an organizing perspective for research and policy.

Blumstein and colleagues also took issue with Gottfredson and Hirschi's argument that lambda has no value. They suggested that all the dimensions of the criminal career defined and discussed in their criminal career report illuminate different aspects of criminal activity that are worthy of examining. Each of these dimensions, importantly, can tell us different things about crime and can be used to test theories. In other words, they are clear that the criminal career notion is not a theory of crime but a framework. Each of the constituent parts of the criminal career are pieces of that framework. Blumstein and colleagues differentiate themselves from Gottfredson and Hirschi by hypothesizing that one factor (criminal propensity) may not account for each of the dimensions. This would be important information for the development of theory.

The criminal career scholars argued that the relationship between age and crime was misinterpreted by Gottfredson and Hirschi. In some ways this is the key to the debate. If the relationship between age and crime is not the same across time and place and for all offenders, the Gottfredson and Hirschi position becomes less tenable. They go on to show how the pattern of crime across age has varied over time and for different offenses, following Farrington's 1986 paper. They also, in this section, take some interesting shots at Gottfredson and Hirschi, including calling their arguments "enigmatic" (p. 8) and pointing out a typo in their abstract in which they describe the "decline in age with crime" (footnote 7). In some ways the invariance of the age-crime curve is in the eye of the beholder.

Blumstein and colleagues (1988) make the case, again, that what the age-crime curves show in the aggregate is not that frequency of offending declines with age, but participation. Blumstein and colleagues argue that Gottfredson and Hirschi had misinterpreted data from the Gluecks they had used to demonstrate that frequency does decline with age. While it was true that raw arrests declined with age, when the data were broken down into prevalence and frequency, the former declined with age while the latter did not. In this 1988 paper the authors also respond to the Gottfredson and Hirschi critique of the Blumstein and Cohen (1979) paper. Whereas Gottfredson and Hirschi asserted that Blumstein and Cohen had defined their sample in such a way as to guarantee the results they obtained, Blumstein's team says they only meant to target "active" offenders and this choice did not require frequency to be stable. Yet that is what they found.

With respect to lambda and Gottfredson and Hirschi's argument that, because in Farrington's data lambda did not vary across age, it was "without theoretical or policy significance" (Gottfredson & Hirschi, 1986, p. 229), Blumstein and his collaborators come to the opposite conclusion. They suggested the finding that lambda is flat *is* evidence for their position and it is important because it shows that people do not slow down in crime frequency. Active offenders are active. The age-crime curve reflects decline in participation. In this way Gottfredson and Hirschi's best argument might have been a shot in their own foot.

One of Gottfredson and Hirschi's most searing critiques of the career criminal literature was that it cannot lead to sound policy. As noted above, identifying career criminals must by necessity occur after the fact and thus cannot be used for selective incapacitation. First Blumstein and colleagues argue that identifying career criminals does not necessarily mean we need to incapacitate them. If we could identify them early in their careers we may be able to direct rehabilitation or prevention programs toward them before they engage in a life of crime. That it is difficult to identify them prospectively does not mean we should not try. Selective incapacitation would be a more sensible policy than simply increasing incarceration rates for all offenders. This position seemingly contradicts earlier criminal career work that suggested selective incapacitation was not likely to bear fruit. The situation is clear, though, that rigorous analyses should dictate policy, not *a priori* beliefs. They come down hard on Gottfredson and Hirschi here: "Regardless of one's policy preferences about selective incapacitation, developing knowledge about criminal careers should be an important objective of research in criminology. Mocking such knowledge or railing against its pursuit, or obfuscating results because of one's policy preferences, strikes us as a fundamental assault on scholarship in criminology" (p. 27).

Finally, Blumstein and colleagues address the Gottfredson and Hirschi critique of longitudinal research. They admit longitudinal research has drawbacks but disagree that it is useless for establishing causality. They say: "Longitudinal data are most clearly superior to cross-sectional data in testing causal hypotheses, for two main reasons. One is that the time ordering of events can be determined more precisely in prospective than in retrospective longitudinal data, which makes it easier to resolve problems of causal order. The second is that there is better control of extraneous variables in longitudinal data, because each person acts as his own control" (p. 29). They turn Gottfredson and Hirschi's argument on its head and suggest that cross-sectional research can result in misleading conclusions (paying particular attention to Hirschi and Gottfredson's misinterpretation of the aggregate age-crime curve).

Gottfredson and Hirschi, in the same issue of *Criminology*, responded. The piece was considerably shorter than the previous two and simply suggested that criminologists would soon lose interest in the idea of criminal careers and career criminals. The paper was largely, though, a response to the essay described above. Gottfredson and Hirschi stated that Blumstein and colleagues' response did not resolve the issue and sidestepped "research whose conclusions argue against the application of career terminology" (Gottfredson & Hirschi, 1988, p. 38).

Gottfredson and Hirschi begin with a dissection of the term "career." They say that it is a fine concept for occupations, but ill-equipped to describe crime. They note that the Gluecks were the first to talk about criminal careers and it seemed novel at the time— but now (the 1980s) we know enough about crime to know that criminals do not operate in anything resembling a career. To Gottfredson and Hirschi, the sticking point seems to have been in the notion that careers imply specialization. That is, offenders would learn a trade and commit one type of crime over their career. The research, they say, contradicts this idea (note, though, we do not see anywhere that Blumstein and colleagues interpret the term career this way, and so in our view Gottfredson and Hirschi's complaint seems semantic).

Gottfredson and Hirschi next turn to whether differentiating between participation and frequency is defensible on logical and empirical grounds. They say that what really matters is distinguishing between offenders and non-offenders, not between an offender who commits two crimes per year and one who commits seven. They then analyze Hirschi's Richmond Youth Project study (Hirschi, 1969/2009) and produce calculations for incidence, participation, and lambda. Then Gottfredson and Hirschi suggest that lambda is nothing more than a count of offending, and as such "it would hardly seem to justify its own research agenda" (p. 42). A key point is that lambda, as typically measured, provides *one* overall measure for a group and thus cannot be used to examine variation across that group (to identify, for example, career criminals).

They then tackle the idea that criminal career dimensions may have different correlates. Using race, smoking, drinking, delinquent peers, Grade Point Average, and dating, Gottfredson and Hirschi argue that there is no meaningful difference in the correlations of these variables by incidence, participation, and lambda. They find largely the same thing when dividing the sample up between serious and less serious offenses.

Again, the subject of age comes up. Gottfredson and Hirschi argue that Blumstein, Farrington, and other criminal career researchers are focused on their invariance hypothesis, even though if proven wrong it would not necessarily support the criminal career idea. They say that the criticism that there is variation in the age-crime curve over time is not the issue—it is that those variations are unexplained. They note "it is an unreasonable caricature of our position to suggest that it denies the possibility of change in the level of crime between 1965 and 1980 or trivial shifts in the modal age for a particular 'crime type'" (p. 48). It comes down to perception: "We tend to see similarity where they see difference" (p. 48). With respect to whether the age-crime curve illustrates a decline in crime frequency or participation, Gottfredson and Hirschi do not fall back on data analysis but rely on the words of other scholars (such as the Gluecks) who were clear that they found criminality declined with age, not just participation.

Finally, Blumstein, Cohen, and Farrington (1988) in the same issue of *Criminology* responded one last time. With three papers now in the fold, things start to get a little confusing in keeping track of who said what. Blumstein et al. (1988b) argue that Gottfredson and Hirschi misunderstand their criminal career terminology; they also take on Gottfredson and Hirschi's (1987) critique of longitudinal methods.

First, in explaining dimensions of the criminal career, Blumstein et al. (1988b) suggest that "it has become clear that they [Gottfredson and Hirschi] do not understand the basic constructs and the conceptual issues involved in using those constructs. . . . We will try one more time to clarify the conceptual distinction that is at the heart of a criminal career framework" (p. 58). They then define participation and frequency, or lambda, suggesting that Gottfredson and Hirschi mistake lambda for a frequency distribution, not a rate of offending per time. The numbers Gottfredson and Hirschi (1988) present in their Table 1, then, are not lambdas, to Blumstein and colleagues.

Blumstein and colleagues also deny ignoring research contrary to their framework. They say, rather, they interpret such research differently than do Gottfredson and Hirschi. For example, they say that the career nomenclature says nothing about specialization or trajectories of offending, as Gottfredson and Hirschi claimed. They also say, with respect to correlates, that while we may know about predictors of participation/incidence, "Few researchers have even attempted to measure the correlates of λ" (p. 60). Using Farrington's Cambridge Study in Delinquent Development data, they find that the correlates of participation are different than those of lambda. They even suggest that Gottfredson and Hirschi's own calculations using the Richmond data do not show support for the thesis that the correlates of participation are the same as for lambda.

On to age. Blumstein and colleagues remain steadfast that what declines with age is not frequency, or lambda, but participation. Further, the only way to know whether crime or participation declines over time is to decompose the criminal career into dimensions, which Gottfredson and Hirschi do not find value in doing. Blumstein and colleagues also note that the reason they harp on the invariance hypothesis is because the only way to know what causes variation in age-crime curves over time is to find variation in such curves.

Next Blumstein and company take on the budding theory Gottfredson and Hirschi are building. Sensibly they question how their theory can account or be reconciled with the age-crime curve if it is based on stability. They then surmise that what Gottfredson and Hirschi are building is a biological theory of crime. Such a theory, we suspect, would be anathema to the criminal careers approach that views different factors as having differential impacts across the life-span. Blumstein and other criminal career researchers simply do not believe that the same factors predict participation (or distinguish between offenders and non-offenders) and lambda.

With respect to methods, Blumstein et al. repeat their claims that longitudinal designs are useful for examining development of offending over time. This does not mean that cross-sectional designs should be tossed aside—each has its own merit. Prospective longitudinal studies are superior to retrospective ones (in which people are asked to remember events from the past) primarily due to memory/recall deficiencies. This is a common complaint of self-report surveys. They also disagree with Gottfredson and Hirschi that studies using observational designs are not valuable. To Blumstein et al. these designs can lead to hypotheses that can be tested in experiments. In addition, examining the natural development of behavior can be useful. Gottfredson and Hirschi had argued that longitudinal studies cannot improve upon causal inference from cross-sectional studies. Temporal ordering, correlation, and a lack of spuriousness were the keys to causality on which Gottfredson and Hirschi focused. Blumstein et al. say that these are fine for cross-sectional designs, but what longitudinal designs allow is an examination of whether changes in a particular variable lead to changes in another. Cross-sectional studies allow examination of variables that vary only between subjects; longitudinal studies permit the examination of variables that vary both between and within individuals, they say.

Interestingly, this 1988 issue of *Criminology* included papers by Charles Tittle and John Hagan and Alberto Palloni. Tittle's piece does a nice job of summarizing the various points of view and arguments made by the two camps. He wrote that both have taken extreme positions and neither has conceded much. Gottfredson and Hirschi are convinced that the age-crime curve is invariant when we don't have enough information to claim that, and Blumstein and colleagues are too quick to assert there is a chronic offender who does not slow down. He argued that part of the debate was unnecessary: for example, "whether longitudinal data are preferred over cross-sectional is something like asking whether hammers or saws are more useful to carpenters. Any overall choice between the two is likely to inhibit progress. Both are useful tools appropriate for specific jobs" (Tittle, 1988, p. 76).

With respect to theory, Tittle argued it is "astonishing" (p. 78) that Gottfredson and Hirschi would deny the theoretical relevance of the criminal career paradigm. It is also strange, he suggested, that Blumstein and colleagues avoided bringing theory to the table in the debate. Thus "We have theorists who refuse to theorize and we have researchers who acknowledge they should theorize but don't" (p. 78). In a foreshadowing of Moffitt's developmental taxonomy, Tittle said that the age-crime curve in the aggregate may tell us that most people decline in crime with age, but some (a small group) do not. He then wrote that labeling and social bond theory may be able to account for these divergent trajectories. His injection of theory into the debate was refreshing.

In the end Tittle awarded neither side with a medal, but simply said that they were being too stubborn. Hagan and Palloni (1988) take a different stance and try to show how the debate can be thought of in a different manner. They noted that both sides of the debate have political views and those views were shaping the discourse. Thus far the entire exchange had focused on street crimes to the exclusion of white-collar crimes, for example. Both sides of the debate have different biases that prevent them from seeing the possible intersections and common ground from which they could plant seeds of collaboration.

Hagan and Palloni then direct attention to what is known as "studies of the life-course" (p. 89). Rather than only examining parts of the life-course, researchers could and should study it in its entirety. They recommend using the term "social events" rather than "criminal careers." This, to Hagan and Palloni, would open up the research arena to a more comprehensive look at the lives of offenders and non-offenders. Thus examining lives over time and conceptualizing crimes as social events bridges the gap between the criminal career side and the criminal propensity side. How? Because such a focus would satisfy Blumstein and colleagues' desire to examine longitudinal sequences of offending and also satisfy Gottfredson and Hirschi's desire to not focus solely on those who commit many crimes over long periods of time.

It is interesting to note that part of the criminal career vs. criminal propensity debate did eventually find its way to a life-course perspective. There is now an entire subfield of criminology devoted to the life-course, complete with its own journal and division of the American Society of Criminology. From which of the two camps does this new life-course criminology derive? We will touch on that below, in the "tale-of-the-tape" section, but we will say here that the foremost proponents of life-course criminology (indeed, the scholars who developed that label) were two of Gottfredson and Hirschi's students.

POLICY IMPLICATIONS: SIDE-BY-SIDE

Criminal career

The research on criminal careers was meant to be specifically policy related. Understanding the dimensions of the criminal career, such as frequency, participation, and chronic offending, was in part intended to focus attention on where criminal justice programs can have the most impact. The policy that has received by far the most attention from the criminal career perspective is that of selective incapacitation. Even 30 years ago, before the term "mass incarceration" became ubiquitous in criminal justice writings, scholars recognized that the increasing rate of imprisonment in the US was not sustainable. Thus a call to simply increase incarceration overall was likely to fall on deaf ears. Perhaps, scholars surmised, a more targeted approach could work. That is, targeting those chronic offenders, for whom a long career was still ahead of them, seemed like a useful strategy. Perhaps it might also be profitable to target chronic hotspots of crime where those who engage in the most crime are likely to reside (for examples, refer to Braga, 2001).

The idea of selective incapacitation seems like a good one in theory, but falls apart at the level of implementation. As Gottfredson and Hirschi (1986) pointed out, it is not easy to identify career criminals until they have already led a life of crime. More recent work echoes this sentiment, noting that predicting such individuals in advance is notoriously difficult (Auerhahn, 1999). Variants of these policies—such as "three strikes and you are out" strategies, aimed at locking people up for life after a third (give or take) felony—also appear faulty, as research has indicated they do not impact crime (Stolzenberg & D'Alessio, 1997).

As mentioned above, however, the criminal career camp did not claim that the criminal justice system is the only policy arena consistent with their approach. It is not clear from their writings, though, what programs they would advocate. A review of both volumes of the 1986 criminal career report reveals mostly appeals to criminal justice policies. The report suggested that "prevention, career modification, and incapacitation" (p. 109) were the three strategies supported by the criminal career paradigm. The report did review prevention programs focused on families and schools, however, suggesting these would be consistent with the criminal career view, but then notes the research does "not establish that any approach tested to date effectively reduces subsequent criminal participation" (p. 113). The authors were no more optimistic of "career modification" programs meant to reduce recidivism. While they argued incapacitation could reduce crime, they were circumspect whether these approaches would have substantial effects and recommended targeted or selective strategies.

Criminal propensity

The criminal propensity camp spent little time in the 1980s discussing the development of crime and more time critiquing what they felt were misguided approaches. The genesis of the approach was the age and crime paper, which convinced Gottfredson and Hirschi that crime always declines with age and thus social variables are not likely to be of much importance after childhood. In 1990 Gottfredson and Hirschi spelled out their theoretical position much more clearly, arguing that self-control, an individual-level trait, is generally established by early childhood (age eight) and that it is the major cause of all crime. Self-control, they argued, is a relatively stable trait, meaning that, in absolute terms, self-control may fluctuate over the life-course but people high or low in self-control relative to others remain that way. Thus the best way to reduce crime is to instill self-control in people, starting in childhood.

Gottfredson and Hirschi (1990) wrote that parents instill self-control in their children by doing three things: 1) supervising or monitoring their children; 2) recognizing deviance; and 3) correcting deviant behavior. Prevention programs therefore should focus on parenting skills and helping parents with these tasks. Research suggests that parenting programs are effective in reducing antisocial behavior on the part of children (Farrington & Welsh, 2007), and that programs meant to increase self-control can also work (Piquero et al., 2010; 2016).

However, Gottfredson and Hirschi also felt that situational factors could reduce crime by preventing opportunity. They were not altogether clear on this point and later dismissed opportunity as an important variable (see Gottfredson & Hirschi, 2003). Yet it may be the case that situational approaches, such as situational crime prevention, may be advocated from the propensity perspective. Situational crime prevention refers to approaches to increase the effort and decrease the opportunity for criminal behavior. It is linked to the routine activities and rational choice theories in criminology; interestingly, in the 1980s Hirschi wrote on the compatibility of control and rational choice perspectives (Hirschi, 1986). Research does seem to indicate that situational crime prevention can reduce crime (Clarke, 1995).

CONCLUSION: TALE-OF-THE-TAPE

The "great debate" of criminal careers vs. criminal propensity was one of the most epic in all of criminology. Numerous pieces were written, responses to essays were quickly penned, and little love was lost between the two camps. Declaring a "winner" in this debate is also not a simple task primarily because the debate has not concluded; it has merely changed form. In many respects, criminal career research continues. Books and empirical studies continue to be published to this day examining the vista of concepts Blumstein and colleagues introduced. However, in another sense the criminal career perspective has morphed. As Hagan and Palloni (1988) recommended, scholars began to turn to life-course studies, examining lives over time, including pathways, trajectories, and turning points. As we hinted at above, the two scholars most responsible for this turn were Robert Sampson and John Laub, both students at the University of Albany when Hirschi and Gottfredson were professors there. Their "life-course criminology" does not necessarily focus on frequency and prevalence, but rather pays attention to the longitudinal sequence of offending over time, noting that the age-crime curve is similar for most offenders (in that they all desist) but that social factors do predict changes in trajectories. In fact Sampson and Laub have taken seriously the criminal career call to examine different facets of the criminal career and have contributed a wealth of information to desistance from crime (see Laub & Sampson, 2001).

On the other side of the debate, as mentioned, the criminal propensity perspective matured into the "self-control" view. In 1990 Gottfredson and Hirschi published *A General Theory of Crime* which put together the theory that they had been building in large part in their contributions to the criminal career debate. This theory, now nearly 30 years old, remains one of the most popular in all of criminology. Tests of the theory,

TABLE 4.2 TALE-OF-THE-TAPE. PROPENSITY THEORIES VS. CRIMINAL CAREERS

Theory	Propensity theories	Criminal careers
Theorists	Travis Hirschi; Michael Gottfredson	Al Blumstein; David Farrington; Jacqueline Cohen; Joan Petersilia
Main arguments	Crime is natural, people will engage in it unless they are restrained; there are individual-level characteristics that are persistent across the life-course that lead to crime	Criminal careers contain several components; each component should be studied separately; there is both continuity and change over time in behavior
Period of popularity	1980s–present	1980s–present
Seminal pieces	*A General Theory of Crime* (Gottfredson & Hirschi); various *Criminology* articles	*Criminal Careers and Career Criminals* (Blumstein and colleagues); various *Criminology* articles
WINNER		✓

refinements, and improved methodologies are published on a regular basis. A Google Scholar search of "self-control and crime" produces 1,960,000 results.

While much support has been garnered for the theory, with most tests of self-control finding some statistical relationship with crime and what the authors call "analogous acts," as we noted at the conclusion of the last chapter the strength of that research is not altogether impressive. Several of the pronouncements regarding social factors, the stability of self-control, and the origins of self-control remain controversial and empirically less supported (see Rocque, Posick, & Piquero, 2016). Nonetheless, it seems fair to say that the criminal propensity side of the debate was successful in refocusing criminology on individual traits and identified an important correlate (if not cause) of crime and delinquency.

Both sides of this battle have not withered and died, but remain, in their own ways, vibrant. Both have, by any measure, had remarkable longevity in the field. Yet when push comes to shove we would argue that the criminal career perspective must be declared the winner. Part of this judgement comes from the new findings that continue to be published using the dimensions identified 30 years ago; part of the judgement comes from the recognition that the criminal career framework spurred a large amount of theoretical and methodological advancements in the field. In the end there are very important changes, both in biology and the social environment, that alter over time and vary with criminality (see Rocque & Posick, 2017).

For example, one of the more popular analytic techniques of the last 20 years, group-based trajectory modeling, was developed in part to examine criminal careers. Nagin and Land (1993) introduced the technique, which allows researchers to identify a number of groups (including chronic offenders) in a sample and plot their trajectories over time. Other analytic techniques have become popular in criminology in order to examine crime over the life-course, such as multi-level modeling. The use of the life event calendar (Roberts & Horney, 2010) is also an advancement that attempts to capture experiences of individuals over the life-course. All of these methods require longitudinal data, data which the propensity camp was adamant were not necessary.

With respect to theory, several fresh perspectives have taken shape since the criminal career debate, all with a focus on explaining crime over time. Perhaps foremost among these is Sampson and Laub's (1993) age-graded theory of informal social controls, which views crime from childhood through adulthood to be a result of a lack of social ties from family and other social agents. In addition, desistance from crime has become a field of study on its own, complete with a body of research and theory to explain it (see Rocque, 2017).

In other words, it appears that while the criminal propensity perspective is valuable, it overly simplifies the world. And while self-control theory remains of interest and is likely an important part of the criminal equation, the criminal career perspective has arguably led to more developments in the world of criminology—only some of which we touched upon here. We have no doubt both camps will continue to inspire new theoretical and empirical work in the pursuit of understanding crime and antisocial behavior. This can only be viewed as a positive. However, the edge, even if slight, we give to the criminal career perspective.

One scholar who has been involved in criminal career and propensity research is Alex Piquero. In a conversation,[1] he said that he entered graduate school after the criminal career debate of the 1980s, "but Gottfredson and Hirschi's book had just come out and then Moffitt's piece came out in 1993." He also took a course with Ray Paternoster on testing theory and he and his friends wrote papers examining the criminal career. When asked who he thought "won" the debate, he claimed neither has: "No side has won, and no side will ever win. The great thing about that debate is that it touches theory, policy, and methods—and that last one is very important." In the end he favors a "mixed perspective, one that lies within the spirit of Sampson and Laub's perspective. I think there are aspects of both continuity and change that support and refute, at the same time, both perspectives."

In the next chapter we turn to a focus on theory building and testing. In the 1970s, with theoretical developments reaching new heights, there came a point in criminology in which scholars felt something must be done. Should we combine theories to reduce their number? Subject them to a fight to the death? Should theories be parsimonious in order to be more useful, or more sophisticated to account for the complexity of human behavior? While the origins of these debates began long ago, they continue to this day.

NOTE

1   Email conversation, July 5, 2017.

Who is right?
Theory testing and construction in criminology

5

CHAPTER OUTLINE

THERE ARE PICKY EATERS, and then there are *picky* eaters. Some people don't like veggies, others don't enjoy seafood. However, for some it isn't so much types of food that matter but combinations of food or whether different types of food should even touch each other. We might call these the "no mixing" crowd. If you are eating greens with potatoes and steak, they each would need to be in their own compartments and eaten separately. Researchers have only begun to look at this phenomenon, but it is more common than one might expect.[1]

According to Hana Zickgraf, who has studied this form of eating, it is a "rigidity of presentation" that leads some to reject "foods that have touched other foods." In one study she conducted, more than a quarter of "picky eaters" would not allow different foods to touch. Yet, she says, it may not just be about how the food looks on the plate, but the mixture of flavors together. Again, Zickgraf:

> Another possibility is that it isn't about how the food looks but about being very sensitive to small differences in taste; picky eaters might notice—or worry that they will notice—slight transfers of flavor from one food to another. It is very common for picky eaters to not like mixed foods like salads, soups, or stir-fries. If two foods touched to the extent that they really mingled, most picky eaters would probably be bothered. Many picky eaters don't even like different foods to mix in their mouths, and some eat the different foods on their plate one at a time.

So here we have a situation in which some people feel that foods are meant to be separate, to stand on their own. If you like to eat collard greens, you want to eat them alone. Any sort of mixing of greens and, say, nuts would denigrate not only the greens but also the nuts. The whole is not more than the sum of its parts.

Of course, with food, some things go together better than others. A lot of folks enjoy spaghetti and meatballs, which combines noodles, meat, spices, and tomatoes among other things. Yet some foods just do not belong together—ketchup and ice cream, for example. They are simply too different in terms of taste, texture, and purpose. Putting them together creates an incoherent whole that leaves everyone worse off. One non-mixer, a news person for Charlotte's WLNK radio station, discussed his particular quirks. "I eat very few different foods," Chad Bowar tells us. "When it comes to main courses it's basically steak, hamburger, chicken, and hot dogs. No ethnic foods at all. I also don't use condiments. Everything is plain: no ketchup, no cheese, etc. No mixing, so that means pizza, soup, salads, sandwiches, etc. are out. I also don't like my foods to be touching on the plate, which of course creates mixing."[2]

Why this digression into food preferences? There's a parallel with criminological theory—some people like mixing, others don't. Some scholars believe that a dish served with a dash of social learning and a heaping of social control, cooked at just the right temperature, produces a more powerful theoretical recipe of behavior. Others, however, are picky theorists—they oppose any mixing and prefer theories to remain "separate and unequal" (Hirschi, 1979). Does putting together different theories result in inedible mush? Or does it help us build more comprehensive theories? That is the topic of this chapter. Theoretical integration, as a specific focus in criminology, emerged in the 1970s as a way to improve existing theoretical accounts and reduce the sheer number of theories that exist. It seemed intuitive but was met with instant resistance. The debate has been raging ever since.

TO MIX OR NOT TO MIX? THAT IS THE (THEORETICAL) QUESTION

To this point in the book we have given the impression that only a few theoretical perspectives have dominated criminology. We have spent time on control and social learning theory, with a bit of strain theory sprinkled in. A field with only three theories might be viewed as a highly organized field. Unfortunately, theoretical organization and order have not characterized criminology for decades, if ever. By the 1990s so many unique theories and variations of others were on the criminological landscape that it began to be difficult to keep track. Several scholars lamented this state of affairs (Bernard, 1990; Bernard & Snipes, 1996) and proposed changes. One of these included theoretical integration, meant to reduce the raw number of theories in the field by taking disparate theories and combining them into a coherent whole.

Theoretical integration includes the combining of distinct perspectives into one comprehensive theory of crime. One of the first formal attempts at theoretical integration was proffered by Delbert Elliott and his associates in 1979. We will focus on this piece shortly. However, informal integrations were prevalent throughout the 20th century. In *Delinquency and Opportunity*, Richard Cloward and Lloyd Ohlin combined insight from Sutherland's differential association, Merton's anomie theory, and Shaw and McKay's social disorganization. They explicitly state in the introduction that their theory of gangs draws ". . . upon two theoretical perspectives. The first, initiated by Emile Durkheim and greatly extended by Robert K. Merton, focuses largely upon the sources of pressure that can lead to deviance. The second, developed by Clifford R. Shaw, Henry D. McKay, and Edwin H. Sutherland, contains germinal ideas about the way in which features of the social structure regulate the selection and evolution of deviant solutions" (Cloward & Ohlin, 1960, p. x).

Shaw and McKay themselves later combined elements of social control and social learning. They argued (1972) that breakdowns in social institutions made it more difficult for communities to regulate behavior. As we saw from Kornhauser's interpretation of social disorganization in Chapter 3, this is a pure control model. However, it was not the entire story of how delinquency comes about for Shaw and McKay. They wrote that "Children living in such communities are exposed to a variety of contradictory standards and forms of behavior rather than to a relatively consistent and conventional pattern. . . . A boy may be familiar with, or exposed to, either the system of conventional activities or the system of criminal activities, or both. . . . His attitudes and habits will be formed largely in accordance with the extent to which he participates in and becomes identified with one or the other of these several types of groups" (Shaw & McKay, 1972, p. 172). This is very clearly the same perspective espoused by Sutherland in his differential association theory. Shaw and McKay note as much.

Other theoretical frameworks in the 20th century also combined perspectives. In 1955 Albert Cohen's classic *Delinquent Boys: The Culture of the Gang* made the case that delinquent subcultures are a primary cause of antisocial behavior. The idea of the delinquent subculture is that there are groups of individuals with different values which allow or even promote antisocial behavior—another social learning/differential association perspective. Yet what separated Cohen's account was that he sought to explain the origins of the delinquent subcultures. For this part of the theory he relied on a strain explanation. Delinquent boys, to Cohen, formed oppositional subcultures because they were unable or unequipped to attain markers of middle class status, such as good grades. They became frustrated with this blockage of their goals and decided to flip middle class morality on its head by adopting values opposed to it (for example, valuing toughness as opposed to scholarship). Cloward and Ohlin (1960) followed with a different version of a strain/social learning theory, applied to the inner city. They viewed both legitimate and criminal opportunities as potentially blocked by structural constraints (not everyone can just become a drug dealer if they get laid-off from their legitimate employer). Therefore there is a more complicated process by which people fall into the categories outlined by Merton and others.

Sykes and Matza's (1957) techniques of neutralization theory has been the subject of a criminological theory tug of war since its inception. Is it a learning theory? Akers (2009), among others, has argued that the purpose of Sykes and Matza's list of five neutralizations was to fill in the "rationalizations" that are learned in a process of differential association, spelled out by Sutherland. Others have made the case that these neutralizations represent a version of control theory, showing how delinquency can spring forth if one justifies away the social regulations typically holding individuals back (see Hirschi's 1969 concept of "belief," for example). It seems fair to say that techniques of neutralization, as a theory, represents an integration of learning and control theories. Sykes and Matza were clear, for example, in the beginning of their essay that "It is now largely agreed that delinquent behavior, like most social behavior, is learned and that it is learned in the process of social interaction" (p. 664). The techniques of neutralization, then, may be learned. But they go on to criticize the view that crime is learned and valued and show that many delinquents feel guilt and are influenced by the prosocial moral order. Neutralizations then "free" them to deviate. So neutralizations are learned but also lift restraint—a social learning/control theory integration.

Thus, when the work of Delbert Elliott, Suzanne Ageton, and Rachelle Canter came on to the scene in 1979, theoretical integration was not a new exercise. Parts of theories or perspectives had been combined for years. But they were more explicit about it (even calling their theory "integrated"[3]). In other words, Elliott and colleagues specifically said that they were combining disparate theories—strain, control, and learning—into one, more comprehensive, whole. Their paper, "An Integrated Theoretical Perspective on Delinquent Behavior," was published in the *Journal of Research in Crime and Delinquency*. The authors started from the premise that criminological theory attempting to explain antisocial behavior was stagnant. Part of the reason why theory had not advanced in the last 20 years, they said, was the recent focus on labeling, which diverted attention away from criminals and on to the state. Why certain people get tagged and labeled as criminal and others don't was the focus. In addition, Elliott and colleagues said most theories at the time presupposed that criminals came from the lower classes. This was so because most data used to formulate theories came from official sources (for example, prison records and arrest statistics). However, self-report surveys in the 1970s demonstrated that class was not as intrinsically tied to crime as criminologists had thought.

After reviewing integrations of strain and learning theories (such as Cloward & Ohlin's in 1960), Elliott and colleagues argue that these theories are improved, but still leave much to be explained. They suggest that the traditional strain approach—that lack of resources (among the lower classes) leads to an inability to obtain goals (strain), and thus to crime as a way to improvise goal attainment—is made more powerful when one enters deviant groups or associations into the equation. This theoretical integration assumes that the strain by itself is not enough to lead to crime—strain in the absence of delinquent role models will not lead to antisocial behavior. But these models are not enough either, they argue.

Thus Elliott and colleagues turn to control theories to help fill in the gaps. Their model begins with control logic, suggesting that strong relationships and socialization experiences are the first link in the chain—if these bonds are weak, deviance will result. But they could be strengthened in adolescence through positive social experiences. If bonds are weak to begin with, and individuals begin to associate with delinquent peers, they are likely to become delinquent themselves. If strong bonds are established initially, they may be weakened later by such things as involvement in the criminal justice system or strain. Weak bonds, however, are not likely by themselves to lead to crime. Thus, in the absence of delinquent peers, crime has a low probability of occurring. They say that most adolescents have been exposed to criminal norms, but most do not internalize or engage in them.

> Those committed to conventional goals, although they may have been exposed to and learned some delinquent behaviors, should not establish patterns of such behavior unless (1) their ties to the conventional social order are neutralized through some attenuating experiences and (2) they are participating in a social context in which delinquent behavior is rewarded (Elliott et al., 1979, p. 14).

It is interesting to note that in Elliott and colleagues' formulation each theory retains its individual logic (that is, there are direct links from bonds to crime, from strain to crime, and so forth) but other perspectives are added to account for situations in which individual theoretical pathways are insufficient. However, they argue that there are "two dominant etiological paths to delinquency" in their theory (p. 17). First is the social bond→social learning path in which weak bonds lead to crime/delinquency through delinquent peers (they argue that weak bonds are not enough to explain crime on their own). The second is the strain→social learning path in which blocked opportunities lead to strain, which leads to delinquency via delinquent peers. In this second path, bonds are initially strong—the strain weakens them.

On its face, this new formulation makes sense. Elliott and colleagues note that, when looked at separately, control and strain theories do not really explain enough of the variance in crime. This, to them, indicates that other pathways are needed. Weak bonds may lead to crime without any further motivation, but perhaps additional motivation is needed for some (most?). Not everyone who has poor relationships with their families will automatically turn to crime, for example. What explains the difference between a person with poor bonds who does not engage with crime and a similarly situated person who does? The answer, exposure to delinquent norms or groups.

Given our extensive discussion in Chapter 3 of assumptions of human nature inherent in theories, one may argue that Elliott and his collaborators must have overlooked them. After all, each of the three theories they integrate paints a vastly different picture of what people are really like. They did not overlook those assumptions, but discussed them rather clearly throughout. However, they did not seem to address the inconsistencies between the theories in these assumptions.

That shortcoming was seized upon in a response article by Travis Hirschi. His essay, entitled "Separate and Unequal is Better," argued that theories with different assumptions cannot be mixed. That Elliott and colleagues recognize this but still go forward is interesting to Hirschi. "Their solution," Hirschi noted, "is to use the terms and ignore the claims of control theory. This allows them to divide the child in two, giving the larger half to differential association and the remainder to strain theory" (Hirschi, 1979, p. 34).

Hirschi then gave a name to several types of theoretical integration. The first he called "end-to-end." End-to-end theoretical integration involves putting theories together such that the variables of one theory lead to the variables of the other, which then leads to delinquency. As Hirschi wrote, "The dependent variables of prior theories become the independent variables of subsequent theories." Yet this simply describes the process and does not do much to improve theories' ability to explain delinquency, he argued, because in effect the subsequent theories mediate the prior ones. Thus the last theory in the causal chain is really the theory that matters. So, to Hirschi, efforts such as Elliott's and others are end-to-end integrations implying that social learning is really the theory that explains crime.

Side-by-side integration is a bit different. Here theories are used to explain phenomenon, but the assumption is not that each theory can explain all phenomena (in other words, there are no "general" theories of crime). Certain theories explain some crimes or behaviors, other theories are better suited to explain different behaviors. In this way the explanatory power of theories can be increased. Hirschi lamented, though, that exercises to figure out how best to divide up behaviors among theories have thus far failed. Different classes of behavior do not need different theories.

Finally, Hirschi described up-and-down integration. In this form of integration, "partial theories become specific applications of a general theory of deviance" (p. 36). Up-and-down integration basically means that one theory, or general framework, is said to subsume other, less comprehensive, theories under its umbrella. The general theory, according to the theorists, can account for the other processes involved in the partial theories. Hirschi, not surprisingly, finds this exercise to be unscientific.

In the end Hirschi disavowed all theoretical integration, but not only because it forces together perspectives with vastly different assumptions of human nature. He also thought that the best way to handle different theories is not to integrate them but subject them to empirical competition—a winner takes all approach. He argued, "I think we should be pleased to find that attainment of the integrationist's goal is so difficult. A 'successful' integration would destroy the healthy competition among ideas that has made the field of delinquency one of the most interesting and exciting fields in sociology for some time" (p. 37).

James F. Short Jr. (1979) provided the third essay in the issue, touching on both sides of the integration debate. Short began by sharing Elliott and colleagues' view that theory in criminology was stagnant. Integration is more complex than their illustration. For example, Short argued, the three theories Elliott and his colleagues combine—strain, learning, and control—all have relevance for social structures and crime rates (macro level), yet the authors do not discuss how their theory addresses this level of explanation. Nor, he wrote, do they attend to microsociological, situational processes. And finally the theory seemed rather blunt, not recognizing that processes and the impact of theoretical variables may differ by social status (e.g., class, race, gender). It wasn't necessarily that he opposed theoretical integration per se, but that this particular one fell short.

And so the lines were set in this debate: on the one side, scholars argued that putting theories together, mixing them up, would create a more comprehensive and powerful theoretical account of crime. On the other side, Hirschi was advocating a different approach. Keep theories separate, do not degrade them by arguing that they don't say what they actually say about human beings, and let the spoils go to the victor. This theoretical competition approach was demonstrated well in Hirschi's 1969 *Causes of Delinquency* in which he set strain, differential association, and control theories against one another with survey data, with control theory (largely) claiming victory. Kornhauser (1978) had done the same, only instead of using survey data she interrogated the logical consistency of the theories and examined how they fared against extant evidence.

The debate lay somewhat dormant through much of the 1980s. However, two criminologists, Frank Pearson and Neil Weiner, renewed interest in the idea of integration in 1985 with their article in *The Journal of Criminal Law & Criminology*. Pearson and Weiner (1985) took stock of criminological theory over the course of the 20th century and found one thing that most would not dispute—there are too many theories and no real mechanisms to trim the fat. In a very real sense, Hirschi's concept of theoretical competition had not worked, since theories that "lost" hung around (more on this argument below). What Pearson and Weiner were concerned with, however, was that criminology seemed to be a field of study under many different disciplines, and that this led to disorganization in criminological thinking. The specters of Michael and Adler from 50 years prior, who lamented that criminology lacked a unifying and central perspective, still haunted the field.

So Pearson and Weiner set out to combine the major theories in criminology into one holistic perspective. But they were not, as most attempts had done to that point, satisfied with integrating two or three theories. Instead they looked at the field and picked out the most cited theories and started from there. In 1985, what were the most influential criminological theories? Pearson and Weiner (1985, p. 118) wrote that 13 had received the most citations:

1. social learning
2. differential association
3. negative labeling
4. social control
5. deterrence
6. economic
7. routine activities
8. neutralization
9. relative deprivation
10. strain
11. normative (culture) conflict
12. Marxist-critical/group conflict
13. generalized strain and normative conflict

Routine activities theory to that point had not been cited as highly as the others, but Pearson and Weiner felt it was important to include.

The reason they argued that integration was useful on a grand scale was that: a) it would expose more criminologists to theories with which they may be unfamiliar; and b) it would allow dissection of theories into their components or concepts. Boiling theories down to their core concepts this way would then strip them of the diametrically opposed assumptions of human nature that make integration untenable. For example, differential association/social learning theory utilizes concepts such as differential association, reinforcement, definitions, and imitation—put together, the picture the theory paints is of malleable humans. But the concept of deviant peers, on its own, says nothing about human nature. It's simply a concept that can be translated into a variable, which is often found to be statistically related to crime.

It should be noted that, in some ways, the exercise Pearson and Weiner were advocating was not *theoretical* integration but "conceptual integration" (Pearson & Weiner, 1985, p. 119). Thus it may not be subject to the same shortcomings Hirschi identified related to theoretical integration. Yet, as he argued theoretical integrationists are wont to do, Pearson and Weiner seemed to use the terms but ignore the claims of conceptual integration. In other words, while they wrote of simply integrating concepts, they go on to stipulate that "Social learning theory is the main component of the foundation" of their integration (p. 119). If it is social learning *theory* that is the basis of their integration, then the integration remains open to logical inconsistency critiques.

Pearson and Weiner's theory had both macro and micro components and incorporated internal and external factors. On the internal micro level, utility (from rewards or punishments), which involves deprivation and demand, behavioral skill, rules of expedience, and rules of morality are concepts that influence behavior. On the external micro level, they listed opportunities and resources. The external factors also included utility reception and information acquisition. The macro-level factors were beliefs about sanctioning practices, utilities, opportunities, and rules of expediency and morality. They then showed from which theories each of these concepts were derived. For example, utility demand is associated with differential association, negative labeling, social bond, economic, deterrence, routine activities, relative deprivation, strain, and Marxist theories. The theory, boiled down to its core though, assumes that behavior that is learned and reinforced will occur.

In the same year Elliott published a chapter in *Theoretical Methods in Criminology* in which he addressed theoretical integration and arguments against it. He wrote that it was time to move on from the past practice of theoretical competition, which never really killed theories anyway. More bang for the buck was likely to be had from efforts to bring theories together to increase explanatory power. One of the reasons theoretical competition seemed useful in prior years, he said, is because univariate, cross-sectional analyses gave the pretense that theoretical variables were strongly related to crime and some variables had stronger relationships than others. Yet with multivariate and longitudinal analyses we see that certain relationships disappear when controlling for important factors and, worse, "the level of explained variance attributable to separate theories is embarrassingly low" (Elliott, 1985, p. 125).

For Elliott, theoretical integration moves beyond this simplistic approach. It does not require there to be one primary or sole factor that explains criminal conduct. Theoretical integration suggests "that there are multiple variables involved in the etiology of the same type of behavior; that there may be more than one set of causal conditions sufficient for explaining involvement in a given behavior; and that there may be more than one temporal ordering for a given set of predictors" (p. 127). He was very clear, though, on the goal of integration: "to increase explanatory power" (p. 128).

Elliott suggested that theoretical integration is distinct from "mixed models" because the former must try to "reconcile" competing assumptions made by constituent theories (p. 130). These approaches are similar to the multi-factor perspectives so disdained by

Sutherland (and discussed in Chapter 2). So the task at hand for the integrationist is to make sense of theories that paint different pictures of humans, before using those theories to develop a coherent explanation. He illustrated this process with control theories. Some have integrated control with learning theories and simply discarded the human nature assumption of control theories—that we are all naturally inclined to antisocial and selfish behavior. This allows control theories to be logically consistent with learning theories, but one might wonder why social bonds would prevent misbehavior if there were no natural inclinations in the first place. Not all theoretical integrations, Elliott wrote, have adequately dealt with competing assumptions.

Next, Elliott addressed Hirschi's (1979) critique of integration in criminological theories. With regard to Hirschi's arguments against side-by-side integration, Elliott wrote that this form of integration does not necessarily ignore theoretical assumptions (they must be reconciled), and that it does not rely on simply broadening the class of behaviors being explained. He says "Hirschi's position appears to reflect the rather limited perspective on multiple causation discussed earlier" (p. 132).

Recall Hirschi's view that, in end-to-end integration, the theorist must choose which theoretical approach or factor really matters. Prior variables in the sequence cannot be causes because they are explained by later ones. To Elliott this represents the mindset of a theoretical competitor. Distal causes, he argues, are just as important to the developmental sequence, and may be vital for crime prevention in the first instance. If self-control leads to crime, we need to know what influences self-control (e.g., parenting practices) even if those influencers aren't "directly" related to crime. In any case, Elliott wrote, "Hirschi's concern that this form of integration might discount or diminish the significance of some particular theoretical perspective is both uncharacteristic of his general approach to theory testing and a questionable basis for rejecting this form of integration" (p. 133). Consistent with Pearson and Weiner's approach, Elliott suggested end-to-end integrations have put variables together from various theories but have not laid the full theories themselves end-to-end. Thus these may be more similar to the notion of conceptual integration.

Finally, Elliott tackled the critique of up-and-down integration. Hirschi had suggested that this form of integration requires the theorist to assume numerous incomplete theories had validity in order for the larger perspective to work. Elliott said this was fair, but the theorist must demonstrate empirical validity; it's not enough to assume it isn't there. He argued that in the literature there does not appear to be many cases of integrations being proposed with elements of disproven theories, however. This form of integration appears to have been the least commonly attempted at the time.

Elliott then reviewed attempts to integrate theories and explained variance. In general, adding components of several theories does increase the explained variance. He noted one example in which Matsueda argued that adding social control variables to a social learning model did not improve explanation. Using data from the National Youth Survey, Elliott showed how explained variance changes with the addition of different theories. For example, adding social control variables to strain increases the explained variance by 10.3 percent. Adding social disorganization to strain and social control adds 1.3 percent explained variance. The total model, with strain, control, learning, and disorganization, explains 36.4 percent of the variance in delinquency. He concluded that theoretical integration has been somewhat successful and will continue to evolve, pointing to inroads for reciprocal integrations in which multiple directions of causality are posited.

ALBANY CONFERENCE AND INTEGRATION BOOK

In May 1987 several luminaries in the field of criminology organized a conference at the State University of New York at Albany to discuss this issue of theoretical integration. Was it worth it? What did it look like? Are there other approaches to consider? The presentations at the conference were then turned into a classic criminological book, *Theoretical Integration in the Study of Deviance and Crime: Problems and Prospects*, edited by Steven Messner, Marvin Krohn, and Allen Liska. The book included 18 chapters and covered numerous theoretical integration issues. Macro integration, micro integration, cross-level integration, and arguments for and against it were just some of the topics covered by the book. In addition to Hirschi and Elliott exchanging their ideas on integration, other well-known criminologists had chapters, including Charles Wellford, Charles Tittle, Peggy Giordano, James Short Jr., Ronald Akers, Robert Bursik, and John Hagan.

The first chapter in the book offered an introduction to the issue of theoretical integration, including the types that have been covered in this chapter, and various arguments that had been made. In addition, they described one of the types of integration that had not received much attention to that point: cross-level integration. Here macro theoretical factors are integrated with micro factors to create a theory that can explain crime at both levels. They also reviewed the two dominant modes of theorizing in criminology—competition and integration. Both aim at reducing the number of theories and clarifying the causes of crime. Competition suggests that the best way to trim the fat is to pit theories against one another.

Integrationists reply that this is all well and good, but it hasn't worked and cannot work because our theories are just too weak to begin with. Theories also are simply not that diverse, they say. If a test shows that bonds have a correlation with crime of .45, and social learning variables have a correlation of .60, who "wins?" Sure, social learning variables have a larger correlation, but can we really just throw away the bonds, which have a moderate relationship with crime? The only way forward, therefore, is to combine them, which will: 1) reduce the number of theories; and 2) increase explanatory power.

Liska, Krohn, & Messner (1989), in the introduction to the book, suggested that both strategies seem to have drawbacks and benefits. In this way, to date, there had not been a clear way forward, but they see more potential in the integration path. They then offered further explication of the three types of integration Hirschi (1979) had identified. One clarification of Hirschi's notion of up-and-down integration was to differentiate between theoretical reduction and theoretical synthesis. In reduction, the theorist sees "that theory A contains more abstract or general assumptions than theory B and, therefore, that key parts of theory B can be accommodated within the structure of theory A." Synthesis "can be done by abstracting more general assumptions from theories A and B, allowing parts of both theories to be incorporated into a new theory C" (Liska et al., 1989, p. 10).

Liska and colleagues suggested that what Pearson and Weiner called "conceptual integration" is not particularly useful if one is using concepts to build a larger propositional framework. Concepts may be put together willy-nilly, but they must be logically consistent for a theory to work. This form of integration becomes deductive integration, related to the up-and-down approach.

In addition to theoretical competition, the camp that opposes theoretical integration also favors what is called theoretical elaboration. In theoretical elaboration existing theories are continually refined, tested, improved, and developed. The theorists who support this type of move are Travis Hirschi, Terrence Thornberry, and Robert Meier. In short, they are arguing that we have done so little work on the existing theories, we know so little about their potential, that combining them into a larger whole seems "premature" (Liska et al., 1989, p. 16). In support of holding off on integration, Liska and colleagues agreed that often integrationists have produced theories with little logical consistency. Integrationists, they argued, must be aware of and address this part of the exercise.

In favor of integration

The book's substantive chapters began with an essay by Ronald Akers. Akers, by 1989, had been working on his social learning theory for more than 20 years. His goal in this piece was to show how concepts from other theories could be viewed within a social learning perspective. In other words, other concepts could be subsumed under his own theory in an up-and-down approach. Akers' essay is a classic, which introduced several terms into the theoretical integration debate. He said that his integration efforts may be called "theoretical imperialism." He also suggested that integration that does not attend to assumptions results in "theoretical mush" and that he was "accused of theoretical illiteracy" for earlier integration attempts (p. 24).

The main argument Akers put forth was that theories in criminology are often "different in name only" (p. 25). This is unproductive for the field. He also wrote that the critique of integration that rests on the notion of "contradictory propositions from two theories" is not a problem because "one is bound to be empirically wrong; thus, it can be dropped in the integration" (p. 25). For him, social learning represents the foundation for all criminological theories. He illustrated this idea using social control and strain/anomie theories.

First, he makes clear that his intention was integration in the sense of "subsuming the concepts of one theory under another, or both under more general concepts" (p. 31). This is clearly the up-and-down form of integration. To show how concepts can be subsumed, he focused on bonds. For example, the bond of belief, to Akers, is a learning variable, a reformulation of definitions. Belief in the validity of the law is a definition unfavorable to the law. With respect to commitment, Akers wrote that this is a form of reinforcement, much like punishment. If one does not commit crimes because of the fear of losing something, that person is being negatively reinforced. The same, he said, was true of involvement. For attachment, the related concept was differential association. The difference for Akers was that the effect of attachment varied by the type of person one was attached to—attachments to prosocial people will produce prosocial behavior and attachments to antisocial people will produce antisocial behavior. Hirschi's understanding of attachments was that the type of person did not matter. Hirschi also wrote of attachments as psychological supervision, meaning that they provided a conscience. In that way, attachment "overlaps with the social learning concepts of *norm qualities, definitions,* and *self-reinforcement* (p. 31, emphasis in the original). Attachments also can be related to imitation, to Akers, since attachment implies significant others that we wish to be like.

With respect to anomie and strain, Akers argued that gaps between wants and expectations (which were said to cause strain) are related to whether one thinks they will be reinforced for behavior or not. The notion from strain/anomie theories that delinquency or crime results when conventional routes to goals are not available is akin to differential reinforcement, from learning theory. When it comes to the driving force for crime, strain, Akers said this is really just a way to say that people are being negatively reinforced—committing crime to avoid negative feelings of strain or anger.

Thus Akers' approach was to view competing theories as simply restatements of social learning principles. Viewing them this way, Akers was able to strip the seemingly irreconcilable differences in assumptions from concepts and show that they were all, at their core, social learning variables. Social learning theory, then, would be the umbrella theory for all of criminology.

Several of the chapters in *Theoretical Integration in the Study of Deviance and Crime* offer attempts at arriving at useful integrations. They include chapters by Gove and Hughes, and Farrell, Wellford, and Bernard. Other chapters are commentaries on the integration examples. In the macro integration section, Charles Tittle's chapter provided justification for integration on that level. He wrote that the goal of "theoretical science" (p. 161) is to "build general theories; that is, to encompass observations of specific phenomena into explanatory schemes subsumed within larger, more general theories that satisfactorily answer questions of how and why posed by critical scholars and can be shown to yield empirically correct predictions. Hence, theoretical science *requires* integration" (p. 162). For Tittle, the way to build really powerful theories, then, relied on combining various theoretical perspectives into a larger whole. He called these "synthetic theories." His basic framework resembled that of up-and-down theoretical integration.

Tittle argued that the benefits of theoretical synthesis are readily apparent, but there are some obstacles. First is the idea that particular theories or ideas cannot be changed. He called this the "immutability" impediment. This impediment arose from the desire to respect the theory in its original form and the theorist who first developed it. To change it, to borrow some elements of it while rejecting others, was a "vulgarization" of that theory (Tittle, 1989, p. 173). Immutability, to Tittle, prevents a science from advancing. "As long as criminologists waste their time arguing about what Durkheim *really said* or meant, or whether a given piece of research is really consistent with what Merton *actually implied*, or if cases of 'real' socialism exist to permit tests of Marxian ideas, then little progress will be made" (p. 174).

Second, theoretical competition, as we've seen, argues that theories should be put to the test, and the winner remains. To Tittle, however, such competition implies "that theories must be either wholly true or false" (p. 174). The sort of theoretical competition in which theories are viewed as right or wrong is not conducive for theory building and for the progression of science. Science is done best when theories are tested and the results are used to improve the theories, not discard them.

Other barriers include what he calls "evangelism" in science, or the practice of protecting a worldview to the detriment of building good explanation. Evangelists have a theory they adhere to or advocate, staunchly arguing that other theoretical perspectives are entirely incorrect. To Tittle this is more akin to political work than science. Perhaps on the opposite end of the spectrum are "particularists" who believe that the social world is so complex that one theory cannot possibly explain it. Each tiny aspect of the world deserves its own theoretical account. Finally, there are "pragmatists" who only want to focus on practical matters, not theory.

Against integration

Travis Hirschi, in the second chapter of the book, wrote an essay arguing that integration was not necessary and specifying what he felt were more appropriate theoretical approaches. He began by describing "classical" theoretical expositions which were developed to oppose other, rival theories. He wrote that scientific progress in criminology was made by the development of theories seeking to better existing ones, such that newer, more consistent and valid theories were continually emerging. Then control theory took center stage and ruined this trajectory because it was not a new theory but a repackaging of old philosophical ideas. And so, with this point of stagnation, something needed to be done; and that something was proposing integration.

But from the view of criminology as comprising oppositional theories, integration is illogical. Oppositional theories were created to oppose, reject, point out the flaws of, and ultimately destroy their competition. They were built to be contradictory—something integrationists ultimately ignore or suggest is only "in the minds of its theorists" (Hirschi, 1989, p. 40). He argued that integrationists assigned variables to particular theories, saw that none completely explained crime (or even mostly), and thus were able to make a case for the necessity of integration. What does this amount to, in reality?

> So now we have theories that combine what were once thought to be opposed theories. And what happens in the process to the original theories? Well, were theory A used to assert X and theory B used to assert not-X, we now have an integrated theory that asserts X. How does the assertion of X and the denial of not-X within the context of an integrated theory differ from the assertion of X and the denial of not-X within the context of an oppositional theory? The answer is, obviously it does not (Hirschi, 1989, p. 41).

After arguing that integrated theories have failed to help us better understand crime (they amount to little more than "shopping lists" of variables (p. 42)), Hirschi discussed what ought to be done next. First he says that oppositional theories were often built to point out the flaws in other theories. Thus they were not well built and much work remains to be done. He even points out the shortcomings of his own social bond theory, noting that he did not spend any time on how it was related to social disorganization theory or consonant with biological research. With a little trouble, one could show how it was consistent with disorganization, routine activities, and rational choice theories in a way that makes integration moot (because they are all the same theory fundamentally). In short, he was arguing that "we should take individual theories as far as we can before we abandon them or try to save what is left of them by adding them to some integrated stew" (p. 44).

Hirschi then wrote that oppositional theorists need to remain steadfast in their opposition. He had learned his lesson earlier: "A major mistake in my original oppositional comparison of social control and social learning theory was to grant a gap in control theory that might possibly be filled by social learning theory. Almost immediately, hordes of integrationists and social learning theorists began to pour through the hole I had pointed out to them, and control theory was to that extent subsequently ignored" (p. 45). He then wrote one of the more quotable statements in the history of criminology, in response to control theory's dismissal in integration attempts: "Therefore, oppositional theorists should not make life easy for those interested in status preserving the quo. They should instead remain at all times blind to the weaknesses of their own position and stubborn in its defense. Finally, they should never smile" (p. 45).

The essay by Terrence Thornberry was also not in favor of integration, but felt that Hirschi had gone a bit too far (as we assume he intended to do). Thornberry wrote that Hirschi's position that theorists never admit flaws is mistaken—"We are after all theorists, not defense attorneys" (Thornberry, 1989, p. 52). Thornberry's chapter is also useful because he actually set out a definition of theoretical integration, as "the act of combining two or more sets of logically interrelated propositions into one larger set of interrelated propositions, in order to provide a more comprehensive explanation of a particular phenomenon" (p. 52). This definition excludes certain exercises we have covered, such as Akers, and Pearson and Weiner's conceptual integration.

Because integration is "costly" for theorists, Thornberry recommended theoretical elaboration in its stead. Theoretical elaboration takes one theory or perspective and attempts to flesh it out, accomplishing the same goals as integration (more comprehensive explanation, more predictive power) but without the headaches of having to reconcile differing assumptions, levels of analysis, or concepts. Thornberry showed how elaboration can be done with social control theory, building on his own interactional theory which includes multi-directional causal structures. Elaboration shares some similarities with integration, but to Thornberry "is theoretically more defensible" (p. 60).

RECENT DEVELOPMENTS IN THEORETICAL INTEGRATION

Many of the key players in the integration debate moved on to other things after the Albany conference and subsequent book. Hirschi, with Michael Gottfredson, would publish their influential *A General Theory of Crime* in 1990 and spend the rest of his career, until his death in 2016, writing about self-control and crime. Delbert Elliott would go on to focus mostly on drug use and violence prevention. However, Ron Akers continued to write about integration after the conference. In 1990 he authored an article showing how social learning, rational choice, and deterrence theories were really the same. Deterrence and rational choice were simply, to Akers, different words for the primary components of social learning theory. For example, deterrence theory is based on the idea that people will refrain from engaging in crime if they fear punishment. This is the concept of differential reinforcement in social learning theory, which states that people will behave based on the expected punishments and rewards of particular lines of action.

So Akers was attempting the same exercise as he had in the integration book, only more formally. He wished to show how "the primary concepts and valid postulates of deterrence and rational choice are subsumable under general social learning or behavioral principles" (Akers, 1990, p. 655). Deterrence and rational choice involve more than just the calculation of the probability of punishment, though. They also incorporate loss of valued things such as relationships and social status. To Akers this is still a form of differential reinforcement (negative reinforcement is the form of reinforcement applicable here, which is when someone does not engage in behavior because of anticipated negative consequences). Akers then argued that this clear linkage of social learning and rational choice/deterrence theory had been ignored or overlooked in criminology.

A year later Akers took on Gottfredson and Hirschi's self-control theory. Among other things, he claimed that the theory was tautological, defining self-control via misbehavior, which self-control was meant to explain. This was perhaps the key point that was taken from his essay. But relevant to the integration debate, he argued that while Gottfredson and Hirschi's self-control theory was meant to be a pure control model, they incorporated elements of social learning into it. For example, Gottfredson and Hirschi argued that self-control was instilled by parents who supervised, recognized deviance in their children, and corrected it. Akers had earlier argued that socialization in social bonding theory is a form of reinforcement. He also suggested that, while Gottfredson and Hirschi had wanted to distinguish their theory from others, "there is no clear-cut qualitative distinction that can be drawn between self-control theory and all other theories in their choice of explanatory variables" (Akers, 1991, p. 208).

The most interesting and pertinent section of the essay began on page eight, where Akers compared self-control theory to social learning theory. Akers argues that Gottfredson and Hirschi go too far in trying to differentiate their theory. They do not admit conceptual overlap. Akers found it in the self-control theory idea that crime is avoided because of anticipation of punishments and the socialization aspects of self-control theory. In his 2009 book *Social Learning and Social Structure*, Akers made a similar point when discussing Sampson and Laub's theory of informal social controls. Akers argued that Sampson and Laub base part of their theory on Gerald Patterson's (1982) coercion theory, in which he made the case that parents who "(1) notice what the child is doing, (2) monitor the child's behavior, (3) provide good models for the child's social skills, (4) clearly state rules and standards of behavior, (5) administer consistent and sane punishment for rule violations, (6) provide consistent reinforcement for conforming, and (7) negotiate disagreements and conflicts with the child" (Akers, 2009, p. 350) are unlikely to produce antisocial children. Akers wrote that Patterson's was a clear social learning theory, yet one can instantly see the similarities between it and Gottfredson and Hirschi's notion of good, effective parenting.

Hirschi, who most vehemently opposed theoretical integration, was accused of engaging in the very practice he disdained more specifically in a later article. Sorenson and Brownfield (1995) wrote "Despite previous opposition to theoretical integration, Travis Hirschi has joined the ranks of integrationists by combining classical theory with the concept of 'self-control' " (p. 20, citations omitted). By classical theory, they were referring to Beccaria and Bentham's early rational theories of behavior. Gottfredson and Hirschi were actually direct in their book that they were reviving classical theory in their new framework. Sorenson and Brownfield's analysis, using the Seattle Youth Study, did not indicate that this integration appreciably improved explained variance over other theories.

In 1996 Thomas Bernard and Jeffrey Snipes, the team that had continued George Vold's book *Theoretical Criminology*, wrote an essay in *Crime and Justice* on theoretical integration in criminology. Earlier Bernard had written of his disdain for theoretical competition, arguing that, "Despite the enormous volume of quantitative research, there has been no substantial progress in falsifying the criminological theories that existed 20 years ago" (Bernard, 1990, p. 326). He then made the case that no theory had ever been defeated in criminology. If that was the purpose of Hirschi's notion of theoretical competition—it had failed miserably. While he offered a way forward for theory, he favored integration as an approach—even offering his own integrated theory in the 1989 book (Bernard, 1989).

Bernard and Snipes' essay reviewed the debate described in this chapter on theoretical integration, including the positions of Elliott and colleagues and Hirschi. Then they offered their own views. In short, they felt that competition could not work because criminology had no way of falsifying theories. They thus favored integration. While they were sympathetic to Hirschi's arguments that directly oppositional theories cannot be mixed, they suggested that his interpretation of extant theories was not accurate— it presented a more oppositional portrayal than was actually the case. The view that strain, social learning, and control theories are incompatible "originated with Hirschi . . . and accurately represents only control theory, but it distorts the arguments of 'strain' and 'cultural deviance' theories" (Bernard & Snipes, 1996, p. 322). So integration was possible once one accurately represents constituent theories.

To the Hirschi/Kornhauser characterization of strain, control, and social learning theories described in Chapter 2, Bernard and Snipes suggest they were mistaken. Bernard and Snipes argued that the strain interpretation provided by Hirschi/Kornhauser painted people as naturally good and needing a push into crime in the form of frustration. But they do not see frustration in any form of classical strain theory. Rather, strain theories suggest structural forces influence motivations, much like control theory asserts. A similar mischaracterization was applied to Hirschi/Kornhauser's discussion of cultural deviance theories. Bernard and Snipes wrote that in no cultural deviance theory was there a description of a person as a blank slate, and the notion that culture and structure could not be disentangled was an invention by Hirschi/Kornhauser. To Bernard and Snipes these learning theories simply said that the social structure influences cognitions, and cognitions lead to prosocial or antisocial behavior. Thus one can see similarities and compatibility between the three theories, if painted in a different light.

Bernard and Snipes then argued that theorists should "identify the location of independent variation and the direction of causation" (p. 330) in theories. "Thus, both 'strain' and 'cultural deviance' theories locate independent variation in structural characteristics and propose a direction of causation that moves through 'cultural' ideas to criminal behavior" (p. 330). With respect to levels of analysis, they suggested that we should think of criminological theories as either structural/process or individual difference theories rather than on macro/micro levels. This must be kept in mind when testing theories (*"the level of data analysis must correspond to the level of theoretical argument"* (p. 338, emphasis in the original)). Then, because of their arguments made in the essay, they state that *"competitive testing of criminological theories, which aims at the falsification of at least some of those theories, may only rarely be appropriate"* (p. 339, emphasis in the original). It is not appropriate to test strain or cultural deviance theories (which are structural/processual) against individual level theories, as an example.

One way forward for Bernard and Snipes is the development of "a single theory of crime that incorporates the structural conditions that are associated with higher crime rates, the processes that explain why normal individuals who experience these structural conditions are more likely to engage in crime, and the individual characteristics that make it more or less likely that an individual will engage in crime regardless of structural conditions" (p. 342). They also wrote that they were unsure this would be a positive move because it would be complex. They did favor some form of integration, however, and earlier in the essay had stated that the best research strategy involves "simply throwing a whole bunch of variables into one gigantic regression stew" (p. 303).

POLICY IMPLICATIONS: SIDE-BY-SIDE

Unlike previous chapters, this chapter has not discussed competing theories but rather competing approaches to theory building and theory testing in criminology. The policy implications of each side of the debate are not necessarily straightforward. However, we can say this: for the most part, primary or traditional theories focus on one or a few causal factors (differential association, social relationships, structural inequality) and are much easier to test and to derive policy prescriptions from than integrated theories. Integrated theories, such as the one proposed by Elliott and colleagues (1979), utilize strain, social learning, and control theories together. The policy implications of all three theories would need to apply, not just one. This adds a layer of complexity that may not be beneficial.

At the same time, approaches to reduce crime using only one theoretical perspective may limit preventative effectiveness if in fact crime is multi-causal in nature. Certain crime prevention programs, for example, rely on more than one theory. The Seattle Social Development Project (Hawkins et al., 2005) was based on the social development model (Hawkins & Weis, 1985), which drew on both social control and social learning theories. The program was given to elementary school children, and evaluations have indicated benefits to participants up to age 21 in terms of mental health and development (some effects were found for crime). Another crime prevention program which used more than one theoretical perspective is the Nurse-Family Partnership program (Olds, 2006). This program targeted at-risk soon-to-be mothers and provided assistance with education, parenting practices, and employment. While not based on any specific criminological theory, elements of strain, learning, and control are evident. The program helped reduce negative life circumstances of the mothers' children in the long-term. This indicates that, regardless of the theory, the intervention proscriptions are not all that different.

CONCLUSION: TALE-OF-THE-TAPE

In some respects this is not a fair fight. While the 1989 theoretical integration book did include some work by authors who opposed integration, none have been as vehemently against it as Hirschi. He has remained a bit of a lone voice when it comes to preserving the integrity of theories as they were devised by theorists. Theoretical integrations, however, continue to be developed, despite his warnings. In fact one of us is guilty of this exercise, devising a multi-faceted, integrated theory of desistance (Rocque, 2015; 2017). And so it would seem that integrationists have come out ahead of the traditionalists.

But things are not that simple. Recall the reasons that integrationists gave for initially moving in that direction. First was the "embarrassingly" low level of explained variance for traditional theories. Yet more recent work has not been kind on this score. The Weisburd and Piquero (2008) study on explained variance explicitly found that "Examination of empirical tests of criminological theory in *Criminology* between 1968 and 2005 yields three key findings. The overall level of variance explained is often very low with 80 or 90 percent unexplained. There has been no improvement over time" (p. 453). The other reason given was that there were simply too many theories in criminology and that integration was the only way forward—competition had failed at

TABLE 5.1 TALE-OF-THE-TAPE. THEORETICAL COMPETITION VS. THEORETICAL INTEGRATION

Theory	Theoretical competition	Theoretical integration
Theorists	Travis Hirschi; Terrence Thornberry	Delbert Elliott; Suzanne Ageton; Rachelle Canter; Frank Pearson; Neil Weiner; Ronald Akers; Thomas Bernard; Jeffery Snipes
Main arguments	Criminological theories contain assumptions about human nature that are incompatible; theories should not be combined; theories should be tested "head-to-head"	Criminological theories only tell part of the story; they can be combined to create a more comprehensive explanation of crime
Period of popularity	1960s–present	1980s–present
Seminal pieces	Separate and Unequal is Better (Hirschi); Exploring Alternatives to Theoretical Integration (Hirschi)	An Integrated Theoretical Perspective on Delinquent Behavior (Elliott and colleagues); A Social Behaviorist's Perspective on Integration of Theories of Crime and Deviance (Akers)
WINNER		✓

trimming the fat. After nearly 40 years of integration, is the state of affairs any better? Have we reduced the number of theories in the field? The answer is resoundingly no. Strain, control, and learning theory exist and are as vibrant as ever. Integrations continue, with old ones not dying out. On top of that there is no shortage of "new" theories of crime and antisocial behavior, with little end in sight.

So both sides in this debate have failed in their mission to reduce the raw number of theories and to expand our understanding of crime. How then to determine a winner? In our opinion, that integrations continue to be developed and tested indicates that the traditional view, that theories which say different things about the world cannot be mixed, has withered. Very few studies in criminology provide tests of different theories—most attempt to test one theory, to garner more support. The idea of falsification was to point out where other theories fail, and this does not seem to be the priority of researchers in criminology. In some ways the notion pointed out by Agnew (1995), that theoretical competitions generally do not appropriately identify where theories diverge, is still applicable. Agnew argued that theories, particularly the "seminal trio" of strain, learning, and control, "share many of the same independent variables in common" (p. 365). What differentiates them is motivation. Unfortunately, most researchers in the theoretical competition sphere choose independent variables, assign them to theories, then determine which have the most support. Not surprisingly this exercise has not provided much headway in distinguishing theories. Agnew suggested we focus on motivational questions, such as the "moral evaluation of crime," the "rational evaluation of crime," "negative affect," and "freedom." These mechanisms are what differentiate learning (which views crime as positive, or likely to bring benefits), strain (which views crime as arising from negative emotions), and control (which views crime as arising from lack of restraint). Unfortunately, it does not appear that tests of these theories have accepted Agnew's advice—were they to do so it may have become clearer which theory is superior.

In the end we give the edge to theoretical integration. This does not mean, however, that theoretical integration has overcome the obstacles identified by those in opposition to the practice. Understanding which theories make fundamentally different assumptions about human nature remains an important task, one that integrationists have not dealt with entirely. In addition, developing integrational theories that are testable remains a formidable task. Pearson and Weiner's (1985) theory appears to have been little tested in the literature, and it is no wonder, given its complexity. It is reasonable to question the value of theories that rely on the explanatory power of constituent theories but are difficult to test in their entirety.

The question of what to do about the mass of distinct theories in criminology is an intriguing one. Theoretical competition advocates never really provided a blueprint for how to know when a theory should be dismissed. Does such a critical test even exist in criminology? Several problems arise when thinking about ways to falsify theories. For example, it is well-known that null findings are difficult to publish. It is also unlikely that analyses will completely support one perspective and completely fail to support another. Meta-analyses do seem to offer a way forward, though. As such we recommend more meta-analyses of primary criminological theories as a method of discerning theories that are well-supported, those that are promising, and those that should be discarded.

In the next chapter we make a move to some theories that fall outside of the seminal trio. Critical theories challenge mainstream accounts of crime and criminality and offer some of their own perspectives on the causes of crime, as well as who gets labeled as criminal. This buck against traditional criminology does not come easy. There are those who believe that critical theories are more political than scientific and that they are not adequate to explain behavior. These debates are among the most heated today—and are explored in the next chapter.

NOTES

1   The information and quotes from Hana Zickgraf are from www.attn.com/stories/10014/what-hating-when-your-food-touches-says-about-you (accessed June 29, 2017)

2   Email interview, August 5, 2017. We learned about Chad's proclivities (and the non-mixing crowd in general) from WLNK's Bob and Sheri show, where the hosts have had Chad on from time to time to discuss his eating habits

3   Note, this was not the first theory to call itself "integrated," as Wolfgang and Ferracuti (1967) had previously published "The subculture of violence: Towards an integrated theory in criminology." However, their definition of integration was different, in that they were not referring to mixing together different theories, but rather disciplines: *Integration in this context means bringing together empirical data relative to the same phenomenon, that have been collected by independent disciplines and interpreted within their limited parameters of orientation so that an analytical synthesis becomes minimally the combination of the parts and maximally a new perspective*" (Wolfgang & Ferracuti, 1967/2001, pp. 2–3, emphasis in the original).

Beyond the "seminal trio"

Critical vs. traditional and conservative criminology

CHAPTER OUTLINE

O N A LATE SUMMER day in Paris, 1844, two young budding philosophers met in the Café de la Regence. One had just written a book on the working conditions of the lower class and wanted to share his ideas with his new acquaintance, who would become his lifelong friend and collaborator. The author of this new book, Friedrich Engels, told his friend, Karl Marx, all about how the working class would lead a major revolution and be the catalyst for sweeping social change (Kirov, 2016).

Marx was convinced. He would himself go on to write extensively on the role of labor and work on human behavior and collective action. He, too, believed that the oppressed working class would eventually be "awoken" and rise up against the oppressive ruling class. While most of Marx's writing was not focused on crime or criminality (almost none of it was), he did write about the constant conflict in society between the upper and lower classes and believed that crime was the direct result of oppression by the upper class over the working class. It is these ideas that inspired and directed a subset of criminology focused on social conflict and class oppression.

This subfield of criminology, which acts as somewhat of an umbrella term for differ- ent but related areas of study, is called critical criminology. These theories, at their core, are all critical of traditional society and of mainstream criminology. Following from this base, critical criminologists often focus on the role of income inequality, social class, and socioeconomics in criminal behavior and when explaining differences in crime rates. But they are also critical of traditional criminology's focus on state-defined criminal acts and seek to shine the spotlight on *who* defines crimes and *what acts* are defined as such (see Schur, 1973). Thus critical criminology focuses on the state and power dynamics that traditional criminology ignores. In addition, critical criminology's focus on the state has led to an examination of so-called state crimes, including war-time activities. Critical criminologists have also moved recently to focus on the role of race and gender in criminal behavior and in criminal justice processing. Many consider critical criminology "radical" criminology. In this way it is a very liberal take on the causes of crime as well as the policy implications that flow from the perspective. The critical perspective can be juxtaposed with that of traditional criminology and certainly with a recent resurgence of "conservative criminology" (Wright & DeLisi, 2016; Wilson, 1985).

While this chapter will focus broadly on critical criminology, it is worth noting some of the major facets of the perspective. Unsurprisingly Marxist criminology is a type of critical criminology. Most criminologists do not consider themselves pure Marxists but do tackle issues that were brought to light by his work (Schwartz & Hatty, 2003). Chief among these are the roles of the economy and social class on crime and that of the capitalist social structure on crime rates. Marxist criminology also explores the contri- bution of the capitalist structure on the operation of the criminal justice system—in particular, how the power elite can define and selectively enforce crime to keep the lower classes powerless in order to maintain their gloried position in society (Sparks, 1980).

As critical criminology moves toward a stronger focus on women and crime, feminist criminology is often subsumed under the critical criminology umbrella. Feminist cri- minology explores the role of females in criminal behavior, as well as how the criminal justice system defines female criminality and treats women involved in the system. Importantly, feminist criminology first made headway by (rightfully) recognizing the near-complete absence of gender in crime theory and research during most of the 20th century (Smith, 1995). Critical race theories are very similar but, instead of focusing on girls and women, the focus is on racial minorities. Recent efforts have begun to investigate the many ways that several streams of disadvantage come together to influence criminal behavior and treatment by the criminal justice system. This is referred to as intersectional criminology (Burgess-Proctor, 2006).

Postmodern criminology is concerned with how certain behaviors become criminalized, as opposed to why people commit crimes. Postmodern criminologists often point to those at the top of the power structure when discussing how language and discourse is used to subjugate certain groups (Arrigo & Bernard, 1997). Constitutive criminologists are included in this group as they are also concerned with how people create their social reality as well as being shaped by it. These scholars are likewise concerned with how society itself can victimize those who are deemed to be criminal by constructing definitions of crime and determining the punishment for committing crimes (Henry & Milovanovic, 1991).

While many of these types of critical criminology might seem rather ambiguous and overly complex, some critical theorists take a more practical approach and focus on the many ways that victims and offenders are intertwined and how victimization is a cause and effect of harm at the hands of others and society as a whole. This view is espoused by those who consider themselves "left realists." They are "left" in that they tend to be more liberal or radical than mainstream criminologists, but are also "realists" in that they focus on immediate issues around harm and implementing short-term policy solutions as opposed to grand initiatives such as overthrowing capitalism in favor of socialism (Schwartz & DeKeseredy, 1991).

In terms of policies and practices, critical criminologists almost uniformly reject the utility of incarceration and harsh laws in reducing crime. Instead many subscribe to efforts such as peacemaking and restorative justice. Peacemaking criminology is not particularly interested in *why* people commit crime but how society *responds* to crime. Peacemaking efforts include nonviolence, social justice, social inclusion, and restorative justice (Pepinsky & Quinney, 1991). Restorative justice, in particular, has made some inroads in criminal justice practice. Restorative justice seeks to connect society by bringing together those parties affected by crime to seek a collaborative solution to healing (Braithwaite, 1989). It is sometimes used not as a replacement of traditional criminal justice practices but alongside it.

THE NEED FOR CRITICAL CRIMINOLOGY

Proponents of critical criminology believe that the perspective offers advantages over traditional theoretical approaches in explaining criminal behavior and the response to that behavior. In fact many reject traditional criminology outright in favor of a more radical orientation. Therefore critical criminologists believe that their perspective is needed if we are to truly understand the causes and consequences of crime.

First, critical criminologists argue that traditional criminology has ignored crimes of the powerful (e.g., white-collar crime, cybercrime, fraud, insider trading) while concentrating almost solely on crimes disproportionately committed by the poor and disenfranchised (e.g., robbery, theft, assault). These theorists suggest that the crimes of "criminal governments" are much more dangerous than street crimes—however dangerous these may be (Friedrichs & Rothe, 2012; Kramer, 2012).

Specific types of crime, especially if there is a clear power differential between perpetrator and victim, fall squarely within the critical criminologist's wheelhouse. For example, hate crimes are generally committed by a person with some power over the victim. The perpetrator feels that he/she has the authority to define the victim as "deviant" and subject that person to punishment. Those who commit white-collar crimes such as consumer fraud or insider trading do so at the expense of others who are often lower in socioeconomic status. In true Marxian fashion, critical criminology views crime as the product of class struggle and social conflict.

TRADITIONAL VS. CRITICAL CRIMINOLOGY

Traditional criminology is exemplified by the "seminal trio" theories that we have discussed elsewhere in this book. Social learning/differential association theory, strain/anomie theory, and control/social disorganization theory are all considered traditional, mainstream theories of criminal behavior. They are all also considered general theories of crime as they are intended to explain the bulk of crime across time and place. Often traditional theories and theorists butt heads with critical theories and theorists. In this section we discuss the debate between these groups, tracing its intellectual lineage.

Critical criminology emerged from a somewhat benign place. Traditional criminologists were (and still are) mostly concerned with why people commit crimes or acts of deviance. They treat the definition of deviance as relatively unproblematic. Everyone, for example, sees murder as bad. But some scholars began to disagree—killing someone isn't always considered murder, for example; it depends on who the killer is. If it is the state, in response to a criminal act? It's a form of legitimized punishment. If it is a soldier carrying out orders, not in the streets of Los Angeles but in a foreign land? It's battle. These scholars began to view deviance not as an objective thing, a set of acts that everyone agrees upon, but rather as a function of somebody in power defining particular acts as such. Cultural conflict theory in criminology (Sellin, 1938), for example, rested on the insight that some acts seen as perfectly normal by particular cultures may be sanctioned by others, labeled as deviant, and subject to social control. Suddenly the spotlight was not on the deviants themselves, seeking answers to why they would do such terrible things, but on the processes by which some acts are considered deviant, who has the power to determine what is deviant, and who gets punished.

Flavors of critical criminology vs. traditional criminology

Critical criminologies often deal with different questions than traditional criminology, but sometimes the two camps tread on similar ground—here is where certain conflicts emerge. For example, a major focus of critical criminology is that of gender and/or sex. Sex mostly refers to a person's biological sex determined at birth. Male sex is determined by XY sex chromosomes while females are determined by XX sex chromosomes. Gender generally refers to a person's socially constructed relationships, experiences, and expectations which are associated with biological sex characteristics but not exclusively associated with biological sex. This is an important distinction because it plays a role in how people see the etiology of human behavior. Individuals who believe that sex influences behavior often look to the role of biology, such as hormone levels, brain structure and function, and evolutionary psychology (for example, see Daly & Wilson, 1988; Ellis & Walsh, 1997). Those who believe gender assignment and self-identification is a primary driver of behavior will look to social interactions between those who identify as male and female as well as to the overall social structure which influences behavior through expectations placed on men and women (Simpson, 1989).

Critical criminologists fall squarely within the gender construction argument. The extent and types of crimes committed by women are different than those committed by men because of their social experiences, societal role expectations, and subjugation by patriarchy. For instance, feminist scholars have suggested that it is gendered victimization that leads to specific forms of female offending. When females do act violently, it is to protect themselves or their children from male violence. When females steal, it is not for personal gain but for self-survival or to meet the needs of their children.

Again pointing to social structure, other criminologists suggest that society expects men to be aggressive, reasoning, risk-takers. They are expected to "do masculinity" (Jewkes, 2005; Miller, 2002). Women and girls, however, are expected to be feminine. This means to be caring, nurturing, and acquiescing. Naturally this leads males to be more violent than women and for male crime rates to be higher than those for females.

Feminist criminologists also suggest that patriarchy influences male and female criminality. Power-control theory (Hagan, Gillis, & Simpson, 1985) specifically discusses the role that patriarchal practices have on the criminality of men and women. From the standpoint of power-control theory, girls are under more social control from their parents than boys. Girls are to be protected and, as such, are more likely than boys to be closely supervised and subjected to more rules. Boys are expected to establish independence early and engage in risk-taking that will prepare them for the workforce later in life. Furthermore, females react differently to punishment than males (Blackwell, 2000). Females experience more guilt and shame, particularly in relation to their family, than males, which influences their continuation in antisocial behavior.

Due to these issues most feminist criminologists argue that gender-specific theories need to be developed to account for male and female criminality. The general theories will not do (see Daly & Chesney-Lind, 1988). In this way women should be considered central to criminological theory and not be invisible from theorizing about crime and delinquency. In our final chapter we will talk at length about general vs. crime-specific theories. While there is certainly variation among feminist scholars, many advocate for more specific attention and theorizing on females and their involvement as offenders and victims of crime.

Not everyone is convinced that societal role expectations and social factors have the greatest influence on sex differences in offending and victimization. Instead, those who adhere more to the argument that sex plays the larger role in behavior believe that it is the biology of males and females that differs and leads to differences in offending. These biological differences are the product of evolutionary processes. One of the most influential pieces of work in this area was written by McMaster University psychologists Martin Daly and Margo Wilson. In their groundbreaking 1988 book *Homicide*, Daly and Wilson suggest that the behavioral differences between males and females can be explained by evolutionary processes. They challenge the cultural argument using data across time and place (across various cultures) and find that male criminality is always higher than female criminality. In other words, the sex difference in offending is a human universal regardless of culture. They explain this sex difference using insight from evolutionary psychology. Briefly (very briefly, as *Homicide* is more than 300 pages filled with in-depth discussion on the evolution of violence), aggressive behavior by males is a worthwhile strategy to acquire females and generate offspring. If males compete with others using aggression they might lose out (through injury or death), but they will *definitely* lose out if they do not compete at all.

Along with Daly and Wilson, psychologist Anne Campbell similarly proposes an evolutionary explanation for the sex difference in antisocial behavior. For her, engaging in potential harmful (or deadly) behavior is just not worth the risk for women. Females must stay alive and healthy in order to rear children. In fact this is often referred to as the "staying alive" hypothesis (Campbell, 1999). They are responsible for feeding and bonding with the child. Males invest much less time and, when they do, it is generally in protecting young—once again highlighting the importance of aggression in males.

Campbell also takes issue with current feminist views—chief among them that men and women are biologically similar and that feminist views are the only ones that support social equality and fair treatment of women. Campbell argues that the feminist view that males and females are biologically similar is indefensible, given the wealth of research showing sex differences in development. She also criticizes feminist perspectives as being overly political and not reliant on empirical research. This comes across clearly in her 2012 article on feminism and evolutionary psychology, where she clarified her use of the term feminism "despite its erroneous implication that it is only they who support the goal of equality of opportunity between the sexes" (Campbell, 2012, p. 137). As an evolutionary psychologist, she very much considers herself an advocate for women but through the use of science and not politics.

The historic gaps between racial groups in criminal behavior have also caught the attention of traditional and critical criminologists. Critical race theory focuses on the ways in which race structures opportunities and influences treatment in the criminal justice system. Critical race theory (CRT), similar to the way in which feminist criminology views gender, does not see race as a natural or biological phenomenon but one that is socially and culturally created. CRT argues that race has and continues to underlie the foundation of American social structure. As Athena Mutua explains, "Its basic premises are that race and racism are endemic to the American normative order and a pillar of American institutional and community life. Further, it suggests that law does not merely reflect and mediate pre-existing racialized social conflicts and relations" (2006, p. 333). Thus, from these perspectives, race is an integral part of not only justice but everyday life in America. It structures behavior and the way particular groups are treated by authority groups.

Some criminologists argue that race is real, biologically speaking, and that these biological factors help explain differences in crime. John Paul Wright, a biosocial criminologist, has written that evolutionary and genetic factors can account for some of the racial differences in crime (Wright, 2009). Wright points to mechanisms such as executive functioning, and selection factors leading to living in disadvantaged social areas, as possibly explaining race and crime differentials in criminal activity. Other criminologists have focused on factors such as culture and epigenetics as important in understanding why blacks have higher crime rates than whites (Walsh & Yun, 2017).

It is also worth noting a larger issue that flows through many critical criminologies which is in stark contrast to positivistic criminology; postmodern and constitutive criminology argue that there is no absolute truth that exists outside the individual. Therefore it is impossible to uncover universal truths about human behavior. This leads many critical criminologists to shun quantitative, positive approaches to criminology in favor of qualitative, idiosyncratic investigations of criminal behavior. Some have even called out quantitative criminology as "voodoo criminology" (Young, 2004).

Critical criminologist Bruce Arrigo outlines the major components of postmodern criminology well. First, postmodern criminologists agree that language is central to our understanding of reality. Language conveys the meaning of everyday situations and one must be immersed in this language to fully understand what is being communicated in social exchanges. Second, knowledge is incomplete and provisional. What we believe is the truth is, at best, relational to our position in the social structure and to our systems of communication. Finally, truth is not absolute. One person's truth is another's fiction. Within any one story of reality it is possible to find implicit assumptions and hidden values. "As postmodernists remind us," states Arrigo, "because our awareness of reality is circumscribed, constantly spawning fragmented knowledges, positional beliefs, and relational truths, there is a certain undeniable relativity to being a human being" (Arrigo, 2003, p. 48). Therefore, unlike the wisdom of *The X-Files,* the truth is not out there.

Positivism, the orientation of most mainstream criminology, can be juxtaposed with the postmodern orientation. Positivism is a philosophical theory that there is a knowable truth that exists in reality and that empirical examination using logic and reason can reveal this truth. The "father" of positivism, Auguste Comte, argued 200 years ago that, just as the Earth is governed by the law of gravity, so too is society governed by absolute laws. Sociologist Emile Durkheim would later formalize this approach for social sciences, positing that the social world is characterized by "social facts" which are knowable and measurable. Survey-based research, common in the social sciences, is an outgrowth of the positivist movement which dictates that researchers can quantifiably measure social phenomena and analyze them using quantitative methods.

CONSERVATIVE VS. LIBERAL CRIMINOLOGY

We would like to begin this section with a caveat of sorts. Both of us see very little to be gained by describing specific theories, methods, policies, and research efforts as liberal or conservative. As social scientists these things are best left to scientific empiricism rather than politics. Additionally, there is nothing inherently liberal or conservative about the majority of theories and methods in existence. However, the dichotomy is apparent in the academy and theories themselves have now been branded by their originators with a nod to particular political affiliations (e.g., left realism, conservative criminology). Thus this debate is fairly easy to trace.

The social sciences have traditionally been a liberal enterprise and this is true, for the most part, today. Criminology is no exception. However, there have been conservative approaches to the study of crime and to the policies espoused by those who claim to be conservative theorists. Often these two camps have not seen eye-to-eye on the science or the morality of their work. Indeed, conservative criminologists are sometimes seen as victim-blaming and racist. Conservative criminologist Richard Kania wrote in 1988: (p. 75)

> Among those who are not Conservative, the label often is used as a perjoritive [sic] to conjure up images of racial bigotry, religious intolerance, apologetics for capitalism, supply-side economics and big business, and a blind preference for the status quo. The stereotypic Conservative is opposed to racial equality before the law, dreams fondly of the antebellum South and slavery, "when the darkies knew their place,"

wants his womenfolk back in the kitchen when he is not using them as sex objects in his bedroom, hates any hint of unionism, socialism, communism, and wants his government—to which he is fanatically loyal—to stay out of domestic social issues unless its policies are firmly based in a Falwellian interpretation of the Bible.

Writing nearly 30 years later, Wright and DeLisi (2016) argued that it is liberal scientists who are misguided, whereas conservatives are seeking objective truth. Liberals, they say, are not using science to discover truth but to "create the truth" (p. 8). Liberal academics are guided by morals which get in the way of scientifically valid findings. Conservatives risk reputational attacks by telling it like it is, rather than like it ought to be.

The most well-known examples of conservative criminology may be the works of Charles Murray, Richard Herrnstein, and James Q. Wilson. These theorists have noted the role of intelligence, self-control, and immorality on criminal behavior and have written at length about conservative policies that could decrease criminal behavior. Much of this work was done in the 1970s and 1980s but has been absent from most theorizing about criminal behavior in the 21st century.

James Q. Wilson was one of the most compelling and influential conservative voices in criminology. In 1974 he published an essay entitled "Crime and the Criminologists," which lamented the sorry state of criminology, dominated, as it was, by ideological rather than empirical theories. This essay was included in his seminal conservative criminology text *Thinking About Crime* (1985). In that book Wilson argued that traditional or social scientific criminology (read "liberal") attributed crime to "root causes" such as poverty and racial discrimination. Not only did Wilson find these explanations wanting in terms of evidence (he spent much time discussing the increase in crime during the 1960s, when the economy was booming), he also thought that they influenced poor policy because some things you just can't change. He argued that ideology drove criminology, rather than objective science.

> What I . . . realized . . . was that many of those seated about me (Task Force on the Assessment of Crime), urging in the strongest tones various "solutions" to crime, were speaking out of ideology, not scholarship. Only later did I realize that criminologists, and perhaps all sociologists, are part of an intellectual tradition that does not contain built-in checks against the premature conversion of opinion into policy, because the focal concerns of that tradition are with those aspects of society that are, to a great extent, beyond the reach of policy and even beyond the reach of science (Wilson, 1985, p. 56).

Instead of focusing on root causes, Wilson argued that we should try to convince would-be offenders that crime is not worth it, that they will be caught and punished harshly, and that they should think twice before harming others. In the concluding passage, Wilson wrote (1985, p. 260), "Wicked people exist. Nothing avails except to set them apart from innocent people. And many people, neither wicked nor innocent, but watchful, dissembling, and calculating of their chances, ponder our reaction to wickedness as a clue to what they might profitably do."

Wilson viewed liberal, social science criminology as wrong-headed. He saw people as good and bad (or something in between), contrary to the sociological view that social context and environment are what largely drive behavior. Soon after Wilson's book was published the criminal justice system seemed to follow his advice, focusing more on punishing the wicked and setting them apart from the rest of "us." Mass incarceration, as has been documented widely, began in the 1970s and continues today, such that the United States has become the world leader both in rates of imprisonment and sheer numbers of prisoners (Pfaff, 2017).

Criminologists did not take Wilson's critiques lightly. One scholar who responded forcefully was Elliot Currie, who's *Confronting Crime* (1985) and *Crime and Punishment in America* (1998) resoundingly made the case for a more liberal view on crime and crime control. In *Confronting Crime*, Currie argued that the conservative criminal justice policy swing led to much damage to communities, families, and individuals. He also argued that the policy prescriptions failed, noting that the massive increases in prison rates did not, it seemed, lead to a reduction in crime.

Currie was clear in who he took to be responsible for this rash of ill-fated policies. The United States, he argued, had embarked on a "decade-long conservative experiment in crime control" (Currie, 1985, p. 10). He further suggested that the conservative commentary—such as Wilson's—prematurely dismissed the liberal view. "Much of what [the liberal view] had to say about the roots of crime and about the potentials of the criminal-justice system remains both remarkably fresh and, more important, correct" (Currie, 1985, p. 13). Notably, though, Currie was a "realist." He understood that crime and violence were serious issues and that the past liberal perspectives, which denied that violence was pervasive or that we should formally punish offenders, were misguided.

The contradictions in the conservative criminological worldview were many, to Currie: "In a world of dramatic national variations in criminal violence, [the conservative view] blames crime on an invariant human nature. In a society that ranks among the most punitive in the developed world, it blames crime on the leniency of the justice system" (1985, p. 49). We should, instead of seeking ever-harsher punishments, turn to alternative methods of crime control. Family support programs, rehabilitation, job training, equitable salaries, early education programs—these are some of the potentially more fruitful avenues Currie identified as directions the US should move toward to reduce crime.

Currie repeated many of these claims in *Crime and Punishment in America*. It's hard to mistake the swipe at Wilson when Currie writes about the unfortunate path criminal justice policy has taken. He characterized the prevailing wisdom this way: "If crime can be said to have causes at all, they are, it's argued, moral and individual, not social and economic; and government is powerless to do much about them." In the next paragraph he then stated "Every one of these assertions, as we shall see, is either flatly wrong or, at best, enormously misleading" (1998, p. 5). His work, he claimed, was meant to "help right the balance," (p. 8) in which policy, scholarship, and the public had been increasingly dominated by wrong-headed conservative views.

Currie made the case that instead of more prisons, more draconian punishments, and more policies that result in harm to already disadvantaged communities, we can use criminological knowledge to reduce crime. He argued that crime prevention programs do work, particularly those aimed at children. He also showed that poverty and inequality are main drivers of crime, contrary to the view expressed by conservatives. One interesting thing to note in this debate is that Currie introduces another element to the discussion: morality. Our policies must not only be guided by evidence and shown to be effective, they must also be the "right" thing to do. Note that conservative criminologists have taken liberal criminologists to task for infusing morals into their work, rather than letting the data speak for themselves.

Recently, a resurgence of traditional criminology has taken place. With the release of *Conservative Criminology* (2016) by criminologists John Paul Wright and Matt DeLisi, the debate between right-leaning and left-leaning criminologies is once again in full swing. Like critical criminology, conservative criminology comes in many forms. In *Conservative Criminology* Wright and DeLisi wrote that "Far from being a uniform political ideology, or dogma, conservatism has many threads that form the core of what it means to be 'conservative'" (Wright & DeLisi, 2016, p. 37). In terms of crime, "conservatism values functional and safe communities, communities where people can form bonds, worship together, engage in exchange relationships, and pursue recreation." They continued, "Conservatism also values communities where individuals, children, and families are safe from criminal victimization. Because of this, conservatism views crime primarily as a threat to social order" (Wright & DeLisi, 2016, p. 48). In this sense there appears to be agreement between critical (at least of the "realist variety") and conservative criminologists. Yet, for conservative criminologists, crime is seen as freely chosen by individuals and criminal actions are deeply immoral acts that threaten the fabric of society. This is in stark contrast to critical criminologists who usually place the brunt of the blame for criminal behavior on the larger social structure and view criminals mostly as victims of the state as opposed to immoral, wayward individuals.

Wright and DeLisi continued their thoughts on conservative criminology in an essay produced for *City Journal*. In their article, "What Criminologists Don't Say, and Why: Monopolized by the Left, Academic Research on Crime Gets Almost Everything Wrong," Wright and DeLisi (2017) lamented the efforts of liberal policies in the 1960s and 1970s that attempted to focus on the "root causes" of crime, such as poverty and racial discrimination. These policies, they said, diverted attention away from the real causes of crime that were avoided by politicians of the time. They argued that alternative policies, including broken windows policing and selective incapacitation, were more effective and were shown to reduce crime. Additionally, they wrote extensively about areas that criminologists do not fully examine, including the benefits of incarceration, the role of individual differences in behavior, and the lack of engagement of criminologists with offenders and victims of crime. Again, while it seems awkward to us to deem certain policy initiatives and theoretical positions as "conservative," some "tough-on-crime" policies are generally supported by conservative lawmakers and shunned by critical (or liberal) criminologists.

Why might everything about academic criminology be wrong? Part of the answer, according to Wright and DeLisi, is the liberal tilt of the academy itself. They point to a survey which indicates about a 30-to-1 ratio of liberals to conservatives in the field of criminology. Quoting the influential mid-1900s sociologist Walter Miller, they state: "When shared beliefs take hold, as they often do in the academic bubble in which most criminologists live, ideological assumptions about crime and criminals can 'take the form of the sacred and inviolable dogma of the one true faith, the questioning of which is heresy, and the opposing of which is profoundly evil.'" The survey also suggests that "Liberal criminologists primarily support theories that locate the causes of crime in social and economic deprivation." Again, this highlights the disjuncture between theories and policies supported by those who are left-leaning and those who lean to the right.

A response to the Wright and DeLisi piece was developed by criminologist Evan McCuish. On the criticism that criminologists ignore the role of incarceration on crime rates, McCuish pointed to early studies by David Greenberg (Greenberg, 1975) and more recent work by Daniel Mears and colleagues that investigate the link between incarceration and crime rates (Mears, Cochran, & Cullen, 2015). On the claim that criminologists do not examine individual differences, he argued that many criminological theories incorporate individual differences and that there is a swath of literature on these issues (see Caspi et al., 1994; Nagin & Paternoster, 1993). Other claims by Wright and DeLisi are not supported by citations or references to others' work. McCuish developed an informal response to the Wright and DeLisi piece which he shared on social media. His response appears (with his permission) in Table 6.1.

An additional concern of conservative criminology is the problem of combining scientific research with social justice. How is it possible to be objective and scientific if the major concern is to promote a social justice political agenda? According to some it is not possible. This is similar to the criticism put forward by opponents of feminist criminology. Both of us question the impossibility of combing objective scientific research while simultaneously promoting laws and policies that achieve fairness and justice in society. One of us (Rocque) has written about this very topic on the conservative criminology blog run by Wright. When talking about good science leading to a more peaceful world, Rocque writes, "Good science, which seeks truth, can focus on social justice in just this way." Good science, he continues, "does not ignore outcomes contrary to preconceived notions. There is nothing inherently contradictory to the marriage of good science and social justice, from that perspective."

In a vein similar to the argument that "social justice" distracts from good science, two criminologists recently took aim at the role of discrimination in the link between race and crime rates. In a paper published in a special issue on race and justice in the *Journal of Criminal Justice,* criminologists Anthony Walsh and Ilhong Yun take a politial stance on race and crime by decrying the "PC mantra" that high violent crime rates among black Americans is partially due to discrimination and a history of oppression. In the very first sentence of the abstract, Walsh and Yun write, "This article examines race, poverty, and criminal behavior ignoring criminological orthodoxy adding two features that spoil the politically correct mantra that black crime results from white racism." To these authors, liberal criminology, focused on issues of social justice and political correctness, has failed to adequately address "real" issues related to race and crime. They also point out the missteps of liberal politicians who seek out policies that hire under-skilled black Americans who are unprepared to compete in the technology-laden workforce.

The picture painted by Walsh and Yun is different than others, especially criminologists James Unnever and Shaun Gabbidon, authors of *A Theory of African American Offending: Race, Racism, and Crime* (whose work is criticized by Walsh and Yun). For Unnever and Gabbidon, the historical and unique experiences of blacks are integral to their involvement in crime, as well as to how the criminal justice system responds to crime committed by African Americans. In their theoretical model, Unnever and Gabbidon place "racial socialization" at the epicenter. Blacks are socialized through their direct and indirect experiences with the police and with racial discrimination and negative stereotypes. This gives African Americans a unique worldview in which they approach the criminal justice system and society as a whole. This specific racial social-ization also increases negative emotions including anger, hostility, defiance, and aggression leading to offending. Unlike Walsh and Yun, Unnever and Gabbidon believe that African Americans have a unique history and contemporary relationship with society that leads to differences in offending.

TABLE 6.1 RESPONSE TO WRIGHT AND DELISI BY EVAN MCCUISH

Statements I think are false or at least not well supported	Reason for my position
Unfortunately, criminologists either lack the tools and abilities to assess the amount of crime prevented through incarceration, or, more likely, they lack the will to do so.	Greenberg's early work and more recent work by Daniel Mears and Michael Mueller-Smith[1]
To understand why many criminologists refuse to acknowledge criminal behavior as a potent predictor of life outcomes—including premature mortality, health disparities, arrest and incarceration, and even being shot by the police . . . liberal criminologists avoid discussing the lifestyles that criminal offenders typically lead.	There are hundreds of articles, written by criminologists, on these topics. While I cannot presume to know the political leanings of the authors of such articles, if the ratio of liberals to conservatives is 30:1[3], that some of the authors would be "liberal" would seem to have "Mayweather vs. McGregor" type odds.
The disciplinary animus toward the study of biological factors extends to other individual factors, including intelligence and personality, and to a range of traits, such as callous and unemotional behavior, psychopathy, and self-control.	Gottfredson and Hirschi developed a theory devoted to self-control and this construct has been the subject of hundreds of papers published in top-tier criminology journals. Temperament, CU [callous/unemotional] traits, and psychopathy have been included in several major longitudinal studies in which a criminologist was the primary investigator (e.g., the Cambridge Study in Delinquent Development, the Pathways to Desistance Study, the Pittsburgh Youth Study). If there was a "disciplinary animus" towards such factors it is difficult to understand how (a) these studies were funded and (b) these studies came to be some of the most widely used datasets within criminology.
Putting predatory, recidivistic offenders in jail or in prison remains the best way to protect the public—especially those who live in high-crime neighborhoods.	I believe that the best way to protect the public from victimization (keeping in mind that these predatory offenders are often victims themselves[2]) would be to prevent an individual from becoming predatory or recidivistic in the first place. This notion emerged in part from the abovementioned research by Greenberg on selective incapacitation. Why wait until the offender can be labeled "chronic" before deciding that it is a good time to protect the public?
Some offenders desist from crime over time but many others simply change the types of crimes they commit.	The majority of offenders desist from crime over time, even when focusing on high-risk populations. See Laub and Sampson's work, work from the Pathways to Desistance Study, work from the Netherlands by Arjan Blokland and colleagues, and work from the Incarcerated Serious and Violent Young Offender Study (among others).

[1] Thanks to John Pfaff for making me aware of this study.
[2] Thanks to Sara Wakefield for reminding me of this point.
[3] The authors did not specify how 'liberal' and 'conservative' were measured
Reprinted with permission from Evan McCuish

POLICY IMPLICATIONS: SIDE-BY-SIDE

Since critical criminologists locate the causes of crime within the social structure of society, their solutions tend to be fairly broad. For many, nothing but a sweeping overhaul of traditional society will have an appreciable effect on crime. For pure Marxist criminologists, the capitalist system must be replaced with socialism. For "soft" critical criminologists, a society based more in social support and welfare, as opposed to the free, capitalist market, will go a long way toward reducing criminal behavior.

The bulk of the efforts of critical criminologists are geared toward the idea of "social justice." Even more moderate critical criminologists, such as left realists, advocate for liberal social policies that aid in a more equitable society. In terms of addressing crime when it happens, critical criminologists often support proposals that do not harshly punish offenders but repair harm and improve community togetherness. Often these proposals include restorative justice.

At the heart of the policy debate between conservative and critical criminologists is the retributive vs. restorative philosophies. Conservatives tend to come down on the side of retributivism. While not all conservatives will have the same approach to justice, Howard Zehr (2005: p. 65) writes that "We expect conservatives to demand quick, sure, and stiff punishment, to decry the rules which protect offenders' rights, and to emphasize offenders' choices to offend while downplaying their circumstances." This is not far off from the expectations given by Wright and Delisi (2016). Retributivists believe that crime must be punished, the guilty must be subjected to some form of "pain," and that "just deserts" are achieved when the punishment is severe enough to deter the crime.

Critical and more liberal criminologists tend to have another focus. While offenders need to be punished and the harm caused by the offense must be repaired (or attempted to be repaired), the circumstances surrounding the crime are weighed more heavily toward restorativists than retributivists. Zehr (2005, p. 181) describes the restorative angle by describing crime as ". . . a violation of people and relationships. It creates obligations to make things right." He continues with the view of justice as ". . . involv[ing] the victim, the offender, and the community in a search for solutions which promote repair, reconciliation, and reassurance." In this way justice is achieved when society can come together to make the situation better for all parties involved. Often critical criminologists consider this paradigm as "social justice."

Most conservative-oriented criminologists take umbrage with the social justice angle and argue that it takes the science out of social science. One cannot be both an "advocate" for victims and offenders as well as an objective scientist. Some have used the term "social justice warrior" to describe individuals who they feel need to consistently push for liberal policies—many of which are radical in nature.

Jonathan Haidt is one critic who has written on the issue of scientific truth vs. social justice. In his view, "no university can have Truth and Social Justice as duel teloses." When social justice becomes the main goal of a university (and of research), results almost always conform to preconceived notions and promote falsehood merely because they are in line with social justice efforts (e.g., equality). These efforts lead to what Haidt calls a "culture of victimhood" and fragility where students are "triggered" by exposure to any idea that does not conform to their view of society. Overall, a social justice focus results in value-laden research, a hive mentality, the rejection of diverse ideas, and limits on free speech.

One of us (Rocque) has responded to this viewpoint publicly (so it should come as no surprise where we stand as we both share very similar views on this issue). For Rocque, there is no contradiction between social justice and good research. He concedes that any effort to "create" a problem where one does not legitimately exist *is* contrary to good science—yet this is not the intent of a social justice agenda, at least for most people. In the end, quoting sociologist Christopher Uggen, he writes that he (like Posick) is "firm in the belief that good science can light the way to a more just and peaceful world."

CONCLUSION: TALE-OF-THE-TAPE

Critical criminology encapsulates many forms of criminology which all follow a similar line of thinking—that mainstream criminology fails to consider culture conflict and the role of postmodern thought in theorizing about crime and justice. Mainstream or traditional criminology also ignores the way that society is structured, such that crimes by the "powerful" are ignored and crimes by the disadvantaged are amplified. Even the language we use has consequences: calling an individual a "felon," "offender," or "inmate" guides the way they are viewed and treated.

Critical criminology is to be commended for shining the light on issues traditional criminology has long ignored. There is no question criminology is enhanced by the contributions of feminist and critical race theories. However, some flavors of critical criminology tend to obscure issues and wade into territory that is not easy to follow. At times we are struck by the notion that critical criminology sometimes introduces unnecessary complexity in what is, at its core, a simple issue. Acts of force or fraud (to use Gottfredson & Hirschi's (1990) definition of crime) are everywhere condemned and not difficult to identify. Further, intentionally ambiguous and pretentious writing is commonplace in the work of postmodernists, leading some, such as Martin Schwartz, to claim "I really do not know what the hell they are talking about" (Schwartz, 1991, pp. 121–122, as cited in Einstadter & Henry, 2006, p. 303). Unfortunately, we believe this distracts from real issues that confront offenders and victims who suffer from the very real consequences of crime.

Conservative criminology also introduces some important insights. It is not debatable that criminology (like much in the social sciences) is dominated by liberal-minded scholars. We could, if we wanted, debate *why* that is the case, but that is for another volume. The potential for politics to interfere with good science is real, and diversity of thought and ideology is only a positive for the field; similarly, the idea that crime has real victims and that focusing on their well-being should not be controversial.

At the same time, conservative criminologies emphasize the type of retributive, tough-on-crime policies that have led to overcrowded prisons and made life worse for those trying to turn the corner (Currie, 1998). The notion that there are "wicked" people is attractive politically but likely hampers re-entry processes. While incarceration likely had some effect of the crime decline of the 1990s and early 2000s, there quickly reached a point of diminishing returns in which the continued expansion of incarceration no longer reduced crime (Spelman, 2000). In addition, we find it curious that a response to the over-politicization of criminology in the liberal direction was met with an opposite politicization in the conservative direction. If politicization of science is wrong-headed, that suggests to us it is wrong-headed in either direction.

IFE-COURSE criminology, researchers are beginning to refocus their attention on idea of maturity. What does it mean to "grow up" or be an "adult?" In criminology's days Sheldon and Eleanor Glueck had found that individuals who had previously enmeshed in a life of crime eventually settled down and became prosocial. They this "maturational reform" (Glueck & Glueck, 1937). The Gluecks were not very on what they meant by maturation, though, and thought future researchers would it out. That question lay somewhat dormant until recently (Rocque, 2017). rity, some began to argue, is not just a physiological phenomenon (e.g., puberty). ils social, biological, and psychological changes as well.

central component of maturation, to some, is the concept of identity. When people up they get a firmer, clearer sense of who they are. According to Steinberg and nan (1996), "Presumably, individuals who are confident, aware of their personal hs and weaknesses, and clear about their values and priorities will exercise more judgment than those who are insecure, not especially self-aware, and confused heir beliefs" (p. 254).

it is with humans and maturation, so it may be with academic disciplines. What a field of study a "mature" discipline? Is it a clear sense of identity or intellectual hroughout the first six chapters of this book we have discussed various perspectives inology and criminal justice that have been embroiled in debates over the past of centuries. All of these debates serve to illustrate that criminology and criminal s a far from unified field of study. Does this fragmentation mean that criminology ninal justice is immature, not quite its own discipline? Or are these disagreements rs of a healthy and vibrant pursuit of the empirical "truth?" Some argue that ogy and criminal justice is not mature enough to have the distinction of being a e but is rather a subfield of other disciplines—in large part because, much like a nager, it lacks a central identity. These individuals often fall back on the fact that ogy and criminal justice does not have unique research methods and is focused mes (e.g., crime, antisocial behavior) rather than specific explanatory mechanisms. continue surrounding the maturity of criminology and criminal justice today. tedly, if criminology and criminal justice is a field of study, not a discipline, to rent discipline does it belong? Is it psychology, as Tarde would have likely Is it biology or criminal anthropology, as Lombroso thought? Perhaps it o sociology, as Edwin Sutherland proposed (as do many contemporary theorists). s it possible that criminology and criminal justice belong to a field all their act this question is itself a debate, and we will focus on this debate in the first e chapter. Some believe that criminology and criminal justice are unique areas vith their own methods and research questions warranting a new field of study. se same individuals view the field as too multidisciplinary to belong to any one cipline such as sociology or psychology. We will review these perspectives oving on to the question of whether or not criminology and criminal justice s are separate fields of study.

hapter considers the study of criminology and criminal justice as a whole. Is Does it have a paradigm? What is its "intellectual core" or driving force? ords, if a scholar considers themself to be a "criminologist," what does this will also examine the question of whether criminology is separate from istice as a focus of study. Often, if one peruses academic departments, y and criminal justice" is the title used for entire programs, which implies re coterminous. Some, however, argue that they are distinct.

TABLE 6.2 TALE-OF-THE-TAPE. CRITICAL VS. TRADITIONAL CRIMINOLOGY

Theory	Critical criminology	Conservative criminology
Theorists	Stuart Henry; Dragan Milovanovic; Walter DeKeseredy; Martin Schwartz; Kathleen Daly; Meda Chesney-Lind	James Q. Wilson; Charles Murray; Richard Herrnstein; John Paul Wright; Matt DeLisi
Main arguments	Traditional criminology ignores the disadvantaged and power structures; discourse shapes how we view crime and criminals	Criminology is dominated by liberal ideology; we cannot solve root causes of crime; criminal justice policy must focus on punishing offenders
Period of popularity	1975–present	1975–present
Seminal pieces	*Women and Crime* (Simon); *Constitutive Criminology* (Henry & Milovanovic); *Feminism and Criminology* (Daly & Chesney-Lind)	*Thinking About Crime* (Wilson); *Crime & Human Nature* (Herrnstein & Murray); *Conservative Criminology* (Wright & DeLisi)
WINNER	*Traditional criminology*	

In the end we believe that criminology is best suited by being cohesive and not branching out into diametrically opposed camps, be they critical or conservative. We have faith that traditional criminology can account for labeling, power dynamics, white-collar/state crime, and street crime. Are there areas in which traditional criminology has failed or has not explored? To be sure. Yet this is not, in our view, a reason to create new branches of siloed criminologies, but rather to push traditional criminology to meet the new challenges. In that sense, specialties, in which scholars focus on particular areas, seem useful and not undermining of the discipline's core mission. Life-course criminologists, for example, study particular questions and use particular methodologies. They do not claim that other forms of criminology are wrong or misguided. We are reminded of criminologist Frank Cullen's American Society of Criminology presidential address in 2010. In that speech Cullen argued that criminology had been too focused on adolescents and should expand its focus to the entire life-course (Cullen, 2011). He was not arguing that traditional criminology was wrong, per se, but that it should simply shift its purview.

Thus we are in support of critical criminology's argument that crimes of the powerful and the way discourse shapes reality are important. And we support conservative criminology's call to restore balance and diversity of perspective. But we think these movements are better served by pushing mainstream criminology, rather than creating their own sub-disciplines, which fracture an already fragmented field of study. In the next chapter we continue our discussion on the state of criminology as a field, investigating the debate on whether criminology is a mature discipline and whether criminology and criminal justice are/should be distinct.

Is criminology/ criminal justice a true discipline?

Criminal justice, crimi and their existence

N
the
early
been
called
clear
figure
Matu
It ent
A
grow
Cauff
streng
matur
about
As
makes
core? T
in crim
couple
justice i
and cri
indicato
crimino
disciplir
fiery tee
criminol
on outco
Debates
Rela
what pa
believed?
belongs t
Instead,
own? In
half of th
of study
Often the
other disc
before mo
themselve
This
it mature?
In other w
mean? We
criminal j
"criminolo
that they a

THE "SOUL" OF CRIMINOLOGY: WHAT IS ITS INTELLECTUAL CORE?

John Laub's Sutherland Address (2006) was entitled "Edwin H. Sutherland and the Michael-Adler Report: Searching for the Soul of Criminology Seventy Years Later." In that piece Laub argued that Sutherland had taken the Michael-Adler report (see Chapter 2) to heart, and sought to provide criminology with an intellectual core based in sociology. As we recounted earlier in this book, criminology would be "owned" by sociology for the foreseeable future. What this meant was that to be a criminologist was to be a sociologist who studied crime.

Nearly 60 years after the Michael-Adler report, Ronald Akers (1992) published a piece in the journal *Social Forces* which was originally given as the presidential address to the Southern Sociological Society. In that paper Akers attempted to review the role of sociology in the study of crime. For much of Akers' professional career, sociology and criminology were linked together. "By the mid-1900s," he wrote, "all criminology and delinquency courses in North American universities and colleges had come to be taught in departments of sociology" (p. 5). Criminology textbooks were also authored by sociologists, not criminologists. It is accurate to say that criminology as a body of knowledge about criminal behavior and criminal justice was defined, taught, and transmitted primarily by sociologists in sociology departments" (p. 6). Yet things were changing. Now students could obtain a criminal justice or criminology degree, separate from sociology. Does that mean that, by 1992, criminology and criminal justice had matured, grown up, and moved out of the house of sociology?

For Akers (1992), the "center of gravity" of criminology remained sociology. Sociology, to him, is the ultimate perspective used in criminology. In large part this was because Akers did not see criminology as mature enough to be on its own. It was, he argued, simply a field, not a discipline. What is the difference? "A field of study," Akers maintained, "is problem-defined. It is differentiated from other fields of study by the object of study. A discipline, on the other hand, is perspective-defined" (p. 4). Therefore, he continued, "sociology is a discipline, and criminology a field of study" (p. 4).

As Akers was careful to note, not everyone will agree with this idea and nor will many agree with his sentiment that sociology is the crux of criminology. In fact he conceded that criminology capitalizes on several disciplines and fields of thought and that criminology cannot be defined *only* by sociology. He was consistent, though, in his belief that "criminology continues to be, and in my view ought to remain, an important part of the sociological enterprise" (p. 4).

Akers' sentiments are not unlike those of sociological criminologists Joachim Savelsberg and Robert Sampson (2002). "Criminology has a subject matter," they contended, "but no unique methodological commitment or paradigmatic theoretical framework. . . ." They continued, "There are no common assumptions or guiding insights. There is no intellectual idea that animates criminology" (Savelsberg & Sampson, 2002, p. 101). For them it is not so much that criminology belongs to sociology (although they note their dismay that criminology has distanced itself from the discipline) but that criminology is just an area of study—subject matter, as they state. It is not a standalone discipline with its own set of rules and principles.

Savelsberg and Sampson's piece was an introduction to a symposium that took place at the 1999 annual meeting of the American Sociological Association. Other papers were included by scholars such as James Short, Diane Vaughn, and John Hagan. The papers interrogated how criminology and sociology were related to one another. The notion that criminology is not linked to sociology, but another discipline, was not considered.

While in 1992 Akers could still claim that sociology was the intellectual core of criminology, things have since changed. As Scott Jaschik (2010) argued, criminology and criminal justice programs are starting to leave sociology behind; criminology and criminal justice is "increasingly standing on its own." He drew on a report by the American Sociological Association that was intended to examine how sociology and criminology are related (ASA, 2010).

The ASA report was written by some of criminological sociology's leading figures, including Steven Barkan, Kimberly Cook, and Marc Riedel. In some ways the report seemed to be the result of a recognition that criminology was no longer tied to sociology and the detrimental effects on both areas that this trend was having. Sociology benefits tremendously from criminology, the authors wrote, noting that criminology is often the most popular student concentration in sociology departments.

Helpfully the ASA report provided a history of the relationship between criminology, criminal justice, and sociology. The authors argued that the 1968 Omnibus Crime Control and Safe Streets Act was a "point of demarcation" (p. 15) after which increased educational attention was paid to criminal justice issues, leading to increased separation from sociology. Criminal justice programs increasingly began to emerge with vocational, not academic, goals. While some criminal justice training programs did exist prior to 1967, many practitioners were trained at community colleges or in departments of sociology.

Because of increasing diversification and separation of criminal justice and criminology from sociology, the authors of the report wrote that "Many sociology departments are concerned that the study of crime and criminal justice . . . is losing its sociological focus" (ASA, 2010, p. 31). In their survey of sociology chairs, the authors found that less than 64 percent of students majoring in Criminology and Criminal Justice were required to take Introduction to Sociology. The task force felt that this is a less than ideal situation, as continued collaboration between criminology/criminal justice and sociology is mutually beneficial. "The Task Force concludes that sociology, criminology and criminal justice have much common ground, and much to gain through collaboration. Sociology as a discipline is enriched by research on crime and one of society's fundamental set of institutions—the criminal justice system. Criminology and criminal justice gain from the theoretical insights and methodological advances of sociology" (ASA, 2010; p. 51).

While Akers, Savelsberg, and Sampson, among others, trace the intellectual core of criminology back to Edwin Sutherland in the 1930s, for some the intellectual core emerged earlier. Criminological anthropology initiated the scientific study of criminality and criminals in the mid-1800s. And, while the bulk of the ideas produced by the "father of criminal anthropology," Cesare Lombroso, have fallen out of favor, the role of studying the human organism through scientific means has a longer historical tradition which places biology as the primary focus of criminology.

This appears to be the case for criminologists who view themselves as "biosocial criminologists." Biosocial criminologists believe that both the environment (which is often the focus of sociology) as well as the brain (the focus of psychology) and biological/genetic makeup (the focus of biology) are all important in the study of crime. In this case, criminology is inherently multidisciplinary and no more "belongs" to sociology as it does to biology or psychology. Scholars have lamented the finding that most graduate students are pigeonholed by sociological perspectives and never learn the role of the brain, body, and genetics on human behavior. Some have even dubbed this "trained incompetence" (Wright et al., 2008). To these scholars, rather than becoming independent, criminology remains tied to sociology, to its detriment.

Beyond the relationship between biological factors and antisocial behavior, biosocial criminologists have made other claims as to why criminology should divorce itself from the idea that sociology is the core of criminology. In an article authored by John P. Wright and Danielle Boisvert—both proponents of the biosocial perspective—five points are made as to why the biosocial perspective is the most profitable for the field of criminology (Wright & Boisvert, 2009). First, biosocial criminology offers the excitement of discovery as it incorporates multiple perspectives to understand human behavior. Second, biosocial criminology uses complex statistical methods that go beyond "standard social science methods" that fail to account for genetic factors influencing criminality. Third, it offers more theoretical specificity by uncovering the most proximate factors influencing behavior. Fourth, biosocial criminology takes into consideration individual differences (biological and psychological factors) that are ignored by sociology. Fifth, and finally, it offers a better basis for public policy because it considers all the mechanisms that lead to behavior—not just societal factors that tend to be difficult to manipulate through intervention.

While some might not take umbrage with sociology's prominence in criminology—nor offer thoughts on the origins of the discipline specifically—they see the profit in criminology as a separate discipline because of the influence it can have on public policy. One criminologist in particular has advocated for a "public criminology." Elliott Currie (2007) suggested that criminology is a field of study and a fruitful one at that. Criminology has great potential to guide good public policy but, in order to do so, it must make some changes. He described the current mindset in academia:

> . . . the modern research university, and the professional disciplines which increasingly drive the university's conception of itself, often institutionally rewards work that (a) is narrowly tailored to the publication imperatives of a few journals in a given discipline, that (b) focuses on the generation of new, even if narrow, research findings, usually ones that address questions within already well-furrowed fields, as opposed to analyses of the meaning or import of those findings, and that (c) often actively penalizes work explicitly designed to broaden and deepen the audience, and hence the impact, of what we do (p. 186).

So is criminology its "own" discipline, or a field tied to parent disciplines? According to Thornberry (2012, p. 47), criminology is a discipline but one "in its childhood, moving toward adolescence, not yet a mature discipline." One reason why some scholars argue that criminology is not a mature discipline is that it has no guiding paradigm (Savelsberg & Sampson, 2002). John Laub, in his Sutherland Address (2006), argued that the life-course perspective should be criminology's new "soul" or paradigm. This "core" includes five principles, such as: 1) social ties; 2) continuity; 3) change; 4) human agency; and 5) prevention and reform. These principles should guide research in criminology, according to Laub.

Others have argued that biosocial sciences should represent the new paradigm for criminology (Wright & Boisvert, 2009; Cooper, Walsh, & Ellis, 2010). Cooper and colleagues, after reviewing data on a survey of criminologists, argued that biological factors are becoming more accepted in criminological work and that this may portend a paradigm shift away from environmentalism and the sociological vantage that had, according to Cullen (2009, p. xvi), "exhausted itself as a guide for future study on the origins of crime." To Cullen, sociology as a paradigm was vastly important in moving criminology forward and creating a discipline from loose strands, but it was time to either find a new paradigm or reinvigorate the old one.

As we wrote recently, we do not feel that a focus on the environment or a focus on biology represents a "paradigm." Instead, they represent a "theoretical orientation" (Rocque & Posick, 2017, p. 293). In our view paradigms are best expressed as guides to studying crime and justice. In that sense, both environmentalism and biosocial research fall under the umbrella of positivism as opposed to constructivism. As we wrote (p. 294):

> Both biosocial criminology and positivist sociological criminology have the same aims—to discover what accounts for variation in criminal and criminal justice outcomes. While there are differences in methods, such as the twin study used in much behavior genetic research, methodological variation has existed within positive criminology since its inception. New methods, such as hierarchical linear modeling, semi-parametric group models, and hotspot mapping have all added to criminologists' methodological repertoire but do not constitute a paradigm shift. As Turkheimer and Harden (2014: 180) state, '[b]ehavior genetics is ordinary social science'. We argue, therefore, that biosocial and social criminology are already partners in the quest to answer criminological questions; both bring different strengths and weaknesses, both also complement one another very well.

In the end we view criminology as representing a discipline (though perhaps less grown up than others). Sociology is not the parent discipline of criminology and criminal justice, but rather a discipline that informs criminology. With that said, we also recognize that, within sociology, scholars specialize in crime and deviance. While we both received our graduate degrees in criminology, one of us works in a sociology department (Rocque) and views himself as much a sociologist as he does a criminologist.

CRIMINOLOGY AND CRIMINAL JUSTICE—SAME OR DIFFERENT?

Throughout this chapter we have been using the term "criminology and criminal justice" as if the two components reference the same broad area of study. Generally speaking, this is how academia treats the discipline. In fact, if you sign up for classes in the discipline that is the topic of this book, you will most likely be looking at courses offered in a "criminology and criminal justice" (or vice-versa) program. Yet some institutions of higher education do have simply "criminology" or "criminal justice" programs. This implies that the two may be, while related, separate. We have both received similar questions from our students; "what is the difference between criminology and criminal justice?" This is a good question and it is the topic of the second half of this chapter.

What is criminology?

To begin our discussion we must revisit the work of Edwin Sutherland. Sutherland (1934, p. 3) defined criminology as "the processes of making laws, of breaking laws, and of reacting toward the breaking of laws." For this pioneering criminologist, the system of designing laws and responding to crime through rehabilitation and punishment (often considered the domain of criminal justice theory) was a part of *criminology*. Rightly, in our view, he thought it difficult to understand criminal behavior without also understanding how laws are made and how those who break laws are treated. Thus what is perhaps the most utilized definition of criminology also includes a focus on criminal justice.

Though Sutherland provided his definition more than 80 years ago, defining criminology remains a tricky task. Entire books have been written seeking to answer the question "What is criminology?" One, going by that title, was published in 2011. In the introduction to the book, editors Mary Bosworth and Carolyn Hoyle wrote that, while criminology was "booming," "there is little agreement within the field over the contours of the discipline itself" (pp. 1–2). Their book included 34 chapters by some of the world's leading criminologists, each presenting their own perspective on what the discipline is or is not. Just one example comes from Al Blumstein (2011), who wrote that "Much of criminology involves research into the behavior of individuals. Criminologists are particularly interested in those individuals who end up committing various kinds of crime. They also study the behavior of the elements of the criminal justice system" (p. 475). Marcus Felson, in the same volume, offered an even more complex definition (Felson, 2011, p. 171):

Criminology is the study of crime, including: its regularities and variations; how it is carried out and how it is avoided or thwarted; when it occurs and where; its precursors and consequences; its targets and modus operandi; how it is intertwined with other activities; and its diverse participants, including offenders, victims, police, bystanders, witnesses, and anybody else whose presence or absence affects crime occurrences or who are impacted by those occurrences.

What about criminal justice?

We see from these various definitions that criminology is often thought to include both crime and justice. At the same time criminology is sometimes referred to as the study of crime and deviance from an academic point of view. Criminal justice, on the other hand, may be related to what the ASA report (2010) described as vocational in orientation. That is, criminal justice programs are often geared toward practice, educating students to be police officers or work in the field of corrections. Husson University, located in Bangor, Maine, does not have a criminology program. However, Husson does have a criminal justice program, which aims to provide students "employment as a full-time law enforcement officer upon graduation."[1] Contrast this with the University of Southern Maine, which has a department of criminology rather than criminal justice. Their website describes the discipline as research-oriented and, when criminal justice is involved, it is because criminologists "assess the enforcement of ... laws, such as the differing organizations associated with violations of the criminal law (police, courts, and prisons), and the regulatory agencies (such as the Environmental Protection Agency, the Food and Drug Administration, the Federal Trade Commission, among others) that enforce violations of regulatory law."[2]

For Posick, his department at Georgia Southern University was, not so long ago, part of the political science department. In fact the department had just moved into a separate department the year prior to him starting his position. When the department moved it had adopted the name "justice studies." A few years later the faculty voted to change the name to "criminal justice and criminology," which was more in line with the academic orientation of the faculty and scholarly mission of the department. Currently the program describes its mission as:[3]

> The Department of Criminal Justice and Criminology provides a comprehensive examination of justice, crime, and the law. Our classes foster a broad understanding of the nature of justice, crime, and the law, in addition to the social, political, legal, philosophic, and historical context in which questions of justice are addressed, both in the United States and around the world. Students are expected to develop not only knowledge but a commitment to public service, ethical consciousness, and leadership abilities. Through the course work in Criminal Justice and Criminology, students are equipped to become proficient writers, critical and independent thinkers, and effective communicators.

It seems fair to say, then, that criminal justice programs are demonstrably different than criminology programs. One views its goal as training future law enforcement officers and the other as studying crime and justice from an academic vantage point. In some ways this is not a new development. The ASA (2010) report argued, for example, that "Criminal justice as a discipline is usually viewed as having its origins in the development of a police training program by August Vollmer at the University of California, Berkeley in 1916" (p. 17). They traced the emergence of other law enforcement training programs, often in community colleges, thereafter.

But what about the "study of" part of the equation? Is criminology and criminal justice one large entity in pursuit of knowledge about crime *and* justice, as Sutherland would have had it? Or do criminologists study fundamentally different questions than criminal justice researchers? On the one hand, the criminologists' domain is criminal behavior—why does crime happen? Why and how does it wax and wane over the life-course? A glance at a typical criminology theory textbook will often show that each chapter is a theory about why people commit crimes. Akers, Sellers, and Jennings' (2016) *Criminological Theories: Introduction, Evaluation, and Application* includes 14 chapters on perspectives on criminal behavior but none on the criminal justice system. Similarly, in their 13 chapters covering criminological theory, Einstadter and Henry (2006) do not include any discussion of criminal justice perspectives. So perhaps criminal justice is *not* part of criminology?

And yet some criminology theory books *do* include theories of criminal justice, typically of punishment strategies. For example, Cullen and Wilcox's (2013) *Oxford Handbook of Criminological Theory* has three chapters on "Theories of the Criminal Sanction." In this section are chapters on deterrence and the consequences of incarceration. Similarly, in *Taking Stock: The Status of Criminological Theory* (Cullen, Wright, & Blevins, 2011) the last section covers "theories of societal reaction." Theories included in this section range from deterrence to effective correctional programming. So the picture is not entirely clear.

In his presidential address at the Academy of Criminal Justice Sciences, criminologist Todd Clear (2001) tried to make the case that criminal justice research had "come of age." He described his academic journey obtaining a (then) new criminal justice graduate degree in 1977. While the field has burgeoned, Clear argued that criminal justice "is typically seen as an academically 'weak' program, attracting below-average students who are taught by questionably prepared instructors. The worst epithet tossed at these programs is 'cop shop'" (Clear, 2001, p. 711). However, in examining members of the Academy of Criminal Justice Studies, Clear showed that the scholars were very productive in terms of publications and that the field is continuing to expand. Clear ended his address with four conclusions (pp. 723–725):

1) Academic criminal justice today is an established area of study which has come of age.
2) A body of scholarly output and venues now exists for criminal justice.
3) Criminal justice higher education needs to be developed and strengthened.
4) Criminal justice needs to increase its policy-relevant profile.

In terms of recent work on the topic, two separate texts have made the case that *criminal justice* theory is just as important as *criminological* theory and deserves its own treatment. The first of these books is Eastern Kentucky University criminologist Peter Kraska's (2004) *Theorizing Criminal Justice* and the follow-up second edition in 2011 with John Brent. In the preface, Kraska laments that most programs offer criminology or criminal behavior courses (and most *require* these courses) while few offer criminal justice theory courses, let alone require students to take them. He and Brent make the intent of the book clear. It is to ". . . emphasize the obvious and clear distinction between the two objects of study" (Kraska & Brent, 2011, p. xi), referring to the separate disciplines of criminology and criminal justice. While Kraska and Brent believe that criminal justice is its own discipline, they still believe that it has certain "deficiencies" (p. 1). Chief among these is the lack of a theoretical infrastructure to establish organizing concepts, guide research questions, and interpret the results of criminal justice research. Their book is one attempt to do just that.

Chapter 1 in *Theorizing Criminal Justice* sets up the rest of the book with an interrogation of "why" we need criminal justice theory. As they argue, "despite over 30 years of research and development, criminal justice studies and criminology do not have a recognizable body of theoretical scholarship *about the criminal justice system and crime control* (2011, p. 1, emphasis in the original). They suggest that when one thinks of criminological theory, what comes to mind is explanations of *criminal* behavior, not behavior of those in the criminal justice system. They then set out eight theoretical lenses through which to examine the justice system: criminal justice as rational/legalism; criminal justice as a system; criminal justice as crime control vs. due process; criminal justice as politics; criminal justice as socially constructed reality; criminal justice as growth complex; criminal justice as oppression; and criminal justice as late modernity.

Another book, the authors of which have similar sentiments as Kraska and Brent, which is intended to advance criminal justice theorizing is *Criminal Justice Theory: Explaining the Nature and Behavior of Criminal Justice* by David Duffee and Edward Maguire. "The book is intended," they state, "to advance the study of criminal justice by focusing on the role of theory in enhancing the *discipline*" (2007, p. xv; emphasis added). Important to their view is that theory is essential for a blossoming discipline and theory is what can lead to effective public policy. However, like Kraska and Brent, Duffee and Maguire have witnessed the challenge that criminal justice has experienced with respect to establishing a solid theoretical foundation.

Duffee and Maguire's (2007) text is a bit different than Kraska and Brent's in that it is an edited volume and covers different components of the criminal justice system. For example, the first section discusses criminal justice theory overall, the second section discusses policing theories, the third theories of courts, and the fourth covers corrections. However, the two books are complementary and reinforce the other's position. Kraska himself offered praise on the back cover of Duffee and Maguire's book, noting that "*Criminal Justice Theory* is a *tour de force* that will undoubtedly strengthen the recent movement toward finally establishing Criminal Justice theory as essential to our field."

Despite the shortcomings of criminal justice theory, these two sets of authors believe that criminal justice is its own discipline capable of guiding an understanding of the criminal justice system and leading to influential public policy. Indeed, there has been a proliferation of empirical work on criminal justice decision-making, functioning, and effectiveness. It is our opinion that this area is likely to continue to grow.

POLICY IMPLICATIONS: SIDE-BY-SIDE

Generally in this section of the chapter we review policy implications stemming from various theories or perspectives. However, in this chapter we did not cover particular theories but rather views on the state of the field or discipline as a whole. Nevertheless, there are certain implications that arise from each of the points of discussion.

First, whether criminology is a field of study or discipline has implications for how students are trained. If criminology and criminal justice is a (maturing) discipline, students can and should take core courses in criminology departments which reflect the multidisciplinary nature of the study of crime and justice. If criminology is a field of study, not yet mature enough to guide students on its own, then programs should be housed within parent disciplines. This would mean, for example, if sociology is criminology's discipline, programs should be placed within sociology departments and students receive a sociology education with a focus on crime and deviance.

This is clearly not the case, with hundreds of criminology and criminal justice programs across the United States. Yet it remains true that, if criminology is not a discipline, these programs will retain the flavor of their parent discipline. This sort of situation is what John Paul Wright and colleagues (2008) were referring to as "trained incompetence." Students in criminology programs are not exposed to biological and genetic research. They are fully enmeshed in the environmentalist paradigm, which hampers the advancement of knowledge. In their study Wright and colleagues found that 2 percent of professors in Ph.D. granting criminology programs "had any training or expressed interest, broadly defined, in the biology-crime link" (Wright et al., 2008, p. 330). They argue that this limits science and also forces students who want to study biology and crime to pursue other disciplines.

With respect to whether criminology and criminal justice are similar or distinct, this question also has implications for education (and also for scholarly work). Can a student who is interested in examining how police operate share a classroom with a student who wishes to become a police officer? Are criminal justice programs really academically "weak" compared to criminology departments?

In terms of theory, the question remains whether criminology perspectives can be applied to criminal justice issues. Do we need new theories to understand the behavior of criminals vs. the behavior of the law? Is criminal justice a unique discipline with its own methodologies, paradigm, and intellectual core? These questions clearly have implications for the structure of higher education.

There may also be more direct implications of this divide for policy and practice. Should criminologists be sought out for research and evaluation of criminal behavior and questions surrounding the analysis of self-report victim/offender data, while criminal "justicians" be sought out to explain the operations of the system and its impact on victims and offenders? Should part of the role of individuals in the field be to promote a "public criminology" concerned with guiding and influencing public policy? If so, a separate field of criminology, and even separate fields of criminology and criminal justice, would promote such activities.

CONCLUSION: TALE-OF-THE-TAPE

Declaring that criminology and criminal justice is a young subject is not controversial. Compared to its counterparts such as psychology, economics, and biology, criminology is certainly not long in the tooth. But does this mean criminology is not a "discipline?" Akers (1992) had argued that criminology is simply a "field of study." The difference, as we described above, is that a field is guided by the subject or problem it is trying to address while a discipline has a unique perspective or paradigm. Using this analysis, criminology is not a discipline. But we disagree with Akers here and argue that criminology and criminal justice does have guiding perspectives or intellectual cores. Environmentalism is certainly one, but so too, we submit, is the life-course and developmental orientation.

However, as we spelled out in an earlier essay (Rocque & Posick, 2017), we believe that positivism vs. constructivism is what ties criminology together. Certainly there is a robust critical and constructivist criminology, but the "dominant" paradigm, judging by what is routinely published in the top-ranking criminology journals in America, is positivistic in nature. By this we mean most criminological work seeks to understand "causes" of crime and what differentiates criminals from non-criminals between and within the life-course. By and large, the definition of crime is taken for granted and the world, while socially influenced, is not seen as entirely constructed.

This observation may not hold outside of the United States, however. As noted by Jock Young 30 years ago (Young, 1988), British criminology in the 1960s was dominated by what he called administrative scholarship; work for the state. A paradigm shift occurred, moving British criminology from positivist to radical. Thus Young was stating that, in Great Britain, positivism had been the paradigm but it had changed. This indicates that criminology's "paradigm" may be geographically and culturally specific. But, in any case, it does not appear that criminology, whether in the United States or across the pond, lacks an intellectual core.

In the end we think the notion that a discipline is only such if it has one guiding perspective is an oversimplification. Sociology is incredibly varied, with dozens of subspecialties and competing approaches (micro, macro, symbolic interactionism, conflict, consensus, etc.). If sociology is a discipline with this much fragmentation we see no reason to argue criminology does not fit that bill.

We spoke to Steven Barkan,[4] sociological criminologist at the University of Maine (and one of the task force members who authored the ASA (2010) report). He suggested

TABLE 7.1 TALE-OF-THE-TAPE. CRIMINOLOGY: DISCIPLINE VS. FIELD

Theory	Criminology as a discipline	Criminology as a field
Theorists	John P. Wright; Danielle Boisvert; Terrence P. Thornberry; John H. Laub	Jerome Michael; Mortimer Adler; Ronald Akers; Joachim Savelsberg; Robert Sampson
Main arguments	Criminology is young, not yet mature, but is its own discipline, with an intellectual core	Criminology has no intellectual core or paradigm; criminology is a field of study under a larger discipline
Period of popularity	2000–present	1930s–present
Seminal pieces	Laub (2006); Thornberry (2012); Wright & Boisvert (2009)	Michael & Adler (1933); Akers (1992); Savelsberg and Sampson (2002)
WINNER	✓	

that criminology is its own discipline. "It's certainly separate from/not a field of sociology, if only because so many criminologists these days do not have sociology Ph.D.s and would not call themselves sociologists. Having said that, it's still a subfield of sociology, as the ASA Crime, Law, and Deviance Section's existence suggests. I would consider criminology an interdisciplinary discipline, even though that sounds like an oxymoron." We fully concur with this assessment.

With respect to whether criminology is separate from criminal justice, while we find much to like in the criminal justice theory scholarship we do not necessarily view that work as demarcating a *separate* field or discipline. Certainly particular theories may be needed to better understand the operation of the justice system as opposed to the operating of a career criminal, but both topics fall under what we see as the umbrella of criminology and criminal justice. In that, we agree with the definition put forth by Sutherland (and by Felson and Blumstein, above). For us, in terms of education and scholarship, criminology and criminal justice are simply two sides of the same coin. There is no criminal justice without crime, and it is hard to address crime without criminal justice. Thus we think whether one wishes to study to become a criminal justice practitioner or to simply study those practitioners, their education should be similar. Practitioners would benefit from sociology, psychology, and economic perspectives on crime and justice, and academics would benefit from a more intimate view of the field that criminal justice programs afford.

Barkan takes a somewhat different approach on this question: "Sutherland famously said that criminology is 'the study of the processes of making laws, breaking laws, and reacting toward the breaking of laws.' Following this definition, the study of criminal justice is part of criminology. However, criminology and criminal justice have more or less developed over the past several decades as two relatively separate, though still

TABLE 7.2 TALE-OF-THE-TAPE. CRIMINOLOGY VS. CRIMINAL JUSTICE

Theory	Criminology and criminal justice as the same discipline	Criminology and criminal justice as distinct
Theorists	Edwin Sutherland; Alfred Blumstein; Marcus Felson	Todd Clear; Peter Kraska; John Brent; David Duffee; Ed Maguire
Main arguments	Criminology entails the study of crime *and* justice	Criminology and criminal justice are guided by different questions and need different theories
Period of popularity	1930s–present	1950s–present
Seminal pieces	Sutherland (1934); Bosworth & Hoyle (2011); Cullen & Wilcox (2013); Cullen et al. (2009)	Duffee & Maguire (2007); Kraska & Brent (2011); Clear (2001)
WINNER	✓	

overlapping, fields. Because I can see arguments on both sides of the 'should they be separate' question, I am eclectic on that issue."

In the next chapter we move on from the state of criminology/criminal justice as fields—or disciplines—of study and consider different perspectives on policy. For theory to be useful it should be used. Which perspectives have had the most impact on public policy? Which seem to lead to the most effective approaches to control crime? These are the topics we address next.

NOTES

1   www.husson.edu/college-of-business/school-of-legal-studies/criminal-justice/
2   https://usm.maine.edu/criminology/overview
3   http://catalog.georgiasouthern.edu/undergraduate/liberal-arts-social-sciences/criminal-justice-criminology/
4   Email interview January 2, 2018

PART III

Great debates in criminology methods and policy

What should we do about crime?
Debates around policy issues in criminal justice

8

RICHARD CLARKE CABOT was not a criminologist.[1] But he was interested in the welfare of youth and had increasingly come to realize that the current state of delinquency treatment in Boston, and more broadly in the Commonwealth of Massachusetts, was not working. In the early 20th century Cabot worked as a professor at Harvard University, where he had also studied as a student. Later in his life he became interested in reform and social work. But it was the work of his former student, Sheldon Glueck, that pushed him to try his hand at developing a crime prevention program.

Sheldon Glueck had taken a course with Cabot in 1925 which inspired him (and his wife Eleanor, also at Harvard) to study crime and delinquency. They conducted some of the most well-known longitudinal studies in criminology, beginning with a follow-up of 500 individuals who had been in the Massachusetts reformatory. The results of that study (Glueck & Glueck, 1930) and the next one (Glueck & Glueck, 1934) were abysmal. Cabot wrote that the youth involved in the second study (1,000 boys who had been in reform school or on probation) "after treatment . . . were as bad as before or worse" (Cabot, 1934, p. 38). In both studies most of the individuals continued their criminal ways.

Cabot felt the time was ripe for a different approach. He believed that once delinquency began to take root in youth it was like an incurable disease. Prevention, before any crimes had occurred, was therefore the only way forward. Cabot began work on the program in 1935, raising money through a foundation he initiated himself. He then began recruiting boys who had shown signs of trouble, eventually ending up with a sample of 650 boys aged five to 13. Half were assigned a treatment, the other a control condition. The treatment, through which Cabot sought to provide "directed friendship" (Zane, Welsh, & Zimmerman, 2016, p. 143), relied heavily on mentoring via counselors. The counselors were quite involved in the youths' lives, visiting their homes, taking them on trips and to summer camps, and offering a friendly ear. The Cambridge-Somerville Youth Study (CSYS) lasted from 1939 to 1945.

The program was not based on any one particular criminological theory—after all, the CSYS was initiated during the same time period in which Michael and Adler were releasing their report on the lack of scientific value of criminology (see Chapter 2). Yet one can discern elements of mainstream theories in the program. For example, the counselors were mentors, offering support and friendship to the boys, thus providing a link to differential association/social learning theory. In addition, part of the program aimed at providing the boys with structured activities. Thus control theory and routine activities theory are also relevant.

It is no exaggeration to say that the CSYS was one of the most rigorously planned and evaluated crime prevention programs to that point in criminology. It was the first randomized experiment to assess whether a particular approach to crime prevention worked or not over time. And, as shown, the approach was not haphazard but was based on what today are thought to be significant factors in the development of crime. How did the program do?

Initial evaluations comparing the treatment to control boys found that they were pretty similar in terms of how they had fared early in life. All that work and all that money seemed to be for nothing. However, the CSYS is known today not as a program that did not reduce crime and delinquency but one that had a large impact on participants—only in the opposite direction than intended. Joan McCord, in the 1970s, conducted a 30-year follow-up and found that the men in the treatment group fared considerably worse on seven measures (including death, crime, and health). In other words, not only had the program not done what it was intended to do, it had a lasting, negative effect on the participants (McCord, 1978; 1980).

The CSYS took place 80 years ago, when crime prevention knowledge was nascent. Surely we have a better handle on how to deal with crime? In some ways, yes. The so-called "what works" movement has indicated that certain approaches do seem more effective than others. At the same time, however, recent work has shown that a fair number of well-intended prevention programs still lead to not just null, but negative (often referred to as iatrogenic), harmful outcomes (Welsh & Rocque, 2014). Several scholars convincingly made the case that nothing could be done for offenders, short of locking them up and separating them from the rest of us. Today, though, most researchers feel that crime prevention and offender rehabilitation programs can work, but they often disagree on the particular type of approach to take.

There is at least a modicum of support for individual-level programs. The same cannot be said for macro-level policies. For example, it is not a controversial statement to say that the United States has a gun violence problem. More than 33,000 people are killed by guns in America every year. This includes suicides, homicides, and accidental shootings.[2] In 2016 more than 15,000 people were killed by guns (not including suicides).[3] Gun violence is not a new phenomenon either, but one which the country was essentially founded upon. Many approaches to reduce gun violence have been offered, but none is without controversy. Even a simple question such as "do more guns lead to more crime?" remains cloudy.

In this chapter we dive into debates about crime control policy. What can we do about it? Should we lock up offenders and keep them out of the general public? Can we do things to reduce crime before it starts? What about hardened criminals? Are they a lost cause? In some ways these questions are among the most important that criminologists can answer. After all, finding out why people commit crimes or why some offend over long periods while others don't is not useful information if it cannot inform efforts to improve public safety. This chapter will not cover every policy debate but will provide a broad overview of historical and contemporary issues that have been tackled in criminology and criminal justice.

THE FOUNDING FATHER AND CRIME CONTROL

In order to give adequate coverage of crime control policy debates in criminology, it is necessary to start at the beginning. Many consider Cesare Bonesana di Beccaria to be one of, if not *the*, founding father of criminology. In 1764 he published *An Essay on Crimes and Punishments* which proved to be a revolutionary treatise for several reasons. Beccaria forcefully rejected the approach to crime and justice that had prevailed up to that point in history—which was supernaturalism. In supernatural thought, crime and deviance was often considered to be the result of evil spirits or the devil inhabiting the soul. The best-known example of this kind of thinking is the infamous Salem Witch Trials in 1692–93. During this ordeal 19 men and women were accused of victimizing others through witchcraft and hanged. A number of others also died during incarceration.[4]

Before Beccaria's time heinous actions were thought to be largely irrational. Why would someone purposely take another's life? Why would they steal, when they knew it was immoral? Some irrational force must then be at work. But the Enlightenment changed this sort of thinking about the behavior of human beings. Philosophers began to argue that all human behavior was explainable using logic and rationality. Beccaria took these ideas to heart and argued that humans are driven by pleasure and pain (a desire to increase the former and decrease the latter). To Beccaria the criminal justice system was not designed with that conception in mind. He wrote, "Surely, the groans of the weak, sacrificed to the cruel ignorance and indolence of the powerful; the barbarous torments lavished and multiplied with useless severity, for crimes either not proved, or in their nature impossible; the filth and horrors of a prison, increased by the most cruel tormentor of the miserable, uncertainty, ought to have roused the attention of those, whose business is to direct the opinions of mankind" (Beccaria, 1764/1819, p. xiii).

Laws are necessary because people are passionate creatures and are continuously seeking to improve their lot. Laws provide a guiding structure so that society can exist in equilibrium. But punishments must take a particular form to be effective. They must be necessary and they must be on par with the level of offense. "Therefore," he wrote, "there ought to be a fixed proportion between crimes and punishments" (p. 28). Too much or too little would be counterproductive. Why? "If an equal punishment be ordained for two crimes that injure society in different degrees, there is nothing to deter men from committing the greater, as often as it is attended with greater advantage" (p. 32).

Particular forms of punishment, such as the death penalty and torture, were, to Beccaria, irrational. With respect to torture, Beccaria argued that as a form of punishment prior to the admission of guilt it is not justified. In addition it would only result in the "weak" being found guilty while the strong (even if they actually were guilty) got off. The death penalty was equally irrational. If we assume it is wrong to kill, it does not matter who does the killing. Further, though, capital punishment does not work—it does not reduce crime in the manner of deterrence. Beccaria's argument was that the thing which really dissuades us from a line of action is not the thought of a momentary imposition but a long-standing one. "The death of a criminal is a terrible but momentary spectacle, and therefore a less efficacious method of deterring others, than the continued example of a man deprived of his liberty, condemned as a beast of burden, to repair, by his labour, the injury he has done to society. *If I commit such a crime,* says the spectator to himself, *I shall be reduced to that miserable condition for the rest of my life.* A much more powerful preventive than the fear of death, which men always behold in distant obscurity" (p. 100).

Interestingly, while criminologists have often written of Beccaria's prescription for a fair and effective criminal justice system, which punishes offenders swiftly, with certainty, and proportionally to the crime, he did not think that was the best approach to reduce crime. In Chapter 41 he wrote, "It is better to prevent crimes than to punish them" (p. 148). He knew it was impossible to prevent all criminal behavior. But one way to reduce its incidence would be to ensure "the laws be clear and simple" (p. 149). They should be supported by the public and clearly made to protect everyone equally, not just the ruling classes. The implication was that if people knew the laws, understood that they were for their benefit, and supported them, they would be less likely to engage in behavior contrary to the laws. These notions were supported hundreds of years later by scholars such as Tom Tyler (see Tyler, 2003).

Beccaria's thoughts had tremendous influence in Europe and in the United States, which would form shortly after publication of his book. The United States' criminal justice system was in part developed with some of Beccaria's ideas in mind (Massaro, 1990) (clearly, though, not all of them, as capital punishment has been on the books in

America since its inception). His ideas also continue to influence criminology, which has grappled to this day with the question of whether laws are a deterrent. Newer iterations of Beccaria's theories are often called neoclassical because his and his contemporaries' views were labeled the classical school of criminology. We will discuss this newer school later in this chapter.

THERE IS SOMETHING WRONG WITH THEM

While some see criminology as being founded by Beccaria, others are more circumspect about that conclusion. Nicole Rafter, for example, observed that "Introductory textbooks, in their obligatory two-and-a-half page genuflection to the past, often identify Cesare Beccaria as the first criminologist. This is nonsense if we define 'criminology' as scientific efforts to understand crime. Beccaria's small volume *On Crimes and Punishments* is not a criminological text, nor does it attempt to be scientific" (Rafter, 2011, p. 144). Who might be the first scientific criminologist then? To Rafter and others it was an Italian scientist, Cesare Lombroso, who was "widely recognized as one of the first scholars to bring scientific methods to bear on the study of crime" (Rafter, 2006, p. 33).

Lombroso helped usher in positivism in criminology, which focused on the search for causes of crime. No longer was it assumed that rational people would choose to commit crime if the price was right; now it was assumed (much like the time period before the classical school) that, in order for crimes to occur, there had to be something "wrong" with the offender. For Lombroso and others during the time (the mid-1800s) in which he was writing, that something often had to do with biology. Some persistent offenders, to Lombroso, were simply born differently; they were not as evolved as others (he called them "atavists").

Lombroso's ideas on crime and criminals were more nuanced than most textbooks have portrayed them. He did not argue that all offenders were atavists or even that most offenders were atavists. He included in his typology alcoholic offenders, occasional offenders, and insane offenders. He also afforded a significant role to the environment in crime causation. Nevertheless, for the purposes of this chapter, his thinking on crime was different than the classical school in that there was a "cause" and that cause could be a target for policy. In the introduction to the English edition of Lombroso's book, *Crime: its Causes and Remedies*,[5] criminologist Maurice Parmelee wrote (1911) that the classical school had argued for punishments to fit the crime. Two individuals who committed armed robbery were to be treated the same, no matter what else differed between them. With the advent of the positive school of criminology, though, "The treatment of the criminal is being based more and more upon his own characteristics rather than upon the character of the crime he has committed. How has this great change come about? The largest credit for it is undoubtedly due to the great Italian criminal anthropologist, Cesare Lombroso" (Parmelee, 1911, p. xi).

In *Crime: its Causes and Remedies* Lombroso discussed many environmental or social factors that could help reduce crime, including education, legalization of divorce, distribution of goods to prevent hunger and inequality, and healthcare. Yet he argued that "Measures for the prevention of crime are unhappily, with our race at least, a dream of the idealist" (Lombroso, 1911, p. 331). Perhaps surprisingly, however, Lombroso's ideas on policy were not all that distinct from the classical school. He decried overly harsh penalties, arbitrariness in sentences, and inequalities in punishment. He wrote that where crimes were caused by factors outside our control "we ought to make punishments more swift and hence better adapted to affect impressionable minds" (p. 247). Lombroso was vehemently opposed to prisons, which he felt only made the situations in which offenders found themselves even worse. He favored instead, "for minor offenses, . . . confinement at home, security for good behavior, judicial admonition, fines, forced labor without imprisonment, local exile, corporal punishment, [and] conditional sentence [probation]" (p. 388).

Lombroso was at first anti-death penalty but came to see that it may be the only recourse for repeat offenders (Gibson & Rafter, 2006). He favored reforms and preventative measures instead, to try to help the offender who, after all, was not "choosing" to commit crimes, as the classical school had assumed. Yet positivists in the 20th century came to support less humanistic and more repressive measures as they began to view the causes of certain crimes as due to genetics and therefore impenetrable by social reforms. Two studies in particular seemed to suggest that criminality (and other social ills) were passed down from generation to generation. One was written in 1877 by Richard Dugdale (see Rafter, Posick, & Rocque, 2016). Dugdale traced the lineage of six people in New York jails all the way back to 1750. The family, which he called "the Jukes," was responsible for an inordinate amount of crime and vice. Yet, interestingly, Dugdale favored reform or correctional treatment. He suggested that, even for the Jukes, "a change in the environment may produce an entire change in the career" (Dugdale, 1895, p. 113).

The other influential study, published in 1912 by Henry Goddard, examined the "Kallikak" family in New Jersey, purportedly showing the heritability of low intelligence or "feeblemindedness." The quasi-experimental nature of the study proved intriguing: the "sire" of the family, Martin, had initiated two branches of progeny—one with his wife and one with a feebleminded woman. The family descended from his wife was relatively normal; the family descended from the feebleminded woman was full of criminals and the mentally ill (Rafter, Posick, & Rocque, 2016). With Goddard, unlike Dugdale, however, reforms were not enough. In fact he suggested we forget about the "idiot" who is "indeed loathsome; he is somewhat difficult to take care of; nevertheless, he lives his life and is done. He does not continue the race with a line of children like himself" (Goddard, 1912, p. 101). The "moron," though, must be dealt with. Locking these people up so they don't reproduce is expensive. And "asexualization," or removing reproductive organs, is sure to be met with public resistance. So Goddard recommended sterilization, which "does not have any effect on the sex qualities of the man or woman, but does artificially take away the power of procreation by rendering the person sterile." The operation, he reassured readers, "is almost as simple in males as having a tooth pulled" (Goddard, 1912, p. 108). Yet Goddard did *not* think that criminals should be sterilized, only the feebleminded (whatever that meant). He suggested that criminality may not be heritable, and "that if criminals were sterilized there was a much greater probability that they will be promiscuous and thus spread venereal disease" (Fink, 1938/1962, p. 208). This is not to say, however, that he felt sterilization would not be a useful crime control policy. In fact he thought that feeblemindedness was "The easiest material out of which to make criminals" (Goddard, 1912, p. 9), and that "if we could make our law apply to the feeble-minded and say nothing about the criminal, we would get, under that head, probably all of the criminals that need to be considered" (Goddard,

1912, p. 10). In other words, sterilization of the feebleminded would take care of the crime problem on its own.

The prevention of particular individuals from reproducing in order to improve the stock was known as eugenics. According to Arthur Fink (1938/1962) the notion to sterilize offenders came from Orpheus Everts in an article published in 1888. Eugenics, though, was a more widespread movement, aimed at leveraging "newly discovered scientific laws of heredity to perfect humanity" (Cohen, 2016, p. 2). It was supported by doctors, judges, and reformers alike to address social ills such as mental illness and crime. Eugenics was a short-lived form of crime control, falling into disrepute in the 1920s (Rafter, Posick, & Rocque, 2016). The reasons were many, but included the lack of reliability of mental testing and the rise of the sociological school of criminology in the 1930s. The notion that offenders, not offenses, should be the focus of the justice system was taking root, though. In 1910, for example, the federal prison system introduced parole, which would allow inmates to be released early if they demonstrated reform (Stith & Koh, 1993). This move demonstrated an interest in treating the individual rather than the offense, which is based squarely in the positivistic tradition.

Sociological positivism

With sociological positivism came the notion that what sets criminals apart from non-criminals was the environment in which they found themselves. Pioneering work by Shaw and McKay, Sutherland, Merton, and others (discussed earlier) indicated that the source of criminality lay not in biology but in disorganized neighborhoods, inequality in society, and association with delinquent peers. Thus the focus of crime policy should be on the macro (societal) rather than micro (individual) level. One of the first examples of such an approach is found in the Chicago Area Project (CAP), the brainchild of Clifford Shaw. The CAP sought to show residents of disorganized areas how to provide structure and prosocial models for youth. The main thrust of the program was to provide activities for youth to engage in and opportunities to make positive changes to the area (e.g., "school improvement, sanitation, traffic safety, physical conservation, and law enforcement" (Kobrin, 1959, p. 26)). Evaluations of the CAP generally have shown it to have been effective in reducing delinquency (Kobrin, 1959; Schlossman, 1984).

Other sociological approaches to crime control, however, were less successful in the early to mid-1900s. Strain theories were popular, beginning with Merton's classic statement in 1938. They assumed that individuals turn to antisocial behavior as a result of conflict between social situations and larger cultural imperatives. One of the more influential theories was Cloward and Ohlin's theory of differential opportunity, which suggested that crime exists in urban areas because of a lack of legitimate opportunity, and the type of antisocial conduct is similarly dependent on what courses of action are available. Cloward and Ohlin would work on a program called Mobilization for Youth, and Ohlin would become an important voice in the White House on how best to reduce social ills such as poverty (Lemann, 1988).

Mobilization for Youth (MFY) contained the following elements: "(1) the improvement of educational opportunities through teacher training, the development of relevant curriculum and teaching methods, increased parent-school contacts, and pre-school programs; (2) the creation of job opportunities through work subsidies, vocational training, and career guidance; (3) the organization of the low income community through the formation of neighborhood councils and the mobilization of residents for social action; (4) the provision of specialized services to youth through detached gang workers, recreation activities, and rap groups; and (5) the provision of specialized services to families through Neighborhood Service Centers which offered child care, counseling, and assistance in applying for public social services" (Berger & Berger, 1985, p. 139). MFY does not appear to have been thoroughly evaluated, however.

The War on Poverty—the governmental suite of programs which was in part based on MFY—seems to have been a mixed bag, with some programs indicating promise and others being entirely ineffective (Bitler & Karoly, 2015). With respect to impacts on crime, the opportunity-oriented perspective was deemed a failure by some. After all, poverty did decline in the 1960s but, paradoxically, crime went in the opposite direction. The problem, to some scholars such as James Q. Wilson, was that sociological criminologists were too concerned with "root causes" of crime that may have validity but do not translate in any meaningful way into workable public policy. In 1975 Wilson offered his own thoughts in *Thinking About Crime*, a conservative critique of the more liberal sociological theories and policies of that time. With respect to the Cambridge-Somerville Youth Study, referenced at the beginning of this chapter, he wrote "McCord and McCord, for example, draw the lesson from the Cambridge-Somerville study that the true causes of delinquency are found in the 'absence of parental affection' coupled with family conflict, inconsistent discipline, and rebellious parents. They are quite possibly correct; indeed, I am quite confident they are correct. But what of it? What agency do we create, what budget do we allocate, that will supply missing 'parental affection' and restore to the child consistent discipline supported by a stable and loving family?" (Wilson, 1985, p. 48). Wilson was also concerned that sociological theories in the 1960s were based not on evidence but on ideology. This was, to him, a major reason programs stemming from sociological theories did not work.

It was not just sociological crime prevention approaches that came under attack during this time period, but the positivistic view that offenders could be reformed through correctional programming. The most damning of these arguments was put forth by Robert Martinson in a pair of publications in the mid-1970s. Martinson was an author on a comprehensive study commissioned by the New York State Governor's special committee on criminal offenders to evaluate the strength of the evidence for prison programs. The committee, according to Martinson (1974), tasked him and his colleagues with evaluating the state of knowledge on offender programs. Did they rehabilitate? Do they reduce recidivism? Improve coping in prison? Successfully educate prisoners? Which ones worked best? Unfortunately, the report, which was published in full form in 1975 (Lipton, Martinson, & Wilks, 1975), did not provide the answer the committee was looking for. The findings were so critical, in fact, that its "disturbing conclusions posed a serious threat to the program which, in the meantime, they had determined to carry forward." The state not only "failed to publish it, but had also refused to give [Martinson] permission to publish it on [his] own" (Martinson, 1974, p. 23).

What would come to be known as the "Martinson report" (despite his not being the lead author) became a watershed event in criminology. The report was comprehensive. It covered the years 1945–1967 and included 231 studies. The inclusion criteria were very basic: "A study had to be an evaluation of a treatment method, it had to employ an independent measure of the improvement secured by that method, and it had to use some control group, some untreated individuals with whom the treated ones could be compared" (Martinson, 1974, p. 24). Despite variances across studies that made comparison difficult, the team offered the following, now infamous, assessment: "With few and isolated exceptions, the rehabilitative efforts that have been reported so far have had no appreciable effect on recidivism" (Martinson, 1974, p. 25). The death toll for any hope that rehabilitationists had was sounded.

The story of the aftermath of the Martinson report was told best—as most criminological stories have been—by Frank Cullen (2013). He, along with others, were thoroughly convinced by Martinson's work that rehabilitation was a fool's game. The social atmosphere, however, was at that time quite receptive to such a message. As he wrote, "virtually everyone came to forsake the rehabilitative ideal. Through an inter-section of cataclysmic social events and strong intellectual currents, a social movement of sorts had risen up to purge systems of control of the insidious social welfare ideology that used the rhetoric of benevolence to mask the abuse of power. Martinson's (1974) study did not spark such thinking; its publication served only to confirm what we already knew" (Cullen, 2013, p. 302).

So antipoverty programs and rising tides did not seem to have the hypothesized effect on aggregate crime rates, and decades of research on individualized rehabilitation programs had resulted in little support for the notion that we can fix people. With the previous dismissal of biologically oriented policies aimed at eradicating flawed individuals, the positive approach of targeting people who have "something wrong with them" appeared—from a policy standpoint—to be a dead-end.

NEOCLASSICAL APPROACHES TO CRIME CONTROL

In what direction could criminology turn to help policymakers control crime? Why not return to its roots, to the lessons of Beccaria? Indeed, the neoclassical school of criminology arose in response to the perceived failings of the positive school. Crime was once again viewed in terms of decisions, costs and benefits, and rationality. To reduce it, then, one must disrupt that criminal calculus somehow.

Several classic criminological works helped spark a return to classical thinking. Economists pushed their way into the field to show how crime can be reduced to a series of equations based on costs, benefits, elasticities, and utilities (Becker, 1968; Ehrlich, 1975). These quantitative models guided statistical tests of the deterrent effect of punishment and renewed interest in leveraging the criminal justice system in more efficient ways to reduce crime. Becker's paper was theoretical while Ehrlich's attempted to show that using a more sophisticated econometric model can uncover a deterrent effect of the death penalty. That offenders may be rational and may be sensitive to increasing costs of punishment was good news to policymakers, since it seemed that "fixing" these individuals was not going to work.

Policy followed suit during this period, seeking to increase the costs of crime in ways that would tip the cost-benefit scale away from crime. For example, one fear was that criminals were being found guilty of offenses, sentenced accordingly, but then not actually serving out their punishment (e.g., getting out early on parole). In some states, parole was abolished (Maine abolished parole in 1975) and measures were taken to ensure that sentences were mostly served as intended. So-called indeterminate sentencing schemes (such as parole boards deciding the terms of release) were replaced with determinate, or fixed, ones. Such "truth in sentencing" measures required offenders to serve a minimum percentage of their sentence (Ditton & Wilson, 1999). Part of this move was in response to concerns that the justice system was too lenient and needed to be harsher to balance the scales. But also relevant was the classical and neoclassical notions that costs must be raised in order to outweigh benefits of crime and that the penalty for particular lines of action must be clear. Recall the Lombrosian move toward treating offenders differently, not based on the crime they committed but their personal characteristics. In the 1970s, with the rise of the neoclassical school, this line of thinking was rejected. It was not fair, some argued, to treat two people, convicted of the same act, differently. In order to guarantee that offenders were not treated differently, some jurisdictions (including the federal government) devised sentencing guidelines, which basically consisted of a matrix that set a range of penalties that judges could impose for particular offenses based upon an offender's past history. The push for sentencing guidelines began with a sentencing commission which was part of legislation put forth by Ted Kennedy in 1975 (the federal sentencing commission did not emerge until a decade later). This removed any sort of discretion that could lead to variation in treatment. In (classical) theory this should have helped reduce crime, as Beccaria argued that punishments must be clear and certain in order for them to deter.[6]

A new—or, more appropriately, renewed—focus in criminological policy emerged and was called deterrence. This research examined: 1) whether sanctions can dissuade would-be offenders from committing crimes; and 2) what types of sanctions worked best. This research also divvied up deterrence into two models, general and specific. On the research front the criminal career scholars produced a volume in 1978 exploring the impacts of deterrence, concluding that the studies to date were too poorly done to provide an assessment (Nagin, 2013). Since that report, research has found more support for deterrence as a general principle (Cook, 1980; Nagin, 1998; 2013). The types of sanctions that appear to work best are those that attempt to bring the offender back into the community rather than ostracizing him (Braithwaite, 1989). Ensuring punishment actually occurs is also a more effective strategy than increasing punishment severity (Nagin, 2013). Some scholars began to examine risk perceptions of individuals to determine if those who foresaw greater consequences for crime would be less likely to offend. Research here seems mixed (Paternoster, 1987; Nagin, 2013). Finally, researchers made a distinction between broad, general deterrence and more individualized, specific deterrence (Nagin, 2013). General deterrence is the idea that simply having sanctions or highly publicized sanctions will deter people from engaging in crime. Specific deterrence is the idea that a person, once sanctioned for a behavior, will be less likely to engage in it in the future.

Another classic piece in criminology was published around this time, again indicating that offenders seemed to be rational. Cohen and Felson's (1979) routine activities theory argued that crime occurs when the ingredients for crime are mixed together in just the right way. First, motivated offenders must be present. Second, those offenders must be in the presence of suitable or attractive targets for crime (e.g., people, goods, businesses). Finally, there must be a lack of capable guardians. Rather than focus on reducing motivation of offenders, which preoccupied criminologists from the positive school, Cohen and Felson turned their attention on reducing opportunities for those offenders to commit their deeds.

How can opportunities be reduced? Felson and Clarke (1998), in their report entitled "Opportunity Makes the Thief," suggested that this can be done in four ways: first, by increasing the perceived effort of crime; second, by increasing the perceived risks; third, by reducing the anticipated rewards; and, finally, by removing excuses for crime (p. 25).

Clarke's *Situational Crime Prevention* (1997) lists examples of strategies to reduce crime corresponding to each opportunity reduction approach. For example, in what opportunity theorists call "target hardening," attractive targets (nowadays things like iPhones and tablets) are made less so by increasing security. Most smartphones now have passcodes that make them difficult to use by thieves. One of us recalls vividly within weeks of moving to Maryland for graduate school being the victim of a car break-in. The thief or thieves made off with a number of items, but most cherished among them was Rocque's Sirius satellite radio receiver. Determined to not let some ne'er-do-well enjoy his radio, he called up the company and had them permanently disable the receiver so no one could ever use it again. Target sufficiently hardened. Clearly this type of service makes products less attractive for would-be thieves, who would be hard-pressed to find buyers for a non-functioning satellite radio receiver.

Other examples of removing opportunity include increasing surveillance (e.g., with the use of closed-circuit television cameras, or CCTVs) and decreasing excuses. With respect to the latter, sometimes individuals may bend or even break the rules and claim that they "didn't know" they were doing anything wrong. To that end, strategies such as increasing the number of speed limit signs on roads, posting "no littering" warnings, and increasing access to public toilet facilities reduce the readymade excuses ("but there was no bathroom!") for particular offenses that individuals may resort to.

POSITIVE CRIMINOLOGICAL POLICY MAKES A COMEBACK

As we recounted in Chapter 2, in the late 1980s and early 1990s psychological criminoloists were very concerned with the dismissal of "individual trait" theories of crime. They argued that it amounted to "knowledge destruction" (Andrews & Wormith, 1989) and that criminology had much to lose from ignoring psychology and personality as correlates of crime. One of the major concerns, these criminologists argued, was that it ignored how treatment and rehabilitation programs could work by focusing on individual risk and criminogenic needs. Don Andrews, James Bonta, and colleagues began by demonstrating that, contrary to the popular belief at the time, rehabilitation worked. They initiated, along with some other influential scholars, the "what works" movement in crime policy.

In 1990 Andrews and his colleagues published a key study, statistically synthesizing studies examining the effect of rehabilitation programs (a meta-analysis). In that piece, published in *Criminology*, the authors did not hide what they felt about the reasons why rehabilitation was deemed a failure in the 1970s: "The decline of the rehabilitative ideal cannot be attributed to a careful reading of evidence regarding the effectiveness of rehabilitative treatment" (Andrews et al., 1990, p. 370). In fact, they argued, the rehabilitation literature was not short on studies showing effective programs. Not only that, but the neoclassical approach—to simply raise the costs by using more punishments—did not work. In their study Andrews and his co-authors showed that a large share of programs did reduce criminal behavior. When programs are what they called "appropriate" they reduce recidivism by half.

Andrews and Bonta went on to develop the risk-need-responsivity approach, which was a more nuanced and focused way to think about offender rehabilitation than the simplistic view espoused in the past. Rather than apply particular programs haphazardly, these scholars argued that we must pay attention to offender characteristics. What risk factors did they have? What needs must be addressed? What about their learning styles? Andrews and Bonta's "Psychology of Criminal Conduct" was based on this approach, and their tool, the Level of Service Inventory (LSI), became one of the most popular risk/needs assessment tools in North American corrections (Duwe & Rocque, 2016). The LSI has an impressive body of research associating one's score on the tool with his/her level of offending, illustrating the importance of particular risk factors to predict recidivism (Olver, Stockdale, & Wormith, 2009; Smith, Cullen, & Latessa, 2009). In addition, this group of scholars delineated what they called the "principles of effective intervention," which pointed out that not all approaches are equally beneficial. Particular types of programs are likely to have success. "More specifically, correctional programs and interventions should focus on higher risk offenders; deliver cognitive-behavioral or behavioral interventions that focus on relevant criminogenic needs; attend to the qualifications, skills, and values of staff; and evaluate what they do" (Lowenkamp, Latessa, & Smith, 2006, p. 203). Lowenkamp and colleagues found, using the Correctional Program Assessment Inventory (which measures adherence to the principles of effective intervention), that programs more closely aligned to the principles had stronger effects on recidivism (see also Smith, Gendreau, & Swartz, 2009).

Thus positive criminologists argued that the reports of the demise of rehabilitation were greatly exaggerated. An entire movement, under the guise of "what works," emerged during the 1990s to shed light on what sorts of programs help offenders the most. Perhaps the culmination of this work was a report issued by the University of Maryland, led by Lawrence Sherman and co-authored with several prominent criminologists. The report, published in 1997 and submitted to the US Congress, reviewed more than 500 studies in areas such as the family, community, school, work, and criminal justice.[7] Along with illustrating what sorts of approaches work to prevent crime, the Maryland report was influential in another way. It introduced the "Scientific Method Scale" to assess the rigor of a particular study. Firmer conclusions could be drawn with more rigorous program evaluations. The scale ranged from 1 to 5, with higher scores indicating more rigor, and was based on the following (Sherman et al., 1998, pp. 4–5):

Level 1. Correlation between a crime-prevention program and a measure of crime or crime risk factors at a single point in time.
Level 2. Temporal sequence between the program and the crime or risk outcome clearly observed, or the presence of a comparison group without demonstrated comparability to the treatment group.
Level 3. A comparison between two or more comparable units of analysis, one with and one without the program.
Level 4. Comparison between multiple units with and without the program, controlling for other factors, or using comparison units that evidence only minor differences.
Level 5. Random assignment and analysis of comparable units to program and comparison groups.

While the Maryland report did provide evidence of effective and promising approaches, the conclusion argued, much like previous assessments of the evidence, that "the effectiveness of most crime prevention strategies will remain unknown until the nation invests more in evaluating them." Thus, while progress had been made from the days of Martinson's "nothing works," there was still much to be done.

Since that time the government has invested more in evaluating and providing information on programs and approaches that are more beneficial than others. The National Institute of Justice (NIJ) has developed a dedicated website called *Crimesolutions.gov* which lists programs in various areas, along with what is known about the program's effectiveness (e.g., effective, promising, no effect). On the juvenile justice side, the Office of Juvenile Justice and Delinquency Prevention (OJJDP) also compiles lists of programs along with their effectiveness (www.ojjdp.gov/mpg). For those seeking the highest level of evidence, Blueprints for Healthy Youth Development (www.blueprintsprograms.com/) provides a list of programs that have been assessed and found effective experimentally (or quasi-experimentally) in more than one location, and the findings hold for at least a year. Programs that reach this level are labeled "model programs."

Examples of model programs include Functional Family Therapy (FFT) and Multisystemic Therapy (MST). FFT focuses on the family relationships of juveniles who are engaged in antisocial behavior. Parenting skills and communication are addressed within the program. MST is also geared toward juveniles who have demonstrated antisocial behavior, but MST is broader in that it targets neighborhood and peer issues that may be affecting the juvenile's conduct.

POLICY IMPLICATIONS: SIDE-BY-SIDE

Clearly this entire chapter has been about policy implications of competing paradigms, so this section will be necessarily short. The classical and neoclassical schools of criminology suggest that, in essence, the causes of crime are the same for everyone; crime is the result of a decision made by individuals who weigh—however quickly—the pros and cons of competing lines of action. When the benefits of crime are higher than the costs, crime ensues. The solution, therefore, is to affect that crime calculus in ways that tip the scales toward prosocial behavior. Traditionally the policy implications of the classical and neoclassical schools have focused on increasing costs through criminal justice sanctions. Beccaria provided a blueprint for what he thought would be a more humane and more effective criminal justice system—one that would ensure offenders were punished, but only to the degree necessary to deter and no more.

Neoclassical policy took these ideas a step further, assuming that if crime was simply a rational calculus then increasing the severity of punishments would make would-be offenders think twice. Thus truth-in-sentencing policies, abolishment of parole, and sentencing guidelines emerged. During the neoclassical revolution, incarceration rates began their ascent in the United States, which continued unabated until relatively recently. While not solely a function of reformers interested in deterring offenders, it seems reasonable to suggest that the neoclassical school played a role in the movement away from rehabilitation and toward a more punishment-centric system in the 1970s.

In addition to the use of the criminal justice system, opportunity theorists suggest that everyday life can be altered in such a way that the criminal calculus is influenced. Making it more difficult to commit crimes by increasing the presence of guardians and hardening targets by reducing the ease with which they can be victimized should also reduce crime. Neoclassical scholars put the onus on ordinary citizens and business owners to reduce their chances of being a victim of crime, rather than relying on the criminal justice system.

The positive school of criminology, on the other hand, does not see much value in punishment alone, or in simply assuming that there's not much we can do to address motivation to offend. The positive school argues that criminologists can discover the causes of crime and address those causes directly. In other words, positive criminologists believe that there is something which leads people to become offenders that differentiates them from non-offenders. If we ignore that, we run the risk of allowing crime to flourish. Perhaps more importantly, positivists argue we cannot hope to reduce crime or recidivism by treating all offenders alike, for the causes of crime may, and likely do, differ among people and groups.

While biological positivism was associated with nefarious policy (such as eugenics) in the early 20th century, sociological positivism emerged to shine the light on environmental causes of crime such as poverty. The emergence of the "what works" movement has contributed to our knowledge-base about what sorts of programs work for different offenders. This knowledge-base and movement continue to grow. Crime prevention has also emerged as an area of study in its own right and has led to the accumulation of knowledge regarding how to stop antisocial behavior before it begins (see Welsh & Farrington, 2012). Typically crime prevention operates by examining risk factors for antisocial behavior, and attempting to either prevent those factors from emerging or disrupting the link between the risk factors and later criminal behavior.

CONCLUSION: TALE-OF-THE-TAPE

As in previous chapters, there is no one clear "winner" in this debate between positivists and classicists with respect to criminal policy. Both have had their "heyday" and both have remained relevant. After all, it is simultaneously true that corrections agencies in the United States function to punish offenders while also providing treatment or rehabilitation services. In Maine, for example, there is no parole, which means that offenders are given determinant sentences and must serve a substantial portion of that sentence. However, the Maine Department of Corrections, where one of us previously worked (Rocque), offers a wide variety of programming to inmates, including education and cognitive behavioral therapy. The other author (Posick) has taught college-level classes in a maximum-security men's facility in Southeast Georgia for the past three years. Thus programming is relatively strong, even in punitive environments.

Classical and neoclassical school policy

What does the research say? We have reviewed a bit of evidence on both sides of the debate. Deterrence, the linchpin of the neoclassical school, has had a rocky empirical life in criminology. Early reviews indicated that the research landscape was too undeveloped to provide firm terrain for evaluation. More recent reviews (Nagin, 1998; 2013) seem to suggest that there is firmer, smoother ground on which to declare that "deterrence works." Yet the story is not that simple. Let's begin on the macro level.

The most visible criminal justice policies are capital punishment and incarceration. Early research on capital punishment was very clear: it does not deter (Baldus & Cole, 1975; but see Ehrlich, 1975). More recent work seems a bit more supportive of the deterrent effect of capital punishment (Mocan & Gittings, 2003; Shepherd, 2004). In an interesting paper, Durlauf, Fu, and Navarro (2013) showed how different models produce

TABLE 8.1 TALE-OF-THE-TAPE. CLASSICAL/NEOCLASSICAL SCHOOL VS. POSITIVE SCHOOL

Theory	Classical/neoclassical school	Positive school
Theorists	Cesare Beccaria; Jeremy Bentham; Robert Martinson; James Q. Wilson; Ronald Clarke; Lawrence Cohen; Marcus Felson	Cesare Lombroso; Clifford Shaw; Henry McKay; James Bonta; Don Andrews
Main arguments	Everyone is a potential criminal; crime is the result of calculated decisions; good policy/strategies seek to deter offenders	Something differentiates offenders from non-offenders; we should target individual differences to reduce crime
Period of popularity	1760s–present	1870s–present
Seminal pieces	*On Crimes and Punishments* (Beccaria); *Thinking about Crime* (Wilson); *Social Change and Crime Rate Trends: A Routine Activity Approach* (Cohen & Felson)	*Criminal Man* (Lombroso); *Juvenile Delinquency and Urban Areas* (Shaw & McKay); *Psychology of Criminal Conduct* (Andrews & Bonta)
WINNER		✓

diametrically opposed results when examining the deterrence of capital punishment. Despite these ambiguous findings, most criminologists, when asked, believe that the death penalty does not deter offenders (Radelet & Lacock, 2009) and the American Society of Criminology has an official policy position opposing capital punishment.

With respect to incarceration, it seems unequivocal that locking people up does reduce crime either via incapacitation or deterrence. With respect to the crime decline in America that began around 1993 or so, estimates have suggested that the increase in incarceration rates helps explain around 33 percent of the fall (Levitt, 2004; others place this estimate much lower, see Clear & Frost, 2015). Yet there seems to be a point of diminishing returns—the degree to which the United States has committed to incarceration is unprecedented in the world, with incarceration rates and raw numbers far exceeding any other nation. There is a general consensus among criminologists that the use of incarceration has gone too far—which is not consistent with Beccaria's admonition that punishment goes only as far as is needed to deter (Clear & Frost, 2015). In fact some work has shown that mass incarceration has actually made the situation worse in particular communities (Alexander, 2012; Clear, 2009).

One clear and simple test of whether deterrence "works," it seems to us, is whether or not offenders who are caught and sanctioned are more or less likely to engage in future offending behavior. On this point deterrence seems to fail, as those punished are often shown to be at *higher* risk of reoffending (Pratt et al., 2006). Pogarsky and Piquero (2003) refer to this as the "resetting effect," whereby individuals who have been punished believe that their chances of being caught again are diminished, apparently assuming punishment to be a random selection process.

Examining the overall statistical effect of deterrence variables is also a useful way to determine whether a theoretical approach is effective. Travis Pratt and colleagues provided a meta-analysis of the deterrence literature in 2006. The results were not promising for deterrence scholars. Of four measures of deterrence (certainty, severity, a composite variable, and non-legal sanctions) "only the certainty estimates and the effects of non-legal sanctions are large enough to be considered substantively important (ranging from -.171 to -.334, all at p<.05)" (Pratt et al., 2006, p. 379). Further, as was the case when Paternoster (1987) reviewed the literature, Pratt and colleagues found that, when controls were included in the studies, the effect of deterrence variables was diminished considerably, indicating that they do not have a strong, independent relationship with offending.

In a recent piece Pratt and Turanovic (2018) examined the celerity pillar in more depth. Celerity, recall, refers to how "swift" punishment is enacted following an offense. The idea, from Beccaria, is that in order to form an impression, and therefore to deter, punishment must follow as quickly as possible after a transgression. The results of this piece are, again, sobering for deterrence theorists. In the criminal justice sphere, celerity does not seem to matter, and in the laboratory its effects are very sensitive to timing—this led Pratt and Turanovic to argue that "implementing celerity of punishment into the criminal justice system in a meaningful way is a practical impossibility" (p. 10). They suggest that celerity has more of a role in informal punishments. Nonetheless, we cannot help but be struck by the general conclusions regarding deterrence theory: "In general, deterrence theory has not fared very well as an explanation of criminal behavior" (p. 14).

The story is a bit more positive when examining the opportunity approach. Reviews have suggested that particular strategies to deter crime in the form of guardianship seem to work. For example, Welsh and Farrington (2009) conducted a meta-analysis of closed-circuit televsion (CCTV), finding a "modest" reduction in crime. Examining situational crime prevention specifically, Guerette and Bowers (2009) found that there was a positive, crime-reducing effect of several situational mechanisms and that one long-standing critique of such measures, that crime will just move to where prevention techniques aren't being implemented, was not an issue.

Positive criminology policy

It is fair to say that the first wave of positive criminology failed where policy was concerned. Not only were some disturbing policies, such as eugenics, attached to the positive school, but the attempt to treat offenders differently depending on the causes of crime was a failure. It not only failed to reduce recidivism, apparently, but it also resulted in the justified critique that offenders were not treated equitably by the state. In other words, discretion left to the judge to determine the appropriate sanction allowed biases to creep in. All of this added up to the dismissal of rehabilitation and a search for causes of crime in order to prevent it.

The resurgence of positivism in the form of crime prevention and offender rehabilitation has, however, been nothing short of stunning. Entire volumes exist on approaches to prevent crime at all points across the life-course and bodies of literature have emerged describing correctional programs that have succeeded in reducing recidivism (Andrews & Bonta, 1990; Farrington & Welsh, 2009; Welsh & Farrington, 2012). From the "nothing works" paradigm we are now witnessing the "what works" movement.

Thanks to this movement we now know much more about how to address criminogenic risks and needs and what sorts of approaches (e.g., Drug Abuse Resistance Education, DARE) do not work.

In the realm of meta-analysis, work has evaluated whether and what types of programs work for offenders or would-be offenders. In one of the earliest, Gendreau and colleagues (1996) found that "criminogenic needs," which included "antisocial personality, companions, interpersonal conflict, criminogenic needs, and substance abuse" (p. 584) were very strongly related to recidivism, whereas intellectual functioning, socioeconomic status, and personal distress were not as strongly related to recidivism. Meta-analyses have also been conducted for various sub-populations, including sex offenders (Hanson & Bussiere, 1998) and juveniles (Cottle, Lee, & Heilbrun, 2001). The Campbell Collaboration (www.campbellcollaboration.org/) houses systematic reviews and meta-analyses on a host of programs, strategies, and approaches for reducing crime, illustrating the breadth and depth of the knowledge that has accumulated on how to reduce crime from a positivistic standpoint.

We would be remiss to leave the story there, however, as the news for offender rehabilitation or crime prevention is not all rosy. As some biosocial criminologists have pointed out, much remains to be studied with respect to programs addressing offenders. Jaime Vaske (2017) argues that our knowledge-base to date has hinged on examining programs overall, rather than focusing on for whom programs may work or not work. She suggests that biopsychological information may provide some of the information we need to better understand program receptivity. Gajos, Fagan, and Beaver (2016) concur with this assessment: "Evaluations of preventive interventions often fail to identify the mechanism(s) or key components that produce behavioral changes, and the degree to which overall effects are generalizable across diverse populations are often not established" (p. 684). We believe that these assessments are likely to be correct and it should be a focus of future research to identify the biopsychosocial impacts of interventions and for whom interventions work best.

Yet it does not seem far-fetched to predict that the information we are currently missing from treatment programs (e.g., mechanisms, populations who are more responsive to particular forms of treatment, etc.) will soon be discovered. Vaske's (2017) paper, for example (and some of her earlier work (Vaske, Gaylean, & Cullen, 2011)), has shown that biosocial mechanisms may help explain why and how certain treatments work. In addition, the "differential susceptibility" hypothesis in the gene by environment literature may go some way toward helping us understand which populations are more responsive to environmental influences. The differential susceptibility hypothesis suggests that individuals with particular genetic makeups may be more influenced by environments than others. This work helps explain gene by environment interactions, where it has previously been assumed that genetic risk plus environmental risk adds up to increased overall risk. But the differential susceptibility hypothesis suggests that these genetic profiles also lead to individuals being influenced by good environments as well.

If we contrast the body of literature amassed by the positivistic school to the deterrence and neoclassical work it seems that the positivists are the winners of this particular debate. The research on opportunity theory and prevention is a bit more favorable to the neoclassical school than the deterrence research. Viewed as a whole, however, we believe the positivistic school has claimed victory. While we feel justified in this statement, it by no means indicates that deterrence-focused strategies should be removed. We are not advocates for prison abolition and feel that it has its place and does lead to crime reduction—to a point. A more integrated approach, where deterrence is utilized with positivistic treatment, seems to us to be the most valuable of all available options.

After covering all the past debates in this book so far, it might be tempting to ask whether or not such debates continue. We say—yes! Most of the debates we have covered continue in one form or another and new ones have emerged. It is to these contemporary debates we now turn.

NOTES

1   This introduction on Cabot is drawn from Welsh, Zane, & Rocque (2017). The study was also chronicled on the *Freakonomics* podcast: http://freakonomics.com/podcast/when-helping-hurts/

2   https://fivethirtyeight.com/features/gun-deaths/

3   www.gunviolencearchive.org/past-tolls

4   https://www.smithsonianmag.com/history/a-brief-history-of-the-salem-witch-trials-175162489/

5   This book was a translation of the third volume of the fifth edition of *Criminal Man* (Gibson and Rafter, 2006)

6   See www.ussc.gov/sites/default/files/pdf/research-and-publications/research-projects-and-surveys/miscellaneous/15-year-study/chap1.pdf

7   The entire report can be accessed here: www.ncjrs.gov/works/

Are we still debating?

Contemporary and emerging debates

9

MUCH OF THIS BOOK has been historical in nature. It has recounted classic debates in the field of criminology that took place decades ago, while covering some relatively recent issues. The question some readers may have, though, is whether debates are a thing of the past, an historical artifact, or whether they are still taking place. One issue impacting the prevalence of debates is that, more and more, criminology is becoming a siloed field of study where factions break off, socialize with one another, publish in their favorite journals, and do not interact with those who might disagree with them. We see this as problematic for the future of debates and diversity of scholarly thought.

The American Society of Criminology (ASC) lists 12 separate divisions, each with a distinct focus and, often, a journal which publishes material in that area. The Academy of Criminal Justice Sciences (ACJS) also lists 12 sections—many similar but a couple different than ASC. Criminologists also seem to know which journals will be open to their niche and which will not. Biosocial criminologists, who argue that their work is not taken seriously by mainstream criminologists, suggest that particular top-tier journals will not publish their work (Beaver et al., 2015). There are journals for "critical" criminologists, journals for quantitative and qualitative criminologists, and journals for those studying cybercrime, to name a few.

It appears that there is less opportunity for those who disagree with one another to do so in formal outlets, as was the case when the flagship journal *Criminology* hosted the classic criminal career debates in the 1980s. Does this mean the "age of the debate" is dead? Thankfully, the answer to that question is no. Scholarly journals do, from time to time, still host debates. And there has been a proliferation of outlets in which scholars can interact and share their thoughts. One includes personal websites and blogs, in which scholars can write relatively quickly and freely on topics that they feel passionately about. These blog posts are then shared and re-shared on social media sites such as Twitter. In addition, web-based academic outlets have grown, such as quillette.com, theconversation.com, and scholarsstrategynetwork.org. As we wrote this chapter a debate on race and intelligence was being hashed out in various outlets by scholars such as University of Texas psychologist Paige Harden, University of Virginia psychologist Eric Turkheimer, and University of Michigan psychologist Richard Nisbett, who wrote about the topic at vox.com.[1] Several scholars responded to the piece at another website, called medium.com.[2] The original authors offered another reply again at vox.[3] This is in addition to many interactions the authors had with experts and those who wish to be considered experts in the field on social media.

And so debates are still occurring in criminology. In this, the last substantive chapter of *Great Debates*, we wish to take a more contemporary view and focus on recent debates. We will begin in the late 20th century, focus mainly on the 21st century, and discuss such topics as general vs. specific theories, the utility of group-based trajectory approaches, how to measure and analyze desistance from crime, epigenetics, and the use of twin studies in criminology. Because this chapter covers relatively new debates and because there are more topics, each section is shorter than the treatment given to the debates in previous chapters.

THEORY: SHOULD IT COVER ALL BEHAVIORS OR JUST A FEW?

In criminology, particularly toward the end of the 19th century, there was a trend toward "general" theories of crime. General theories of crime are just that—general.

They are not specific to any type of behavior or type of criminal. One of the best known general theories of crime was published by Michael Gottfredson and Travis Hirschi in their book, appropriately named *A General Theory of Crime* (1990). In that text the authors provided a useful definition for a general theory, being one that could "explain all crimes at all times, and, for that matter many forms of behavior that are not sanctioned by the state" (Gottfredson & Hirschi, 1990, p. 117).

Learning theory also falls under the rubric of general theory. Edwin Sutherland's (1947) differential association theory was an example of a general theory, one meant to explain all forms of crime and antisocial behavior, from street theft to white-collar swindling. Ronald Akers later revised differential association theory into his social structure and social learning theory, specifically labeling it a general theory of crime (Akers et al., 1979; Akers, 2011).

Strain theory, particularly Robert Agnew's version, is another well-known general theory. Merton's strain or anomie version was not necessarily general, as it applied to offenses in which a shortage of resources or a personal deficit is driving antisocial behavior; presumably, for those who have enough of whatever they want (be it wealth, status, and so forth), offending would have to be explained via other means. But Agnew transformed strain theory into a social psychological one, specifically equipped to address the shortcomings and gaps left by Merton. And in so doing he relabeled the theory "general strain theory," thus demonstrating his intention for the theory to account for all types of crime.

The appeal of general theories should be obvious. If only one account of crime is needed to understand all forms of antisocial behavior the world will be much simpler. There is no need to develop theories for cat burglars, embezzlers, and phishers. This logic should, if it holds, also apply to policy. If one theory accounts for disparate behaviors, policies do not need to be molded after particular offenses but derive from the one theory, thus reducing the plethora of options available.

Yet it is not the case that every iteration of general theory is necessarily more simple or parsimonious than their non-general counterparts. Sutherland's differential association theory, while composed of nine principles, really hinged on proposition six, which stated that a person becomes delinquent because of an excess of definitions favorable to law violation. Akers, however, expanded the theory to include not only definitions but reinforcement, imitation, and differential association. Agnew's general strain theory also expanded Merton's version, making it more complex. By the time general strain theory was published in book version (2006's *Pressured into Crime*) the theory had become incredibly complex, incorporating elements of several other theories, such as self-control, social control, and social learning theory.

Theory is only useful if it can be effectively applied to understanding and controlling crime. In the 1980s some criminologists began to argue that, rather than engaging in grand theorizing, we should be focused on particular acts of crime, explaining/ understanding those, and then getting to the work of preventing such acts in the future. But how can we know what is the more useful approach? What sorts of evidence would support one or another form of theorizing? Osgood and colleagues (1988) provided a useful overview of these two distinct forms of building theory.

Some scholars have focused on whether offenders are specialists or generalists. By distinguishing between the two they are asking: do people who engage in crime tend to treat it like an occupation where they are trained in one or two types of acts and focus on those behaviors; or do offenders engage in a wide variety of antisocial acts?

Specialization would be expected from the early "professional" criminal literature (e.g., Sutherland, 1937). Yet the research, at least in the late 20th century, is pretty clear on this score—offenders do not specialize. As Gottfredson and Hirschi (1986, p. 218) stated, "There is, then, virtually no evidence of offense specialization anywhere in the life cycle of ordinary offenders." Instead offenders are said to be "versatile," meaning they engage in a number of specific types of crimes. Depending on how specialization or versatility is measured, however, researchers tend to find varying results. Using a calculation called the "diversity index," which provides an indicator across a set number of types of crimes regarding how diverse or specialized offenders are, we found evidence of versatility. In a sample of more than 12,000 youngsters across the world our diversity index could range from 0 (complete specialization) to .667 (complete diversity). Our results showed a diversity index of .13 (Rocque et al., 2015). In other words, there wasn't complete specialization but neither was there evidence that offenders are totally diverse. Other research has found some evidence of short-term specialization (Sullivan et al., 2006).

Yet even if offenders tend to be "polymorphously perverse" (Geis, 2008, p. 43), does that mean an approach that focuses on how crimes are committed is unlikely to be effective? The argument for a crime-specific approach is not necessarily that the motivations are different for different types of crime, but that the opportunities, physical environmental factors, and techniques for each likely vary. As Cornish and Clarke (1986, p. 2) argued about their rational choice perspective, "a crime-specific focus was adopted, not only because different crimes may meet different needs, but also because the situational context of decision making and the information being handled will vary greatly among offenses. To ignore these differences might well be to reduce significantly one's ability to identify fruitful points for intervention." Thus the focus of crime-specific theorists is not necessarily increased explained variance but ability to inform policy (Weisburd et al., 1993).

More recent theoretical explorations have not clarified this debate. For example, general theories still exist and continue to stimulate research. In addition, general theories are being developed to this day, including a theoretical perspective put forth by Matt DeLisi in his recent book on psychopathy as a unified theory of crime (2017) and John Hipp's (2016) general theory of spatial patterns of crime. At the same time crime-specific theories and approaches have continued to grow. Theories have been developed to explain cybercrime (Jaishankar, 2007), female offending (Steffensmeier & Allan, 1996), and desistance from crime (Rocque, 2015; 2017).

A final example of this debate centers on white-collar crime. When Michael Gottfredson and Travis Hirschi were developing their general theory of crime they argued that it could account for all forms of deviance (those illegal and legal). In particular they railed against the study of white-collar crime as a separate area of focus in criminology. Why act as if white-collar crime is different than all other forms of crime? Theirs was "a general theory of crime capable of organizing the facts about white-collar crime at the same time it is capable of organizing the facts about all forms of crime" (Hirschi & Gottfredson, 1987, p. 949). They (Hirschi & Gottfredson, 1987) suggested that crime-specific theories may be useful for policy but not for understanding why crime occurs. To them the only reason white-collar crime became an interesting concept was the fallacious notion that crime is the sole purview of the lower classes.

What is different about white-collar crime? To Hirschi and Gottfredson, nothing. White-collar crimes, they argue, "provide relatively quick, relatively certain benefit, with minimal effort. Crimes, including white-collar crimes, therefore require no motivation or pressure that is not present in any other form of human behavior" (Hirschi & Gottfredson, 1987, p. 959). That there is nothing different about white-collar crime means that heading down the path of treating it as such is a waste of theoretical energy. What has the study of white-collar crime produced? "Its conclusions are not new (citation omitted) and its rewards meager: outside of its obvious ideological value, 'white-collar' crime offers little to criminology that cannot be found elsewhere at less cost" (Hirschi & Gottfredson, 1989, p. 360). Thus the issue is territorialism. They argue "It is perhaps understandable that scholars specializing in a particular crime or offender type would resist efforts to include their specialty in a more general theory" (Hirschi & Gottfredson, 1989, p. 368).

What do the proponents of white-collar crime as a separate area of study argue? Steffensmeier (1989) replied to Hirschi and Gottfredson, showing that their data analysis used to compare white-collar and ordinary offenders was inaccurate. He also suggested that the profile of the white-collar criminal was different than that of ordinary offenders. Steffensmeier first argued that the categories of crime (fraud, forgery, and embezzlement) Hirschi and Gottfredson examined from the uniform crime reports do not represent white-collar crime well. According to Steffensmeier, "The evidence indicates that most arrests for fraud or for forgery are not occupationally related but rather involve passing bad checks, credit card fraud, theft of services, falsification of identification, defrauding an innkeeper, fraudulent use of public transport, welfare fraud, and small con games" (1989, p. 347). Steffensmeier then argued that the demographic profile (e.g., age curve) of white-collar crime looks different than for other crimes, such as burglary. Steffensmeier concluded that his analyses are not definitive in regards to whether general or specific theories are preferred, but Hirschi and Gottfredson's points are dealt a blow.

Other researchers have taken up the general vs. specific mantle with respect to white-collar crime. Michael Benson and Elizabeth Moore (1992) examined whether self-control theory applies to white-collar crime, arguing that the theory implies that white-collar offenders should be versatile and engaged in crime to the same degree as ordinary criminals. They found that many white-collar criminals don't fit these patterns, concluding that the general theory is damaged by these findings. Yet Hirschi and Gottfredson (1987) had stated that their theory would suggest white-collar criminals are less likely than ordinary offenders to be engaged in crime because the characteristics of white-collar employees imply a higher level of self-control. To Benson and Moore a distinct theory of white-collar crime is necessary. Finally, Langton and Piquero (2007) found that general strain theory is moderately useful in explaining white-collar crime but does not fit corporate crime as well.

ARE THERE DISTINCT GROUPS?

A related issue in criminology concerns the question of typologies. One reason Gottfredson and Hirschi dismissed the importance of white-collar crime as a separate area of study is that they viewed it as part of the tendency of scholars to see offenders as belonging to distinct groups. As they clearly argued, offenders differ in degree (of criminality), not in kind (groups). In their 1987 piece they suggested the typological approach was due to the eclectic nature of criminology and of scholars wanting to specialize in their "parent discipline" (Hirschi & Gottfredson, 1987, p. 971). But while the typological or group-based theorizing is similar to the general vs. specific theories of crime debate, it is separated by a focus on types of offenders and not types of crimes.

Typologies of offenders are not new in criminology, but it is fair to say they received their most high-profile boost in 1993 with Terrie Moffitt's publication of a theoretical taxonomy. Moffitt's (1993) typological theory was created to respond to the debate in the 1980s regarding the meaning of the age-crime curve. The age-crime curve is a well-known (and replicated) finding in criminology. In brief, the age-crime curve describes the finding that crime tends to increase with age during adolescence, reaching a peak in the early 20s, and declining thereafter (Hirschi & Gottfredson, 1983). Moffitt argued that the age-crime curve, in the aggregate, masked two distinct types or groups of offenders. The first, adolescent-limited offenders, are relatively "normal" individuals with a lack of disadvantages. They engage in mostly non-serious offending during adolescence when they are exposed to deviant peers. Adolescent-limited offenders also engage in offending when they experience a maturity gap as they are biologically developing into adults but are not afforded social privileges that come with adulthood. When the peer models and maturity gaps vanish with the attainment of social adulthood, adolescent-limited offenders find it easy to become prosocial. Thus their criminal careers are limited to adolescence.

On the other hand, life-course persistent offenders come from disadvantaged backgrounds and are characterized by neuropsychological deficits. They are relatively antisocial throughout life and continue to offend beyond adolescence. Thus we see two groups of offenders and two theories of offending in Moffitt's theoretical scheme. Note that this theory fits neatly with the findings of the criminal career work showing that a small group of offenders (5 percent) accounted for a disproportionate amount of crime (50 percent).

Coinciding with Moffitt's (1993) theoretical exposition of qualitatively different offenders was the development of a statistical tool meant precisely to disentangle groups of offenders (or any other group) over time. In one of the first uses of this type of method in criminology, Nagin and Land (1993) used a semi-parametric approach to model the trajectories of crime over time and to group individuals into clusters. This method eventually came to be known as semi-parametric group-based modeling (SPGM) and was fully described in Nagin's book in 2005. The model relies on the Poisson distribution and does not enforce parametric restrictions on lambda, the crime rate of individuals. The approach allows researchers to find a different intercept or starting point as well as different growth parameters for separate "groups." Interestingly, and usefully, for those in the typology camp, model fit statistics can be leveraged to determine the optimal number of groups that exist in a dataset. Are there two? Three? Just one? In their classic paper, Nagin and Land (1993) uncovered four groups, three of which had some non-trivial level of offending.

In justifying the need for a distinct method of finding and plotting groups of offenders (or any other form of behavior), Nagin and Piquero (2010, p. 107) wrote: "Taken together, extant developmental theories and empirical research raise the possibility of important variation underlying longitudinal crime patterns. Yet, most statistical approaches for analyzing longitudinal data (developmental trajectories) are designed to account for individual variability about a mean population trend, and thus ignore the possibility that there are meaningful subgroups within a population that follow distinct developmental trajectories that are not identifiable ex ante (Nagin, 2005, p. 1). Thus, it becomes necessary to have a methodological approach that permits detection and examination of individuals following distinctive developmental trajectories."

The popularity of group trajectory modeling cannot be understated. Since the development of the model, and the package specifically written for the software program SAS (Proc Traj), the use of the model to plot trajectories of different groups' offending has exploded. The Nagin and Land paper itself has been cited more than 800 times, the Nagin (2005) book on the method more than 2,000. A Google Scholar search (admittedly a blunt way of gauging the popularity of an approach) produced more than 122,000 hits in the summer of 2017. Groups have been calculated for all manner of criminal behaviors, and even for crime "places" (Weisburd et al., 2004).

Not all agree with the approach, however. A debate of sorts was initiated in 2004 when life-course researchers Robert Sampson and John Laub, along with Elaine Eggleston (Doherty), published a couple of papers in the *Journal of Quantitative Criminology* regarding whether groups existed in reality or were a methodological artifact. First, Eggleston, Laub, and Sampson (2004) argued that, despite the group-based modeling approach's increasing use, researchers had been overlooking whether it was the best analytical tool and what happened when robustness checks were implemented. They used the Glueck data Sampson and Laub had analyzed previously (Sampson & Laub, 1993; Laub & Sampson, 2003) to explore the effects of varying follow-up periods, controlling for "street time," and taking account of deaths in follow-ups. They found that each of these factors influence the trajectories that are "identified" by the group-based modeling approach, particularly the length of follow-up.

In response, Nagin (2004) wrote that, first of all, the issues Eggleston and colleagues raise are not specific to the group-based approach. In addition, where Eggleston, Laub, and Sampson had seen differences across varying follow-up periods, controlling for street time and mortality, he saw similarities. Finally, and to us most importantly, he argued that the group-based method is not identifying *actual* groups—it's a statistical tool after all. These groups, he said, are most likely "approximat(ing) an unknown and presumably continuous distribution" (p. 31). Some may suggest a discrete method then is not the best way to plot the distribution. However, he replied "usually there is no good empirical or theoretical basis for specifying that distribution. The cost of approximation is obvious. Approximations are just that—there is a loss of accuracy" (p. 32). In other words, Nagin was careful to state that the method identifies statistical groups but should not be used to reify them.

Sampson, Laub, & Eggleston (2004) then replied to Nagin. They wrote that they had meant to shake things up a bit where group-based methods were concerned. They were afraid popularity had won out over clear thinking about selection of model. Sampson and colleagues clarified that it wasn't necessarily the method itself that they disagreed with but its response and how the results are interpreted. It should come as no surprise that Sampson and Laub critiqued the group-based methodology, considering their 2003 book questioned the theoretical basis of groups. In the 2004 critique they pointed out "One catch in all this is that SPGM begins with the methodological assumption that groups exist, often leading to the notion that a wide array of group configurations is possible. It is then easy for the naïve user to conclude (tautologically?) that groups exist because they are discovered, even though a model cannot be said to discover what it assumes. SPGM will estimate groups from an underlying continuous distribution, a fact that can bedevil even the most sophisticated user" (Sampson et al., 2004, p. 41).

In 2005 Nagin and Tremblay added another log to the ever-growing fire. This time their piece found its way into the pages of *Criminology*, the flagship journal of the field and host of the criminal career debates 20 years prior. Nagin and Tremblay (2005) reiterated their view that groups found in statistical models do not necessarily "exist." That groups are estimated or categories are defined when they may not be identical representations of reality is nothing new, they say (Nagin & Tremblay, 2005, p. 877):

> Categorical groupings are used as basic organizing devices in countless mundane human activities, even though the groups have no more reality than they do in statistical modeling. Everyday communications are filled with queries requiring a categorical response—for example, "did you have a good day?" or "is Smith a pleasant person?" Both the questioner and respondent know that the query is about a fictional category. Days are rarely all good or bad, and people are not entirely pleasant or unpleasant. Nevertheless, such queries remain a staple of everyday communications because both parties understand that a categorical response provides a succinct summary that can be elaborated upon if necessary.

Nagin and Tremblay also noted that the number of groups estimated in a particular sample will vary by sample size and other characteristics (as found by Eggleston and colleagues) but this is to be expected. People change over time and that is the reason we collect longitudinal, within-group data. Finally, they wrote that their method does not assume that each individual identified with a particular trajectory will necessarily follow the path of the group trajectory over time perfectly. In other words, of course there is individual-level variation within groups.

Robert Sampson and John Laub (2005) wrote of their concern for the "seduction" of the group-based method. According to Sampson and Laub, criminology as a field is prone to falling for a new statistical method and often judges the value of scholarship based on the use of that method. The authors were replying to a critique by Nagin and Tremblay (2005) of their work. Sampson and Laub argue that Nagin and Tremblay offered nothing new: "Expecting to learn, we were instead disappointed by the lack of an original contribution" (p. 906).

Sampson and Laub then take on each of the points made by Nagin and Tremblay. Most pointedly, they argue that if Nagin and Tremblay truly believe that individuals do not necessarily belong to trajectories, trajectories are just statistical tools, not reality, and that people do not follow trajectories, then the value of the method and its usefulness for testing taxonomic theories is unclear. To be sure, they are not saying groups do not exist. They simply believe that groups cannot be predicted prospectively and that their causal underpinnings are not distinct. The problem is with the method. "Nagin's model begins with the assumption that groups exist, leading users to then discover groups even though a model cannot be said to discover what it assumes. And, as Nagin and Tremblay correctly note, Proc Traj will estimate ('find') pseudo groups from an underlying continuous distribution" (Sampson & Laub, 2005, p. 909). In a clever footnote, Sampson and Laub respond to Nagin and Tremblay's example of using shorthands every day ("it's a nice day outside") by suggesting that we do so in ways that are often wrong.

Next, taking a leaf out of the book by Gottfredson and Hirschi, Sampson and Laub show how the findings generated by the group-based modeling approach are not new. For example, they show that a higher number of risk factors overall increases criminal behavior; poorly educated and younger mothers more often have delinquent children;

chronic offenders are more violent; there is within-group variation; and changing definitions of terms (e.g., desistance) changes results. All of these findings were known before the group-based method emerged and do not require it to be found.

A few years later other scholars began to weigh in on this methodological debate. First, Torbjørn Skardhamar (2010) analyzed whether the group-based methodology is a statistically useful way to examine trajectories. Skardhamar used a simulation to show that the factors that are said to produce groups do create trajectories, but not distinct groupings of offenders. As he explained: "In the small simulation study reported here, I found that general mechanisms could generate behavioral patterns similar to those usually revealed by SPGM studies" (p. 297). In other words, there are not distinct mechanisms for each group, calling into question just how "real" they are. In an interesting analysis, Skardhamar first simulated longitudinal data purposefully such that there were no distinct groups. He then applied group-based modeling which—aha!—found groups. He concluded that "It is hard to see how [group-based modeling] can *test* for the existence of distinct subpopulations in a sample, and interpretation of group-specific parameter estimates can be misleading" (p. 315).

Two years after Skardhamar's piece, Robert Brame, Ray Paternoster, and Alex Piquero (2012) responded with a defense of group-based methods. To these scholars Nagin's method is useful in testing theories. They began their essay with interesting language, indicating they do not believe Skardhamar accurately comprehends group-based methodology (e.g., "In a recent paper, Skardhamar . . . presented his *understanding* of the purpose and value of group-based trajectory modeling (GBT) in criminology and criminal justice" (p. 470, emphasis added)). They argued that Skardhamar prematurely dismisses group-based methods and that they are used for more than just taxonomic theory testing (they actually identify seven unique ways in which the method has been used in criminology).

Brame and colleagues first reviewed the precursors to the Nagin and Land (1993) paper, work which built the foundation for statistical models to identify or estimate the mixing distribution in criminological data. In a footnote (footnote 4) Brame and his collaborators took aim at a less important point of Skardhamar's but one that has bearing on the accuracy of his claims. In his essay he had stated that Moffitt's theory was influenced or "spurred" by the group-based modeling approach. Yet Brame and colleagues rightly showed that Nagin and Land (1993) had referenced an unpublished version of Moffitt's (1993) theoretical paper, suggesting it existed prior to their work. Thus, they argued, Moffitt's theory could not have been spurred by the group-based approach. Yet at the same time they had previously taken pains to show that the approach did not begin with Nagin and Land (1993).

They then discussed several sticky issues with group-based modeling. With respect to the argument that these models always find groups, Brame and colleagues replied, essentially, "yes, that is what they are meant to do." In their words:

> Even Skardhamar (2010) acknowledged in a previous paper (Skardhamar, 2009, p. 873) that it is "uncontroversial" that semi-parametric group-based modeling (SPGM) identifies groups of offenders and that "SPGM will *always* find groups, whether they truly exist or not" (emphasis in original). Such an observation is "uncontroversial" precisely because GBT modeling strategies are, in fact, group-based. They are explicitly designed to identify points of support in the data that can be thought of as constituting groups of individuals who are similar to other individuals in the

group in their offending pattern over time and dissimilar to those in other groups (p. 479).

To Brame and colleagues, how scholars interpret the identification of groups is a "theoretical" question (p. 480). The lack of theory in the use of group-based models, they concluded, appears to be the source of the largest controversy. Yet that critique applies to all methods. They understood the concern that people may be identified as being part of a "group" and treated unfairly, but believed criminology can responsibly handle that danger.

WHAT IS DESISTANCE?

As an outgrowth of the criminal career debate (see Chapter 4) researchers began to pay more attention to different parts of the life-course. Criminology had, up to that time, been "adolescent-limited" (Cullen, 2011), meaning that most research focused on youth. In a way this makes sense, because youth are a population that are relatively easy to access and for whom criminal behaviors are beginning to emerge. Desistance, the decline in crime over time, has increasingly become an area of focus for researchers.

We have long known about desistance. Adolphe Quetelet, in his *Research on the Propensity for Crime at Different Ages* (1831/1984), noted that crime rates peaked at ages 25–30. The Gluecks (Sheldon and Eleanor), the two Harvard scientists who conducted some of the first longitudinal studies of crime and delinquency, also found that crime declines after early adulthood (for an overview of the history of early desistance research, see Rocque, 2017). It was in the 1980s and 1990s that the decline in crime with age became a focal point in criminology. In 1983 Hirschi and Gottfredson published their piece on age and crime and, three years later, Farrington (1986) published his *Crime and Justice* essay covering research on the topic. The term desistance did not come to be commonly used in criminology until the 1990s. The 2001 publication of Laub and Sampson's "Understanding Desistance from Crime" in *Crime and Justice* unofficially marked the unveiling of desistance as its own field of study. In that paper they note that a peer reviewer of one of their studies told them that desistance was not a word!

Unfortunately, desistance remains a term that is not well defined and, perhaps as a result, is not consistently measured. Is desistance the within-individual decline in crime or does it reflect only a decline on the macro level? Farrington (1986) argued, for example, that the aggregate age-crime curve, which shows an increase over time until the mid-20s followed by a decline, was a result of people at older ages dropping out of the criminal ranks. Those who continued offending were active at the same level. Others argue that crime does decline with age for active offenders, indicating a slowing-down effect (Sampson & Laub, 2003).

So it is difficult to arrive at an agreed-upon definition of desistance if we are unsure of what it actually represents. It should therefore not be surprising that several definitions exist in the literature. As one of us has recounted (Rocque, 2017, p. 57):

Shover, in his *Great Pretenders* (1996), defined desistance as "the voluntary termination of serious criminal participation" (p. 121). Baskin and Sommers (1998) considered the women in their study to have desisted when they had "successfully exited the social world of violence, crime, and drugs" (p. 127). More recent researchers have viewed desistance as the changes and developments that precede termination of offending. For example, Laub and Sampson (2001) defined desistance as "the causal process that supports the termination of offending" (p. 11). Mulvey and colleagues (2004, p. 219) argued that "[d]esistance is a decline over time in some behavior of interest." Loeber and LeBlanc (1990, p. 382) suggested that desistance involves several things at once, not solely a decreasing of offending rates. To them, desistance is defined by "a slowing down in the frequency of offending (deceleration), a reduction in its variety (specialization), and a reduction in its seriousness (de-escalation)."

What about the way desistance is measured? Lila Kazemian (2007), who has written some of the best work on desistance in criminology, listed 13 operational definitions used in the literature. A few years later one of us updated that list to include five more definitions. What are some of the ways researchers measured desistance? The oldest in both lists is Farrington and Hawkins (1991) who measured desistance as the absence of a conviction after having one previously. Aaltonen, in 2016, measured desistance failure as a new conviction, prison stint, or fine in a three-year follow-up (see also Shover & Thompson, 1992; Warr, 1998). These operational definitions of desistance are really getting at termination, or the ending of a criminal career. They are static definitions, in other words.

Dynamic definitions do exist, however. If desistance is the slowing down of offending, static definitions which only capture the absence of offending (or punishment) sometime after having been in trouble don't do the job. Some work has used longitudinal growth models to track declines in crime (Rocque, Posick, & Paternoster, 2016; Sampson & Laub, 2003), thus defining desistance as a decrease in antisocial behavior, even if it did not disappear altogether in the study time-frame. The basic idea behind quantitatively studying desistance as a decrease in crime comes from the work of Bushway and colleagues (2001). They argued that desistance is really a process, not a state, and so it must be modeled as such. Their definition reflects this thinking: "the process of reduction in the rate of offending . . . from a nonzero level to a stable rate empirically indistinguishable from zero" (Bushway et al., 2001, p. 500).

Also on the dynamic side of things, qualitative researchers have queried offenders about whether they are intending to desist. Maruna (2001) asked individuals in his sample about their intentions—those who said they would quit were labeled and treated as desisters. Farrall and Calverley (2006) also used a qualitative approach (in addition to a quantitative one) to measure desistance. Peggy Giordano and colleagues (2002) provided one of the better qualitative measurements of desistance by asking respondents whether they were doing better than they had been in the past. Specifically, they asked "Would you say that the overall amount that you do things that could get you in trouble with the law is about the same, more, or less than when you were interviewed back in 1982?" (Giordano et al., 2002, p. 1008).

It should probably not be a surprise to learn that there is not much on which desistance researchers have come to a consensus. After all, the definitions, measurement, and even analyses of desistance vary widely. Is desistance dropping out of the offending ranks or is it a slowing down? Static and dynamic quantitative methods often come to different conclusions. For example, Bushway, Thornberry, and Krohn (2003) compared two measurements of desistance. In the static form they defined individuals as desisters if they had offended before age 18 but not after. In this scheme, 27.6 percent of the sample were classified as desisters. Using the group-based method described above, they found that the sample could be divided up empirically into seven groups. Of these, one they labeled "bell-shaped desisters" and it was composed of 8.5 percent of the sample—a far cry from the 27.6 percent classified as desisters in the static approach.

A final analytic issue is whether desistance researchers should be focused on official records or self-reports (Kazemian, 2007). Official records include such things as arrests, convictions, and prison stints to determine whether an individual is still engaged in crime (and getting caught). Of course, this method may not capture all criminal behavior and thus provide an inaccurate understanding of desistance. Researchers refer to the measurement of desistance using official records as "official desistance," and desistance measured with self-reports as "behavioral desistance" (Uggen & Kruttschnitt, 1998). Massoglia and Uggen (2007) further delineated the measurement of desistance with self-reports by asking respondents whether they were committing less crime than they were previously (similar to Giordano et al., 2002), which they called "subjective desistance," and whether they were committing less crime than their peers, called "reference group desistance" (Massoglia & Uggen, 2007). A recent study has compared official records to self-reports, indicating that desistance was found at earlier ages when using self-reports rather than convictions (Farrington et al., 2014).

Thus much remains to be determined with respect to the best way to define, measure, and analyze desistance from crime. Until common definitions are achieved, findings will continue to vary, hampering the ability of desistance research to inform policy and practice. At the very least it should be a priority for researchers to determine whether desistance represents a change in prevalence (people just dropping out of the offending ranks) or frequency in offending (slowing down in terms of the number of crimes committed over time).

GENES, HERITABILITY STUDIES, AND EPIGENETICS

A final debate we would like to consider is the most recent in criminology, having been hashed out in the pages of *Criminology* just a few years ago. We should qualify that, in actuality, this debate is not "new" per se; it harkens back to the origins of the field of criminology, and indeed all social sciences, for it revolves around the classic question of nature vs. nurture. In 2014 Callie Burt and Ronald Simons published a paper in the field's flagship journal *Criminology* offering some criticisms of what are known as "heritability" or "h2" studies. Such studies, associated with the field of behavior genetics, try to assess how much of the variance in a trait (i.e., phenotype) across a population is attributable to the environment and how much to genetics. Generally the method of choice to do such work is the twin study, which allows researchers to compare how similar identical (monozygotic) twins are to how similar non-identical (dizygotic) twins are.

Burt and Simons (2014, p. 230) provide a useful summary of how twin studies partition variance to environments and genes. "The basic logic of the twin study is to compare twin concordances for phenotypes and, based on several assumptions, assign the greater phenotypic similarity of MZ relative to DZ co-twins to their greater genetic similarity. Through the formula explained in more detail in the subsequent discussion, heritability is usually estimated from twice the MZ–DZ difference in correlations."

Without getting into the details, Burt and Simons (2014) argued that such designs are not helpful for social scientists trying to understand behavior (echoed by other prominent social scientists recently; for example, see Conley, 2016). They outlined methodological shortcomings of heritability studies and argued that even the exercise of trying to determine how much of, say, criminal behavior is genetic vs. environmental is folly because neither operates in a vacuum and both affect and influence each other. One of the most prominent of critiques of the twin study method is that it relies on what's known as the "equal environment assumption," which necessitates that twins are treated the same way—if they aren't, the method falls apart for partitioning variance accurately. Burt and Simons also discussed several other limitations with such designs, ultimately suggesting (p. 246):

> an end to heritability studies in criminology. In addition, we urge scholars to recognize that existing heritability estimates are the result of models biased toward inflating genetic influences and underestimating shared environmental ones, and that using these rough and biased heritability estimates to undergird specious debates about the irrelevance of shared environmental factors, such as the family, neighborhoods, and SES (citations omitted), does a disservice to both scientific and public knowledge.

This paper did not sit well with some biosocial criminologists, to say the least. A response was published in the same journal, led by J. C. Barnes (and including six others engaged in behavior genetics research). In that paper the authors argued that the criticisms leveled by Burt and Simons were old hat and had been addressed quite well by others. They expressed much frustration with having to "demonstrate the validity of twin studies" and were annoyed that prominent criminologists were, in their view, calling for a ban on such methods. They also took umbrage at what they saw as attacks on their work and a call for "a *de facto* form of censorship" (Barnes et al., 2014, p. 589).

First, Barnes and colleagues reviewed research addressing the assumptions of heritability studies that Burt and Simons had argued were fatal flaws. Barnes and colleagues acknowledge that the twin study relies on assumptions, but they say all statistical methods do. And these assumptions can be tested. The reply was heavy with data and empirical evidence showing what happens when assumptions are violated and that, even when such is the case, the models have generally not produced misleading findings.

Second, Barnes and his co-authors claim that Burt and Simons misinterpreted behavior genetic findings and "presented a misleading portrait" of that work (p. 610). They argued that Burt and Simons engaged in "selective citing" of twin studies and those which they reviewed. Particularly, they questioned the selective quoting of Terrie Moffitt to demonstrate the fallibility of such methods. She would later have her own thoughts published on the debate. Barnes and colleagues also suggest that Burt and Simons suffer from a limited understanding of what heritability studies can offer criminology (e.g., it's not just for partitioning variance). They also respond to Burt and Simons' critique that one cannot partition variance in a trait between environmental and genetic factors because the two are inextricably intertwined. That is true for individuals, they say (one's behavior, personality, and other phenotypes are the result of an interaction between biology and environment and it would be impossible to determine how much of each mattered), but not for groups, who vary across traits. In the end they reject Burt and Simons' arguments and their call for criminologists to stop conducting heritability studies.

Both "sides" were able to respond once again to the initial papers and very little common ground was found. In the first, Burt and Simons (2015) replied that the math in the Barnes et al. piece was all well and good but the issue with heritability studies is that they are not sensible from the standpoint of how the world actually works. The rejoinders were less charitable than the initial papers. For example, Burt and Simons (2015, p. 104) claim that Barnes et al. (2014) "adopted a strategy common to behavioral geneticists, which Panofsky (2014, p. 141) called, 'hitting them over the head style.' This approach involves dodging criticisms by misrepresenting arguments and insinuating that critics are politically motivated."

Burt and Simons (2015) argue that their problem with heritability studies is "conceptual" not mathematical (p. 104). If the concept of heritability studies is flawed then it does not matter how many simulations one runs to estimate various iterations of the method; they remain misleading. Burt and Simons (2015) reemphasize that their largest issue has to do with the *idea* that one can separate genes from the environment. They argue that this is nonsensical since genes cannot have any influence on behavior apart from the environment in which they are found. "Advances in molecular genomics evince that genes and environments are involved in an interpenetrating and interdependent dynamic relationship that renders the attempt to demarcate separate influences—the goal of heritability studies—illogical at both the individual and population levels" (p. 105).

Additionally, Burt and Simons (2015) discussed the field of epigenetics, which explores how the expression of genes varies according to environmental factors. This research (which Barnes and colleagues argued was too new to make any conclusions about) shows that the environment directs how genes influence behavior and is contrary to the way behavioral genetic methods model the world.

Burt and Simons (2015) also wrote that Barnes and colleagues ignored some of their critiques and insufficiently addressed others (such as the equal environments assumption). They stated that there is plenty of evidence about whether this assumption matters and, to them, it indicates that the heritability method remains flawed. They also quibbled over interpretations of genome-wide complex trait analysis (also known as GCTA), which Barnes et al. leveraged to show twin studies are sound and which Burt and Simons argue show twin studies overestimate heritability.

One particular critique that Barnes and his colleagues put forth was that Burt and Simons were political and that they were anti-biology because of it (an interesting assertion as Simons had previously been involved in several biosocial research projects). Burt and Simons (2015) reiterated that they support biosocial research and that they "consider [them]selves biopsychosocial scientists" (p. 108). They seemingly took offense to this charge and the implication that biosocial scholars (however that is defined) consider themselves the only ones capable of appreciating, articulating, and conducting biosocial criminology.

The group of biosocial scholars responded, led by John Paul Wright (Wright et al., 2015). Their title was illuminating: "Mathematical proof is not minutiae and irreducible complexity is not a theory." Wright and colleagues began by refusing to back down from their original claims. They saw the Burt and Simons (2014) article as misleading and cherry-picking. They stood by their empirical demonstrations and lamented that it did not convince Burt and Simons. Wright and colleagues disagree with Burt and Simons

(2015) that theirs was largely a conceptual critique, arguing that their initial piece had been based on statistical and methodological claims.

With respect to that conceptual critique, that one cannot in reality separate biology from the environment, Wright and colleagues responded that, yes, one can, statistically. They admit "Yes, genes and environments do interact in the *colloquial* sense. Indeed, it is impossible to separate a person from his or her environment (genes) to study the 'pure' influence of genes (environment). The two are inexorably linked in a tangled causal network" (Wright et al., 2015, p. 116). Yet the variance of group-based traits or behaviors and the sources of that variation, they say, can be separated. Turning Burt and Simons' argument on its head, they said that if it's true one can't separate biology from the environment then sociological research which does not account for genes is similarly flawed.

Wright and colleagues (2015) dismissed Burt and Simons' arguments as essentially not being well-informed. They stated that "Burt and Simons (2014, 2015) have never worked with twin data, and they show no signs of being familiar with the large and substantial body of work that supports the use of these behavioral genetic methods. And yet they claim to have invalidated the work of statisticians and behavioral geneticists around the world" (Wright et al., 2015, p. 117). Wright and colleagues also claimed that Burt and Simons used "linguistic gymnastics" (p. 118) in making their arguments. It's interesting to point out, though, that somewhere in the midst of these claims the criticism of heritability studies became a criticism of "twin" studies, which, from what we can tell, is slightly different than what Burt and Simons were attacking (of course, the main method used to examine heritability is to use twins, but twin studies can be used in other ways and not just to estimate heritability). We have discussed this debate and some of our own views on biosocial research in a recent article published in *Theoretical Criminology* (Rocque & Posick, 2017).

CONCLUSION: TALE-OF-THE-TAPE

Because these debates are not all theoretical, we will end the chapter with a discussion of who has thus far claimed victory and forgo the usual section on policy implications. Of course, these being newer topics, any conclusion we draw will necessarily be tentative and new evidence may come to the surface swaying the tale-of-the-tape.

The general vs. specific theory debate is an interesting one, but perhaps the most difficult to assign victory. General theories, as we argued, are attractive in their simplicity and comprehensiveness. Yet, if the value of theory is to be found in its practicality, then there is much to like about crime-specific explanations. It is easy to see how examining particular crime types can lead to insights on how they are accomplished and how they can be prevented.

In the end we side with the goal of general theories which, in our view, seek broader understanding of criminal behavior. After all, crime-specific theories may help inform prevention practices but do not get us any closer to understanding why such crimes happen, only how they happen. To us this is akin to continuing to apply aloe to repeated sunburns rather than seeking shade. Typologies and crime-specific analyses have been promoted for decades but we believe the evidence suggests general theories are broadly applicable (Alarid et al., 2000; Gottfredson & Hirschi, 2003; Langton & Piquero, 2007).

TABLE 9.1 TALE-OF-THE-TAPE. GENERAL VS. SPECIFIC THEORIES OF CRIME

Theory	General theories	Specific theories
Theorists	Edwin Sutherland; Ron Akers; Travis Hirschi; Robert Agnew; Nicole Piquero	Ron Clarke & Derek Cornish; Darrell Steffensmeier;
Main arguments	Theories can be constructed to cover all forms of crime and deviance	Certain types of crimes require their own theories; we should examine how crimes are committed to reduce them
Period of popularity	1939–present	1980s–present
Seminal pieces	*Principles of Criminology* (Sutherland); *Social Learning and Structure* (Akers); *A General Theory of Crime* (Gottfredson & Hirschi)	*The Reasoning Criminal* (Cornish & Clarke); *Gender and Crime: Toward a Gendered Theory of Female Offending* (Steffensmeier & Allan)
WINNER	✓	

TABLE 9.2 TALE-OF-THE-TAPE. GROUPS OF OFFENDERS EXIST VS. GROUPS OF OFFENDERS DON'T EXIST

Theory	Groups exist	Groups do not exist
Theorists	Terrie Moffitt; Daniel Nagin; Richard Tremblay	Robert Sampson; John Laub; Torbjorn Skardhamar
Main arguments	Offenders cluster into groups based on trajectories; statistical software can be used to identify these groups	Groups are not meaningful; statistical programs will find groups whether they exist or not
Period of popularity	1990–present	2000–present
Seminal pieces	*Adolescence-Limited and Life-Course-Persistent Antisocial Behavior: A Developmental Taxonomy* (Moffitt); *Group Based Modeling of Development* (Nagin); *Developmental Trajectory Groups: Fact or Useful Statistical Fiction?* (Nagin & Tremblay)	*Shared Beginnings Divergent Lives* (Sampson & Laub); *Seductions of Method: Rejoinder to Nagin and Tremblay's Developments Trajectory Groups: Fact or Fiction* (Sampson & Laub); *Distinguishing Facts and Artifacts in Group-Based Modeling* (Skardhamar)
WINNER	✓	

Perhaps somewhat contradictorily we side with the group-based methods camp over the opposition. This is not necessarily because we believe there *are* groups of offenders who are distinct and real, but because the method itself has value in testing theories (Brame et al., 2012). While Skardhamar's (2010) analyses, and Laub and colleagues' critiques, are convincing in that they reveal problems with the trajectory approach, we view these as cautions rather than signals that the method should be discarded entirely.

Once again we see much about the "losing" side to like, including the warning that a method should not drive the purpose of a scientific study and how exciting new statistical tools can be seductive. We agree whole-heartedly with these arguments and, in fact, are convinced by the Laub and Sampson (2003) findings that groups cannot be prospectively identified or predicted (this is in part why we view typological or crime-specific theories to be of less value than general ones). Yet testing whether groups "exist" is only one of the purposes of group-based models of crime—and perhaps not even the most useful. They can also be used to simply track desistance, as has been done to great effect (Bushway et al., 2003). They are a useful way to visualize data and changes in behavior and do not necessarily need to be interpreted in such a way that groups become reified.

The last two "debates" hit a bit closer to home for us. We've conducted statistical analyses of desistance (Rocque et al., 2015; 2016) and we've written on biosocial criminology extensively (Posick, Rocque, & Rafter, 2014; Rafter, Posick, & Rocque, 2016; Rocque, Welsh, & Raine, 2012; Rocque, Posick, & Felix, 2015; Rocque & Posick, 2017). With respect to desistance, we are partial to Bushway and colleagues' (2001) definition, "the process of reduction in the rate of offending (understood conceptually as an estimate of criminality) from a nonzero level to a stable rate empirically indistinguishable from zero" (p. 500).

With respect to how best to analyze desistance, we feel if it is a process then it must be modeled as such. Binary/static measures do not do the trick. Growth modeling approaches (and even trajectory models) seem preferable. Of course, qualitative methods also can get at a process of de-escalation in offending, but—much as is the case for growth models—they require more than two time-points. As one of us has argued, though, qualitative and quantitative approaches to modeling desistance are not mutually exclusive and are best used to explore different facets of desistance (Rocque, 2017). For example, quantitative models can be put to use examining the correlates of desistance and trajectories over time. Qualitative approaches are best used for gaining a subjective understanding of desistance. What does it feel like? Are offenders aware and making intentional moves to "make good?" (Maruna, 2001). Thus "quantitative and qualitative methods are able to capture different parts of the desistance journey and therefore should be seen as complementary rather than competing" (Rocque, 2017, p. 107).

Finally, perhaps the newest methodological debate, surrounding behavior genetics, is far from settled. Interestingly the second round of debates published in *Criminology* included three other scholars. First, Douglas Massey, a sociologist, wrote about the history of sociology and biology and efforts to join the two in the quest to understand behavior. He showed that Nazi use of biosocial research led to a rejection in the 20th century of this line of work. Recent research, however, has increased our knowledge of biology and how biology matters in the context of the environment. In particular, Massey suggested that epigenetics upsets the apple cart of the traditional understanding of how biology is expressed socially. "The critical insight here," Massey wrote, "is that genes are not simply inherited and automatically expressed, but they are turned on and

TABLE 9.3 DESISTANCE AS STATIC VS. DESISTANCE AS A PROCESS

Theory	Static	Process
Scholars	Mark Warr; Neal Shover; David Farrington; Mikko Aaltonen	Shawn Bushway; Robert Sampson: John Laub; Ray Paternoster; Daniel Nagin
Main arguments	Desistance can be measured by examining whether a previously active criminal has not committed a crime over a certain period of time. For active offenders, frequency of offending remains relatively stable	Desistance is best measured as a process or trajectory in which crime decreases
Period of popularity	1990–present	2000–present
Examples	*Age and Crime* (Farrington, 1986); *Age, Differential Expectations, and Crime Desistance* (Shover & Thompson); *Life-Course Transitions and Desistance from Crime* (Warr)	*Shared Beginnings Divergent Lives* (Sampson & Laub); *An Empirical Framework for Studying Desistance as a Process* (Bushway et al.)
WINNER		✓

*Note, our placing these scholars in the "binary" camp does not mean they necessarily advocate for that construction of desistance, but that they have influential work showing it can be measured that way

off through interactions with the environment, yielding a variety of complex socio-biological processes that we are only beginning to understand" (Massey, 2015, p. 128). This sort of work, to Massey, means that partitioning variance of a trait between the environment and biology "makes little sense" (p. 129). Massey is familiar and supportive of work showing how biology and the environment work together, but, with respect to the debate at hand, argues that Burt and Simons have the upper hand.

Terrie Moffitt and Amber Beckley (2015) also provided a response, this time in favor of Barnes, Wright, and colleagues' view. They first take issue with the call to end heritability studies, arguing that such methods are valuable. Moffitt and Beckley suggest that, contrary to what Burt and Simons indicated, twin studies are able to show "*social causes of antisocial and criminal behaviors*" (p. 121, emphasis in the original). Part of the reason Burt and Simons were skeptical of heritability studies was that their relatively high estimates of heritability (~50 percent) of behavior had "not generated more critical attention in criminology" (Burt & Simons, 2014, p. 224). Moffitt and Beckley stated that behavior genetic twin studies could do what observational social science research could not: rule out selection effects.

Moffitt and Beckley also argue that twin studies have broader applicability than discussed in Burt and Simons' critiques. For example, they argue for the study of "discordant twins." "Because twins in a monozygotic pair are never perfectly identical in their offending behavior despite sharing all their genes, this gives criminologists a special opportunity to study what experiences reduce co-twins' behavioral similarity" (p. 123).

Finally, Moffitt and Beckley urged scholars to pump the brakes on epigenetics, as Wright and colleagues had argued. Moffitt and Beckley feared that epigenetics "has been wildly oversold, particularly in the media" (p. 124). The primary mechanism behind epigenetic effects is called "methylation," which, they say, is not necessarily something caused by the environment. In the end they conclude, somewhat ironically, that epigenetic effects should be examined using twins, which puts the Burt and Simons call to end heritability studies but to focus on epigenetics in a tough position.

Our reading of this debate is that it is complicated and there is no clear victor, as of yet. We agree wholeheartedly with Burt and Simons (2014) that heritability studies for the sake of partitioning variance seem to offer little value. As Eric Turkheimer and Paige Harden have written, "[f]iguring out how 'genetic' traits are, either in absolute terms or relative to each other is a lost cause: Everything is genetic to some extent and nothing is completely so. There is little more to be said" (2014, p. 179). To some extent the Burt and Simons critique was about heritability studies and *not* other uses of twin methods. Their methodological critique of twin models seemingly applies to non-heritability studies using twins as well. We agree with Moffitt and Beckley's arguments about the flexibility of twin designs and feel that they can be exploited to do more than they have in criminology.

For example, a fascinating paper exploring the twin methodology, in particular the use of twins to partition variance into genes, shared, and unshared environment, found that the three components are not independent. Daw, Guo, and Harris (2015) found that the shared environment interacted with the unshared environment components, which implies that the findings of behavior genetic studies pointing to the unimportance of the shared environment have been overstated.

It is very interesting to note that Burt and Simons' position evolved from one opposed to heritability studies to one opposed to twin studies. We expect that Burt and Simons would support the disconcordant twin study method advocated by Moffitt and Beckley, as do we. We also expect that the need for twin models to explore epigenetics would not be seen as a problem from their perspective as, again, they never argued to end *twin* studies, only *heritability* studies.

Where epigenetics is concerned, frankly we are puzzled that scientists would on the one hand decry a call to end studies using a particular method while at the same time seemingly dismissing a new approach simply because we do not know enough about it. This is contra science in our view—science is about discovery and learning what we don't already know, after all! Nearly all the criticisms we have seen about epigenetics is that it is "too new." This is not a legitimate criticism but a call to learn more. Further, the idea that it is dangerous because it has been oversold in the media is a bit like saying twin studies have flaws, but so do all other methods. The media's job is to oversell; that they do so should not impact how scientists operate one whit.

Thus, for this last "great debate," we come somewhere in the middle. Twin studies should be used and they can tell us a lot about how both genes and the environment matter. But heritability studies for purely heritability's sake do not have value. We agree with Burt and Simons on that point, but agree with Barnes and colleagues that the methodological flaws inherent in twin studies are no more dire than the flaws in other statistical methods. At the same time twin studies should be used more creatively than they typically are in the social sciences, in ways shown by Daw et al. (2015) and Moffitt and Beckley (2015).

One final point as regards the heritability study debate. Burt and Simons' (2015) last piece on the matter argued that the real issue was conceptual. That is we cannot separate genes from the environment. Wright and colleagues (2015) responded that, for individuals, that is true, but not for groups. On a theoretical level we very much agree that the notion one can separate the effects of biology and the environment is folly. We have argued (Rafter, Posick, & Rocque, 2016) that the exercise of searching for gene by environment interactions is nonsensical because it assumes that each have "independent" effects, and we have called for a replacing of the term interaction with integration. Yet Wright and colleagues' logic is also convincing—that population variance can be separated for statistical purposes. And in some ways virtually all social science analyses are confounded in some way or the other (aside from true experiments). Thus, when we examine whether marriage impacts crime, we know that we cannot randomly assign marriage to people and so our methods can only be considered incomplete points of support. But the same is true for studies of, say, intelligence, which often does not control for genetic factors. That's the way it works in the social sciences, and if we are aware of those limitations we can work with them rather than dismissing entire bodies of work.

TABLE 9.4 TALE-OF-THE-TAPE. HERITABILITY STUDIES VS. EPIGENETIC STUDIES

Theory	Heritability studies No, epigenetics Yes	Heritability studies Yes, epigenetics No
Theorists	Callie Burt; Ronald Simons; Douglas Massey	John Paul Wright; Terrie Moffitt; Amber Beckley; J.C. Barnes; Brian Boutwell; Eric Connolly; Joe Nedelec; Joe Schwartz; Kevin Beaver
Main arguments	Studies for the sake of examining heritability have run their course; epigenetics is a promising new field for understanding the origins of behavior	Twin studies are meaningful; epigenetic research is too new for sweeping conclusions
Period of popularity	2014–present	2014–present
Seminal pieces	*Pulling Back the Curtain on Heritability Studies: Biosocial Criminology in the Postgenomic Era* (Burt & Simons); *Brave New World of Biosocial Science* (Massey)	*Demonstrating the Validity of Twin Research in Criminology* (Barnes et al.); *Abandon Twin Research? Embrace Epigenetics? Premature Advice for Criminologists* (Moffitt & Beckley)
WINNER	✓	✓

In the end, while it is possible to separate effects, we do agree with Burt and Simons that approaches seeking to study the way the environment and the body work in concert are likelier to bear fruit for understanding behavior. Epigenetics is just one path that can be taken in this pursuit. Gene by environment interactions is another. New and promising lines of work have linked traumatic brain injury to behavior (Kennedy, Heron, & Munafò, 2017; Schwartz, Connolly, & Brauer, 2017; Schwartz, Connolly, & Valgardson, 2017) and environmental lead levels to crime (Lersch & Hart, 2014; Taylor et al., 2016). These types of studies illustrate how environmental factors influence behavior via biological mechanisms. This is similar to a theoretical account of urban crime we developed (Rocque, Posick, & Felix, 2015), arguing that exposure to violence and other forms of stress impact the functioning of the HPA axis (the fight or flight response), which helps explain the quick resort to violence in certain areas. Understanding and ultimately reducing criminal behavior, we believe, will depend on fully understanding how the environment and body work together, not separately.

NOTES

1 www.vox.com/the-big-idea/2017/5/18/15655638/charles-murray-race-iq-sam-harris-science-free-speech
2 medium.com/@houstoneuler/the-cherry-picked-science-in-voxs-charles-murray-article-bd534a9c4476
3 www.vox.com/the-big-idea/2017/6/15/15797120/race-black-white-iq-response-critics

Conclusion
On debates past, present, and future

D EBATE HAS LONG BEEN recognized as an important part of education. At Bates College, where one of us (Rocque) teaches, the debate team—the internationally recognized Brooks Quimby Debate Council—was created almost at the same time that the college was founded (1855). Jeffrey Parcher, in *The Value of Debate* (Parcher, 1998, p. 1), argued that "Debate is a uniquely beneficial educational tool in part because of the value of argumentation theory itself. The creation of an argument is one of the most complex cognitive acts that a person can engage in. Creating an argument requires the research of issues, organization of data, analysis of data, snythesization of different kinds of data, and an evaluation of information with respect to which conclusion it may point.[1]" Abigail Westberry, a lead debater at Bates College, expanded on what debate provides students:

> Debate forces you to listen, understand, and address alternative conceptions of the world. This can remove the ideological blinders that students often place around themselves, and expose them to ideas that they wouldn't have otherwise engaged with. This is incredibly important because it better prepares students for the real world. At its very least, debate teaches students to listen to others. At its very best, debate teaches students to respect each other. These are skills that are necessary for our political and social communities to function.[2]

Recently a debate was held between the Harvard University debate team and, wait for it, the Eastern New York Correctional Inmate team. The inmate team was made up of men from the maximum-security prison in New York. The outcome? The prison team came out victorious. In fact they had previously beat the nationally ranked University of Vermont team and West Point.[3] The inmates expressed their appreciation of the opportunity to develop and use their debate skills because of the usefulness of these tools in the larger society, where most would soon find themselves. We argue that each of us "free folk" should not take such opportunities for granted.

Within academic disciplines, debates are essential, if for no other reason than to prevent the unwarranted dominance of particular viewpoints. In the social sciences, increasing attention is being paid to ensuring that disciplines are infused with viewpoint diversity. One group, calling themselves "Heterodox Academy," was created by social psychologist Jonathan Haidt to promote such diversity. According to their website the members "share a concern about a growing problem: the loss or lack of 'viewpoint diversity.' When nearly everyone in a field shares the same political orientation, certain ideas become orthodoxy, dissent is discouraged, and errors can go unchallenged."[4]

In criminology such debates can ensure that theoretical perspectives remain sharp, informed, and up-to-date. Healthy disagreement ensures that advocates of specific perspectives refine their logic, continually search for empirical support, and, importantly, update their views (or "priors," if you are a Bayesian) when new information is available. Criminology, we submit, is more vibrant, informative, and useful when scholars are engaged in debates. This was true from the inception of the field, with the work of Beccaria and Lombroso, and the sociological debates of Sutherland and Hirschi, to the most recent debates between J. C. Barnes, John Wright, and Callie Burt and Ronald Simons.

As we indicated in the Introduction of this book, there is another reason we believe debates are important in academia. As students we found them compelling and they encouraged us to seek more information about the topics that we were studying. We admit that now, as professors, we still find these debates compelling and, yes, entertaining. While we are both keenly interested in biology, sociology, and how the two disciplines can unite to inform criminology, we admit that we may not have read either Burt and Simons' or Barnes and colleagues' exchanges as carefully or thoroughly as we would have if they were not part of a heated debate. Reading the literature closely in any field is vital for both professors and students. Thus these debates help to make criminology stronger!

In this concluding chapter we review the debates and main points from each. We also expand on our thoughts about the importance of debates for criminology. Finally, we look to the future and provide some predictions about what we think will continue to be debated and what new debates will arise in the field in the years to come.

RECAPPING THE GREAT DEBATES

We hope it has been clear throughout this book that debates between scholars in criminology are not new or isolated phenomena. In fact, from the field's very inception, debates have gripped the study of crime and justice. Whichever Cesare (Beccaria or Lombroso) one considers to be criminology's founder, their work was in part a response to what they believed to be misguided thinking. Beccaria's *On Crimes and Punishments* was written to illustrate the flaws in the way criminals were treated during his time. He wrote of the inefficacy of treating criminals differently depending on who they were, not what they did, and of torture as a way of extracting truth. Lombroso was struck by the shape of the skull of Vilella—a notorious criminal—and thus began his work showing that some criminals were not created by society (as many thought at the time) but were born that way.

Chapter 1: Lombroso vs. Goring; Durkheim vs. Tarde

We started the book intentionally focusing on debates that emerged once criminology was established and where there was evidence of scholars engaging with one another. Shortly after Lombroso's influential work was published on types of criminals he was challenged by Charles Goring in England. Goring's *The English Convict* argued that the physical attributes by which Lombroso had characterized born criminals did not coalesce in his data. Interestingly, however, Goring's work *did* identify traits that differed between criminals and non-criminals and so his findings did not entirely refute Lombroso.

When sociology took root as a discipline in the late 1800s it did not take long for scholars to begin explaining crime and deviance using a societal lens. Emile Durkheim had particular views about how deviance emerges, focusing entirely on the environment and group structures in which individuals find themselves. Society acts as a controlling force for human impulses and, when properly balanced, can help people lead peaceful lives. When social forces are disrupted, however, social ills emerge, such as suicide. Durkheim's views were opposed by Gabriel Tarde, who was more psychological in orientation. Tarde thought that individual behavior was not entirely driven by social factors, but that individual characteristics mattered as well. Whereas Durkheim viewed society as its own entity, something that was made up of people but also distinct from them, Tarde felt that society was just the sum of its parts—what mattered were the people and their inherent characteristics. These differences were explored with respect to the explanation of deviance. Not surprisingly Durkheim felt that these acts can be explained by social facts (such as social integration and bonds), whereas Tarde viewed deviance to be, in large part, the result of imitation and social psychological mechanisms.

Winner: Biopsychosocial theories

Chapter 2: Sutherland v. psychology

The next chapter delved further into the sociological vs. psychological debates surrounding the causes of crime. As we noted, while scholars had been examining crime for decades it was not until the early 20th century that criminology became its own field and was claimed as a social scientific discipline. In fact in the early 20th century, as we recounted, the famed Michael-Adler report (1933) forcefully made the case that criminology was not scientific and had not produced any useful knowledge about crime or its control. The first true move to make criminology a discipline occurred when Edwin Sutherland made the case that crime is a learned behavior and can be understood only via social interactions. To Sutherland, psychological explanations of crime that relied on mental deficiencies were, well, deficient. They could not, for example, account for professional thieves or those involved in white-collar offending.

Sutherland was very successful in co-opting criminology for sociology, which meant that psychologically oriented perspectives went by the wayside for decades. Sutherland also, as argued by Laub and Sampson (1991), was successful in pushing multi-factor perspectives associated with scholars such as the Gluecks to the fringes of the field. It was not until the late 1980s that a group of psychologists from Canada were able to break the sociological stranglehold on criminology and show that psychological principles mattered and could advance our understanding of crime—particularly correctional programming. Today criminology is perhaps more interdisciplinary than at any time in its history, claiming insights from economics, psychology, biology, and, still, sociology.

Despite the interdisciplinary nature of contemporary criminology (and our own personal opinions that this integration of thought is a positive—and necessary), in this debate we awarded the winner to sociology, which continues to maintain its dominance in the field, if somewhat diminished. It is fair to say that most programs in criminology and criminal justice are "traditional" in their approach and the tradition that still holds sway is largely sociological.

Winner: Sociology/Differential Association Theory

Chapter 3: Control vs. learning theories

In Chapter 3 we recounted the debate between control and learning theories of crime, one of the more entrenched areas of disagreement among theorists in the field. Is criminal behavior, like other behaviors, learned in a process of social interaction? In other words, is there no hard-wired "natural" way to behave? Or is criminal behavior simply part of an intrinsic suite of behaviors that benefit the perpetrator and thus need no explanation (or learning)? As criminologists in training, we learn early on that we must identify with one or the other perspective. Even if we reject both theories, the assumptions they make about human nature are likely to guide our thinking on the subject. Sure, we could compromise and say that both make sense, maybe try to combine the theories, but this method has its own drawbacks (see Chapter 5). Learning theory in criminology got its beginning with Gabriel Tarde, but more officially with Edwin Sutherland's differential association theory. In the 1960s (through the present) it was claimed by Ronald Akers, who made some revisions in developing his social learning and social structure theory.

Akers' and Sutherland's main opponents consider themselves control theorists. Travis Hirschi, in his seminal *Causes of Delinquency* (1969), attempted to show how a control perspective is empirically superior to learning theory. Ruth Kornhauser, in 1978, took the logical structure of learning theories to task, arguing that control theories simply made more sense. While Akers and Hirschi would continue their tit-for-tats, others took up the debate. Ross Matsueda wrote in defense of differential association theory while Barbara Costello furthered Kornhauser and Hirschi's critiques of the perspective.

In the end both perspectives maintain sway within criminology, with hardcore adherents continuing to publish on the topics. In a very close contest, we made the case that control theories, because of their logic and internal consistency, are the winner. Some of the defenses of learning theories, we argued, place them closer to control theories in logic. However, empirically, both theories seem at least moderately supported.

Winner: Control theories

In Chapter 4 we covered *the* great debate in criminology (Bernard et al., 2016), centered on criminal careers. Scholars such as Jacqueline Cohen and Al Blumstein began writing about what they called "criminal careers" in the 1970s, seeking to better understand the way criminal behavior changes over time for offenders. One might think this was a rather innocuous, non-controversial endeavor, but that was not the case. Bolstered by their 1983 paper on age and crime, where they came to the conclusion that social factors are impotent in the quest to understand changes in crime over the life-course, Michael Gottfredson and Travis Hirschi took issue with the criminal career approach.

Among other things, Gottfredson and Hirschi did not believe that criminals have careers in the traditional sense, that longitudinal data were unnecessary for studying crime, and that identifying "career criminals" was doomed from the start. What Gottfredson and Hirschi were really in disagreement about, however, was that there is a possible different explanation for different kinds of crimes and criminals and for different periods of the life-span. They also disagreed with the notion that one must divvy up the criminal career into component parts (onset, frequency, participation, duration, etc.). To these "propensity theorists," crime and all its manifestations are readily explained by the same thing—individual differences in self-control. This debate continued through several exchanges in the 1980s and continued thereafter in multiple forms. For example, theoretical advances built on the criminal career and propensity approach (Sampson & Laub, 1993) and new methodologies aimed at examining trajectories of crime over time emerged (Nagin, 2005).

While this debate is by no means over, as criminal career and self-control scholarship has continued into the present, we gave the nod to the criminal career side of the debate. Why? Because criminal career work is still presenting interesting puzzles and is certainly not as complete as the propensity or self-control perspective (at least how it was presented at the time). For example, Gottfredson and Hirschi made very parsimonious arguments about what causes crime (self-control) and where that cause comes from (parenting). There is little room for adjustment or refinement. In addition, the criminal career approach, arguably, led to the development of the propensity or self-control theory and to methodological advances still in use today.

Winner: Criminal career perspective

In Chapter 5 we turned our focus to the issue of theory construction and testing. Because, historically, criminological theories have shortcomings empirically, explaining very little of the variation in criminal behavior, some theorists in the late 1970s began to take strides toward combining distinct approaches into a larger whole. The argument, again, seemed straightforward: in criminology we have three primary orientations to explaining crime; strain, control, and learning. Each separately seems to explain a bit of the behavior but nowhere near all of it. So why not develop a scheme in which we show how the perspectives combine to add up to a fuller understanding of crime.

Not so fast. Once again Travis Hirschi was part of the counter-movement. Theoretical integration, he argued, sullies the original theories that comprise the integrated model. Hirschi not only critiqued the efforts at theoretical integration, he provided a new lexicon describing different styles of integration. He outlined three basic ways of constructing an integrated theory, from side-by-side, to up-and-down, to end-to-end versions. Others began to join the debate and the efforts culminated in a conference in the 1980s which was intended to provide a forum for scholars on both sides of the debate to thrash things out. The exchanges were published as a volume in 1989. Debates continued thereafter, with scholars chiming in with various suggestions for improving theory construction often offering their own theoretical perspectives.

Hirschi's arguments regarding why it makes no sense to combine inherently oppositional theories make logical sense. If people learn crime then it isn't natural, and supplementing that theory with one that sees people as needing to be restrained does not seem to produce a consistent theory. Yet we also agree that the seminal trio theories have not done well in explaining crime. Clearly there is more to be done to elaborate these perspectives. However, we ended up siding with the integrationists and argue that there are ways to combine theoretical variables without imposing the constraints of human nature assumptions. That constituent theories have failed to meaningfully explain crime, and that theoretical competition has not whittled down the sheer number of theories, seems to us to suggest that integration wins the day.

Winner: Theoretical integration

In the next chapter we moved on to discuss critical vs. conservative criminology. In some ways critical criminology can be juxtaposed alongside so-called "traditional" criminology, which is positivistic in orientation and does not as a rule question the government or power structures. Critical criminology has many flavors, from Marxist, to postmodernist, to feminist. Each has a slightly different focus, but at their core shine the light on power dynamics and who controls the discourse surrounding crime and justice.

In this chapter we also contrasted conservative with liberal criminology. Conservative criminology is best represented by the works of James Q. Wilson, John P. Wright, and Matt DeLisi. These scholars argue that we need to be tough on crime, that crime has real victims who we should prioritize, and that sociological criminology is infected by ideology. Liberal criminologists (who conservative criminologists argue make up the lion's share of all criminologists) disagree with most of what Wilson and others wrote.

To them, being harsh on crime not only had little effect on crime but actually made things worse. Further, outcomes like mass incarceration are moral failures, according to scholars such as Elliott Currie.

Much like previous debates, we find value in both perspectives. Critical criminologists pushed traditional criminology to recognize and take seriously power dynamics, discourse, and illegal behavior by governing bodies. Conservative criminologists are correct that much of standard criminology is liberal in nature; diversity of perspective is always a plus. However, we are reticent to endorse fragmentation or perspectives that are siloed into their own scholarly world. We tend to think that traditional or mainstream criminology can be pushed, expanded, and adapted to accommodate the issues raised by right and left criminologies. Thus we award the points to traditional criminology.

Winner: Traditional criminology

In Chapter 7 we introduced perspectives on the status of criminal justice and criminology. Is criminology a field of its own? Or is it a subfield of more developed disciplines like sociology and psychology? Some scholars, particularly those trained in sociology, believe that criminology is still a subfield of that discipline, not established enough in the methods and perspectives it uses to guide research.

Others, many trained in fields outside sociology such as psychology and biology, often consider criminology as a field of its own, not tied to the anchor of sociology. These scholars recognize the diverse nature of the study of crime and criminal justice, conceding that it belongs to no one discipline outside of its own. This is often how those trained in criminal justice and criminology (who generally hold degrees by those names) see the field.

Some of those who view criminal justice and criminology as its own field prefer to go a step further. Criminal justice (the study of making and enforcing laws) and criminology (the study of the etiology of criminal behavior) are considered by some to be separate fields as well. Advocates of this separation believe that the questions asked by the two areas are different and distinct. By considering each as a separate field it is easier to refine theory and impact public policy.

As to the first question, we believe that the questions and perspectives of criminology are unique enough to warrant criminology as a separate field of study. Because criminology is inherently multidisciplinary and interdisciplinary, and focuses on specific questions using diverse perspectives, it is profitable to view criminology as a stand-alone field. It is also important for honing public policies using crime-specific research and policy analysis.

We feel it is best to stop there, and do not see criminology and criminal justice as separate fields. Criminology to us is very similar to the way that Sutherland viewed it—the study of making, breaking, and reacting to laws. It is very difficult (and to us unwise) to separate these aspects of criminological study as they are so intertwined. With that said, we agree that there should be as much focus on criminal justice as criminology and that both are important (and integral!) to the study of crime and behavior.

Winner: Criminology and criminal justice

Chapter 8 focused on the end result of theory—policy. What approaches have been more useful for reducing crime? Which has had more of a policy impact? In this chapter we simplified matters a bit and compared positivism vs. classical/neoclassical schools of crime. This is a useful stratagem as the two perspectives differ fundamentally on the most important factors that produce criminal behavior and the factors most suitable for intervention. The classical school, initiated by the work of Cesare Beccaria and Jeremy Bentham, viewed offenders as rational beings who commit crimes when the perceived benefits outweigh the costs. Thus anyone can be an offender and it is folly to try to determine who among us is most likely to fall from the path of the straight and narrow. Far more effective, according to this school, is to try to change the cost-benefit calculus such that people see that "crime does not pay."

The classical school fell out of favor in the late 19th and early 20th centuries with the rise of the positive school, which attempted to understand what individual factors drive people to crime. The positive school did not see everyone as equally capable of committing crimes, and so the logical way to reduce offending was to figure out what was different about criminals and address those characteristics. In other words, if offenders are more likely to be poor, reducing poverty should result in a decrease in criminal behavior. Thus the positive school's approach to policy is to prevent crime by reducing childhood risk factors and to rehabilitate those already engaged in crime. The neoclassical school made a comeback in the late 20th century and currently both the rational, cost-benefit and risk factor approaches can be found in criminal justice policy.

Both the classical/neoclassical and positivist schools of criminology have had their heyday with respect to influence on public policy. Prior to the 1970s, rehabilitation (the correctional perspective that seeks to fix what caused the offender to commit his/her crimes) was all the rage. In the 1970s through the 1990s a "get tough" on crime approach held firm, which was based squarely on the idea that criminals choose their behavior relatively freely and the purpose of the justice system is to encourage them to see that crime will not pay. Part of the appeal of the get-tough approach and neoclassical turn was the rejection of the rehabilitative ideal; the idea that rehabilitation does not "work" proved convincing.

Yet we have seen a resurgence of the rehabilitative ideal and a strong evidence-base on which to ground the argument that rehabilitation *does* work. While it is undeniable that deterrence has some effect on crime and that mass incarceration lowered the crime rate to a degree, we have been *too* tough in the United States and it has cost us. Thus we side with the positivists with respect to policy.

Winner: Positive school of criminology

The last substantive chapter (Chapter 9) provided a brief overview of several more recent debates. These included discussions on the superiority of either general or crime-specific theories, the use of special methods to identify and track "groups" of offenders over time, the measurement and definition of desistance from crime, and the use of twins to study heritability of antisocial behavior. Some of these current debates resemble older ones, where two sides engage with one another and attempt to illustrate how their position is the correct one. Others, alternatively, have submitted their perspective independent of any real critique. For instance, desistance researchers have not published exchanges arguing for one definition or another. Yet they have published work showing the differences in results stemming from varying definitions or measurement choices.

The discussion of each debate was necessarily brief. However, we found more to support in the general theory camp, the group-based methodologists, and a definition of desistance that is dynamic, while recognizing that quantitative and qualitative approaches answer different questions about desistance. Somewhat anticlimactically we ended the book with a toss-up between heritability scholars and those who see no value there.

Winner: General theories
Winner: Group-based methodologists
Winner: Dynamic/process definitions of desistance
Winner: Tie between heritability and anti-heritability scholars

WHAT DOES IT ALL MEAN?

We want to emphasize that our characterization of the debates, including the winners and losers, is necessarily a subjective exercise and one that is used for the purposes of illustration. In our discussions with scholars engaged in the debates recounted in this book, a couple expressed hesitation regarding naming a "winner" in a particular debate. Al Blumstein, for example, said that our approach seemed "too much like a boxing match looking for a knockout after several rounds. That's not the way different perspectives on analysis work."[5] Alex Piquero, similarly, wrote regarding the criminal career debate, "No side has won, and no side will ever win. There is no checklist of sorts, where we can say; ok, this team has more points so they win." Part of the issue with declaring a winner, for Piquero, is that science is always fluid and dynamic. New methods, new data, new approaches are constantly emerging which allow us to attack questions from a different angle, perhaps leading to discoveries that a particular perspective may have more support than previously thought. "That is what makes science so fun," Piquero adds.

So we feel it necessary to qualify that our awarding a winner in these debates is, first and foremost, solely our judgement and that does not, by any stretch of the imagination, mean the book is closed on the particular topic. In fact we welcome debates on our discussion about debates! In that sense these are not like boxing matches, where one winner is declared and there is no going back, but more like the rounds within a boxing match, each being awarded to one side or the other. Inevitably more rounds are in store. In large measure these are thought exercises, one way to organize exciting and diverse perspectives on criminology and social science. Thus we are not attempting to "reify" these debates or our judgement of the victors. We agree with Blumstein that science does not often work out as cleanly as we have presented it, but we do believe that perspectives come and go, become popular, and then are largely discarded. New paradigms emerge, new ways of looking at the world. This is in part what Kuhn (1962) meant by scientific revolutions. To believe that all perspectives are equally valid, that certain theories cannot "win out," is a sure recipe for scientific stagnation.

In the end our characterizations of the debates remain our interpretations, but we have largely based them on the actual writings of those involved. We also note that we are not the first to label these "debates" (Bernard et al., 2016; Laub & Sampson, 1991). And we are convinced that, as we have mentioned, science is more engaging and interesting when people care about their positions. As our colleague Ray Paternoster used to say in class, "put your stake in the ground." Believe something. Defend your positions.

Doing so makes research much more intriguing. To a large extent the debaters we've covered in this text did just that, and we thank them for it.

THE FUTURE OF DEBATES

We end with a look to the future. What will debates in the field look like in the coming years? As mentioned at the outset of this chapter, debates are still occurring in criminology but the venues have changed a bit. Blog posts and online magazines are increasingly becoming popular and are not restricted by page limitations or the lengthy publication process that is the case for some (most?) academic journals. Scholars can also host their own websites for free or a nominal fee. Both of us do so as a way to expand upon who we are, what we are currently working on, and also to share some thoughts. Rocque's website[6] allows space for blog posts that he can write, edit, or solicit contributions for and publish immediately. In addition, we both belong to the Scholars Strategy Network (SSN), which provides the opportunity for regular opinion editorials in local newspapers. We have also written for online outlets in ways we hope contribute to ongoing debates in criminology.[7]

We also anticipate that debates will continue in academic journals as well. These exchanges remain beneficial for the field and for the journals themselves. Burt and Simons' (2014) piece had reached 48 citations by fall 2017. The article was also ranked in the top 5 percent of all research articles in terms of "attention" by altmetric.com, which is calculated by providing points according to how many mentions the article receives on forums such as Wikipedia, Twitter, and blogs.[8] Further debate was stimulated by online posts referencing to the articles.[9] This is all to the benefit of criminology and to researchers who want to know more about twin methods and their drawbacks/ advantages.

With respect to topics that will be debated in the future, there are endless possibilities. The age-old nature vs. nurture debate, while seemingly setting up strawmen, has evolved over time to boil down to environmental vs. selection effects. One particular topic that seems ripe for future debate is whether social scientific research that has ignored selection is fundamentally erroneous. For example, Judith Rich Harris (2009) argues in her book *The Nurture Assumption* that parenting effects on child outcomes have been wildly exaggerated. Parents, she says, actually do not have that much influence aside from passing down genes and ensuring that their children do not hang out with the wrong crowd. Brian Boutwell, a biosocial criminologist, has spelled out this argument further in several essays[10] arguing that parents may have a very minimal impact on who we are—including helping prevent criminal behavior.

Much of the support garnered for this argument comes from twin studies which are able to partition variance between what is called the "shared environment" (things twins share in common, including household income and parents), the "nonshared environment" (things twins do not have in common, including peers), and heritability. In this kind of work the shared environment is often found to account for a trivial amount of the variance in particular traits and behaviors (Rhee & Waldman, 2002).

As one of us has argued,[11] this method does not specifically measure parenting or parental behaviors. It makes a lot of assumptions as well, both analytically (as all quantitative models do) and logically (e.g., parents treat their twins the same at all times). But more to the point, these models cannot get at causality in that they remain observational methods. The only method that can truly disentangle effects is the true, randomized experiment. Typically, in criminology, such designs are uncommon because it is difficult to randomize individuals into groups that vary according to the factors we find most interesting. Generally with parenting this is also the case, as we would not want to assign children to groups in which their parents ignored them, for example.

Yet interventions to improve parenting skills and communication do exist and have received experimental evaluation in the context of crime and delinquency. The results of these evaluations largely show that parenting programs work—that they positively affect children's outcomes. As noted in Rocque's piece (2017), "Projections of the overall impact of the [Nurse-Family Partnership, a program which helps at-risk mothers with parenting skills], which has been rolled out to other communities, indicate that by the year 2031, it will prevent 90,000 violent crimes by youth, 594,000 property and public order crimes (e.g., vandalism, loitering) by youth, 36,000 youth arrests, and 41,000 person-years of youth substance abuse (Miller, 2015). These are large, and meaningful effects."

And so there is evidence that parenting does matter, but also evidence that standard social science techniques, largely observational in nature, have overestimated the effects. Future research will continue, we believe, to flesh out these issues in new and interesting ways. In particular, the use of twin studies to examine environmental effects in a more nuanced manner (perhaps by incorporating surveys to assess any differences in parenting between twins, for example) will advance this discussion. And far from us bemoaning the work of Harris and Boutwell, seeing it as an attack on a bedrock of sociology, we welcome such exchanges. Critiques of well-entrenched positions, when they come from a neutral and informed place, can only lead to more rigorous scholarship.

It is also clear that the emerging field of epigenetics is not going anywhere anytime soon. As we recounted in the last chapter, current exchanges in criminology have rightly pointed out that we do not know much about how epigenetics works to make sweeping conclusions (Moffitt & Beckley, 2015). Yet interesting and engaging work has emerged, showing how epigenetics may help us understand particular issues, such as drug addiction (see Walsh, Johnson, & Bolen, 2012). It remains to be seen whether epigenetics comes to represent a true fusion of the environment and genes in the social sciences, but one thing is for sure: to the extent that there are adherents of either the social or biological worldview, epigenetics will continue to be controversial.

One last debate we would like to mention here is the one we started this book with—the causes of mass incarceration. We described the position of Michelle Alexander and others regarding the role of race, social control, and the targeting of urban neighborhoods in the War on Drugs during the 1980s. Alexander's (2010) argument is provocative: that mass incarceration was an intentional, colorblind method of racial social control—one that replaced Jim Crow in the United States. Her position is supported by history, statistics that indicate people (particularly men) have borne the brunt of mass incarceration, and the "hidden" reality that mass incarceration continues to control this population well after inmates have been released.

John Pfaff's 2017 book, *Locked In*, took aim at what he called the "standard story," that the War on Drugs is largely responsible for America's incarceration binge. To Pfaff, drugs do not tell the whole story. Most people locked up in this country committed violent crimes, and yet it is not the case that the mass incarceration explosion was the result of a sustained surge in violence (it's true that violence did increase in the 1980s, but it has fallen off the map since the early 1990s while incarceration rates continued

to skyrocket). Pfaff places the blame on prosecutors and a system that rewards punitiveness and not leniency. As we mentioned in the Introduction to this book, this debate
is a bit too new to know which way it will go. It is fair to say, however, that Pfaff's new
perspective has pushed the boundaries of discourse and study on mass incarceration and
led scholars to rethink their former positions.

In late 2017 the Minnesota Department of Corrections' Director of Research, Grant
Duwe, wrote a policy report on prison reform for the American Enterprise Institute
(Duwe, 2017).[12] In that report Duwe, who has worked in corrections since 2004, has a
different perspective than Pfaff and Alexander (both of whom hold law degrees). Rather
than viewing mass incarceration as a "front end" problem, he sees it as a failure of prison
(the back end). Recidivism rates are high by any reasonable standard in the US, with
one report referenced by Duwe showing that 77 percent of released inmates were
rearrested within five years. Duwe brings up a point that has gone largely unacknowledged
in the mass-incarceration debates, which have generally agreed that reducing prison
numbers is a good thing. If prisons are not doing anything to help inmates while on the
inside, decarceration may present a danger to the community (though evaluations of
California's decarceration efforts have not shown that to be the case[13]). Thus he suggests
that we need to take correctional programming seriously and make better use of evidence-
based practices that have been shown to reduce recidivism. He also suggests that we
assess risk and responsivity of all inmates so that we know how we should treat them
while inside. Finally, he argues that overall prison numbers can be reduced by being
more conservative with respect to what sort of probation and parole outcomes lead to
incarceration (technical violations, which often are not criminal, should not lead to
incarceration). Duwe introduces a risk-severity grid (see Figure 10.1) that would help
correctional officials determine who should be incarcerated, depending on the seriousness
of the offense and the risk level of the offender.

FIGURE 10.1 RECIDIVISM RISK-VIOLATION SEVERITY GRID (FROM DUWE, 2017)

Most Serious Severity Level	Low Risk Level	Medium Risk Level	High Risk Level	Very High Risk Level	Total
Low Severity	400	400	400	400	1,600 (16%)
Medium Severity	900	900	900	900	3,600 (36%)
High Severity	700	700	700	700	2,800 (28%)
Very High Severity	500	500	500	500	2,000 (20%)
TOTAL	2,500	2,500	2,500	2,500	10,000

Reprinted with permission from Grant Duwe.

As can be seen in the grid, which was constructed to represent a hypothetical system with 30,000 parolees, 10,000 of which violate their conditions, both the type of violation and the violator are placed into one of four risk categories. One way to guide decisions is to limit who is sent back to prison to only select cells—here, the cells above the black line would be sent to prison, the rest would not. This would be a way of reducing prison numbers without necessarily increasing public danger.

Clearly there is much work to be done in this debate, and we imagine new ideas will emerge in the future. In our view the best way forward is for competing theories and proposals to be put to the test, head-to-head, in a debate. In that way each side will be forced to refine its arguments and address shortcomings. Only time will tell where the debate on mass incarceration and prison reform will lead.

CONCLUSION

We hope you have enjoyed this foray into great debates in criminology. While our focus was on theoretical issues, it should be clear that scholars have and still do debate nearly every issue in the field, from which type of statistical model is best, to how to define and operationally measure key concepts. Debates have characterized the field of criminology literally since its inception (depending on where that line is drawn) and continue to roil to the present day.

As we have tried to make clear, however, our assessment is that debates are not a marker of an immature field or one in chaos, but one that takes ideas seriously (Laub, 2004). Scholars in criminology believe in their theories and the methods they use to test them. Others disagree. These exchanges, we submit, have created a more vibrant and useful body of knowledge. They have ensured that scholars do not become complacent with their ideas and that scholars constantly update their views with the latest evidence— or at least that they are confronted with the latest evidence. Debates can also help students better understand particular ideas and methods so that they can choose which path seems to be the most empirically sound. In the end, one would hope, ideas and techniques with clear flaws would go by the wayside. In any case, debates are, we feel (and hope you agree by now), a collective good for criminology.

NOTES

1 Retrieved from www.pbcfl.net/curriculum/coaching/60general/gc01.pdf
2 Email interview, September 11, 2017
3 See: www.cnn.com/2015/10/07/living/harvard-debate-team-loses-to-prison-inmates-feat/index. html
4 https://heterodoxacademy.org/
5 Email conversation, September 4, 2017
6 http://michaelrocque.weebly.com/
7 See for example: www.psychreg.org/victimology/; http://www.psychreg.org/psychosocial-criminology/; http://jjie.org/2015/08/05/a-biosocial-explanation-for-running-from-police/; http://quillette.com/2017/01/17/saints-sinners-a-dialogue-on-the-hardest-topic-in-science/
8 https://wiley.altmetric.com/details/2218961
9 For example: http://quillette.com/2015/11/13/criminologists-who-study-bio-shunned-by-field/
10 http://quillette.com/2015/12/01/why-parenting-may-not-matter-and-why-most-social-science-research-is-probably-wrong/

11 http://jjie.org/2017/10/23/why-parenting-matters-evidence-from-parenting-programs-and-at-risk-kids/

12 www.aei.org/publication/rethinking-prison-a-strategy-for-evidence-based-reform/

13 https://sentencingproject.org/wp-content/uploads/2015/11/Fewer-Prisoners-Less-Crime-A-Tale-of-Three-States.pdf

References

Aaltonen, M. (2016). Post-release employment of desisting inmates. *British Journal of Criminology, 56*(2), 350–369.

Agan, A. Y. (2011). Sex offender registries: Fear without function? *The Journal of Law and Economics, 54*(1), 207–239.

Agnew, R. (1992). Foundation for a general strain theory of crime and delinquency. *Criminology, 30*(1), 47–88.

Agnew, R. (1995). Testing the leading crime theories: An alternative strategy focusing on motivational processes. *Journal of Research in Crime and Delinquency, 32*(4), 363–398.

Agnew, R. (2006). *Pressured into Crime*. Los Angeles, CA: Roxbury.

Akers, R. L. (1973). *Deviant Behavior: A Social Learning Approach*. Belmont, CA: Wadsworth Publishing Company.

Akers, R. L. (1989). A social behaviorist's perspective on integration of theories of crime and deviance. In S. F. Messner, M. D. Krohn, & A. E. Liska (Eds.), *Theoretical Integration in the Study of Deviance and Crime: Problems and Prospects* (pp. 23–36). Albany, NY: State University of New York Press.

Akers, R. L. (1990). Rational choice, deterrence, and social learning theory in criminology: The path not taken. *Journal of Criminal Law & Criminology, 81*(3), 653–676.

Akers, R. L. (1991). Self-control as a general theory of crime. *Journal of Quantitative Criminology, 7*(2), 201–211.

Akers, R. L. (1992). Linking sociology and its specialties: The case of criminology. *Social Forces, 71*(1), 1–16.

Akers, R. L. (1996). Is differential association/social learning cultural deviance theory? *Criminology, 34*(2), 229–247.

Akers, R. L. (2009). *Social Learning and Social Structure: A General Theory of Crime and Deviance*. New Brunswick, NJ: Transaction Publishers.

Akers, R. L., Krohn, M. D., Lanza-Kaduce, L., & Radosevich, M. (1979). Social learning and deviant behavior: A specific test of a general theory. *American Sociological Review, 44*(4), 636–655.

Akers, R. L., Sellers, C. S., & Jennings, W. (2016). *Criminological Theories: Introduction, Evaluation, and Application*. Los Angeles, CA: Roxbury.

Alarid, L. F., Burton, V. S., & Cullen, F. T. (2000). Gender and crime among felony offenders: Assessing the generality of social control and differential association theories. *Journal of Research in Crime and Delinquency, 37*(2), 171–199.

Alexander, M. (2010). *The New Jim Crow: Mass Incarceration in the Age of Colorblindness*. New York, NY: The New Press.

American Sociological Association (ASA). (2010). *Report of the ASA Task Force on Sociology and Criminology Programs*. Washington, DC: American Sociological Association.

Andrews, D. A., & Bonta, J. (2002/2010). *The Psychology of Criminal Conduct*. New York, NY: Routledge.

Andrews, D. A., & Wormith, J. S. (1989). Personality and crime: Knowledge destruction and construction in criminology. *Justice Quarterly, 6*(3), 289–309.

Andrews, D. A., Zinger, I., Hoge, R. D., Bonta, J., Gendreau, P., & Cullen, F. T. (1990). Does correctional treatment work? A clinically relevant and psychologically informed meta-analysis. *Criminology, 28*(3), 369–404.

Arrigo, B. A. (2003). Postmodern justice and critical criminology: Positional, relational, and provisional science. In M. D. Schwartz, & S. E. Hatty (Eds.), *Controversies in Critical Criminology* (pp. 43–55). Cincinnati, OH: Anderson Publishing.

Arrigo, B. A., & Bernard, T. J. (1997). Postmodern criminology in relation to radical and conflict criminology. *Critical Criminology, 8*(2), 39–60.

Arseneault, L., Tremblay, R. E., Boulerice, B., Seguin, J. R., & Saucier, J. F. (2000). Minor physical anomalies and family adversity as risk factors for violent delinquency in adolescence. *American Journal of Psychiatry, 157*(6), 917–923.

Auerhahn, K. (1999). Selective incapacitation and the problem of prediction. *Criminology, 37*(4), 703–734.

Avi-Itzhak, B., & Shinnar, R. (1973). Quantitative models in crime control. *Journal of Criminal Justice, 1*(3), 185–217.

Baldus, D. C., & Cole, J. W. L. (1975). A comparison of the work of Thorsten Sellin and Isaac Ehrlich on the deterrent effect of capital punishment. *The Yale Law Journal, 85*(2), 170–186.

Baldwin, J. D. (1985). Thrill and adventure seeking and the age distribution of crime: Comment on Hirschi and Gottfredson. *American Journal of Sociology, 90*(6), 1326–1330.

Barkan, S. (2011). *Sociology: Understanding and Changing the Social World*. Boston, MA: Flat World Knowledge, Incorporated.

Barnes, J. C., Wright, J. P., Boutwell, B. B., Schwartz, J. A., Connolly, E. J., Nedelec, J. L., & Beaver, K. M. (2014). Demonstrating the validity of twin research in criminology. *Criminology, 52*(4), 588–626.

Baskin, D. R., & Sommers, I. B. (1998). *Casualties of Community Disorder: Women's Careers in Violent Crime*. Boulder, CO: Westview Press.

Beaver, K. M. (2008). Nonshared environmental influences on adolescent delinquent involvement and adult criminal behavior. *Criminology, 46*(2), 341–369.

Beaver, K. M., Nedelec, J. L., da Silva Costa, C., & Vidal, M. M. (2015). The future of biosocial criminology. *Criminal Justice Studies, 28*(1), 6–17.

Beccaria, C. (1764/2009). *On Crimes and Punishments and Other Writings*. Toronto, Canada: University of Toronto Press.

Becker, G. S. (1968). Crime and punishment: An economic approach. In G. S. Becker, & W. M. Landis (Eds.), *The Economic Dimensions of Crime* (pp. 13–68). London, UK: Palgrave Macmillan.

Benson, M. L., & Moore, E. (1992). Are white-collar and common offenders the same? An empirical and theoretical critique of a recently proposed general theory of crime. *Journal of Research in Crime and Delinquency, 29*(3), 251–272.

Berger, R. J., & Berger, C. E. (1985). Community organization approaches to the prevention of juvenile delinquency. *Journal of Sociology and Social Welfare, 12*, 129–153.

Bernard, T. J. (1989). A theoretical approach to integration. In S. F. Messner, M. D. Krohn, & A. E. Liska (Eds.), *Theoretical Integration in the Study of Deviance and Crime: Problems and Prospects* (pp. 137–160). Albany, NY: State University of New York Press.

Bernard, T. J. (1990). Twenty years of testing theories: What have we learned and why? *Journal of Research in Crime and Delinquency, 27*(4), 325–347.

Bernard, T. J., & Snipes, J. B. (1996). Theoretical integration in criminology. *Crime and Justice, 20*, 301–348.

Bernard, T. J., Snipes, J. B., & Gerould, A. L. (2016). *Vold's Theoretical Criminology*. New York, NY: Oxford University Press.

Bessler, J. D. (2009). Revisiting Beccaria's vision: The Enlightenment, America's death penalty, and the abolition movement. *Northwestern Journal of Law & Social Policy, 4*(2), 195–328.

Bierne, P. (2006). Free will and determinism? Reading Beccaria's *Of Crimes and Punishments* (1764) as a text of enlightenment. In S. Henry, & M. M. Lanier (Eds.), *The Essential Criminology Reader* (pp. 3–17). Boulder, CO: Westview Press.

Bitler, M. P., & Karoly, L. A. (2015). Intended and unintended effects of the war on poverty: What research tells us and implications for policy. *Journal of Policy Analysis and Management*, *34*(3), 639–696.

Blackwell, B. S. (2000). Perceived sanction threats, gender, and crime: A test and elaboration of power-control theory. *Criminology*, *38*(2), 439–488.

Bleyer, J. (2013). Patty Wetterling questions sex offender laws. Retrieved from www.citypages.com/news/patty-wetterling-questions-sex-offender-laws-6766534.

Bloom, P. (2013). *Just Babies: The Origins of Good and Evil*. New York, NY: Broadway Books.

Blumstein, A. (2011). Criminology: Science + policy analysis. In M. Bosworth, & C. Hoyle (Eds.), *What is Criminology* (pp. 475–487). New York, NY: Oxford University Press.

Blumstein, A., & Cohen, J. (1973). Theory of the stability of punishment. *Journal of Criminal Law and Criminology*, *64*(2), 198–207.

Blumstein, A., & Cohen, J. (1979). Estimation of individual crime rates from arrest records. *Journal of Criminal Law & Criminology*, *70*, 561–585.

Blumstein, A., Cohen, J., & Farrington, D. P. (1988). Criminal career research: Its value for criminology. *Criminology*, *26*(1), 1–35.

Blumstein, A., Cohen, J., & Hsieh, P. (1982). Duration of adult criminal careers: Final report. *National Criminal Justice Reference Service (NCJRS) Report*, (89569).

Blumstein, A., Cohen, J., Roth, J. A., & Visher, C. A. (1986). *Criminal Careers and "Career Criminals."* Washington, DC: National Academy Press.

Blumstein, A., & Moitra, S. (1980). The identification of "career criminals" from "chronic offenders" in a cohort. *Law & Policy*, *2*(3), 321–334.

Bosworth, M., & Hoyle, C. (2011). *What is Criminology?* New York, NY: Oxford University Press.

Braga, A. A. (2001). The effects of hot spots policing on crime. *The Annals of the American Academy of Political and Social Science*, *578*(1), 104–125.

Braithwaite, J. (1989). *Crime, Shame and Reintegration*. Cambridge, UK: Cambridge University Press.

Brame, R. (2016). Alfred Blumstein. Oxford Bibliographies Online.

Brame, R., Paternoster, R., & Piquero, A. R. (2012). Thoughts on the analysis of group-based developmental trajectories in criminology. *Justice Quarterly*, *29*(4), 469–490.

Brehm, H. N., Uggen, C., & Gasanabo, J. D. (2016). Age, gender, and the crime of crimes: Toward a life-course theory of genocide participation. *Criminology*, *54*(4), 713–743.

Brown, S. F., Dewender, T., & Kobusch, T. (2009). *Philosophical Debates at Paris in the Early Fourteenth Century*. London, UK: Brill.

Burgess, R. L., & Akers, R. L. (1966). A differential association-reinforcement theory of criminal behavior. *Social Problems*, *14*(2), 128–147.

Burgess-Proctor, A. (2006). Intersections of race, class, gender, and crime: Future directions for feminist criminology. *Feminist Criminology*, *1*(1), 27–47.

Burt, C. H., & Simons, R. L. (2014). Pulling back the curtain on heritability studies: Biosocial criminology in the postgenomic era. *Criminology*, *52*(2), 223–262.

Burt, C. H., & Simons, R. L. (2015). Heritability studies in the postgenomic era: The fatal flaw is conceptual. *Criminology*, *53*(1), 103–112.

Bushway, S. D., Piquero, A. R., Broidy, L. M., Cauffman, E., & Mazerolle, P. (2001). An empirical framework for studying desistance as a process. *Criminology*, *39*(2), 491–516.

Bushway, S. D., Thornberry, T. P., & Krohn, M. D. (2003). Desistance as a developmental process: A comparison of static and dynamic approaches. *Journal of Quantitative Criminology*, *19*(2), 129–153.

Cabot, R. C. (1934). 1000 delinquent boys: First findings of the Harvard Law School's survey of crime. *Survey*, *70*, 38–40.

Campbell, A. (1999). Staying alive: Evolution, culture, and women's intrasexual aggression. *Behavioral and Brain Sciences*, *22*(2), 203–214.

Campbell, A. (2012). The study of sex differences: Feminism and biology. *Zeitschrift für Psychologie*, *220*(2), 137–143.

Carrier, N., & Walby, K. (2014). Ptolemizing Lombroso the pseudo-revolution of biosocial criminology. *Journal of Theoretical & Philosophical Criminology*, *6*(1), 1–45.

Caruso, G. D. (2012). *Free Will and Consciousness: A Determinist Account of the Illusion of Free Will*. Lanham, MD: Lexington Books.

Caspi, A., Moffitt, T. E., Silva, P. A., Stouthamer-Loeber, M., Krueger, R. F., & Schmutte, P. S. (1994). Are some people crime-prone? Replications of the personality-crime relationship across countries, genders, races, and methods. *Criminology, 32*(2), 163–196.

Clarke, R. V. (1995). Situational crime prevention. *Crime and Justice, 19*, 91–150.

Clarke, R. V. (1997). *Situational Crime Prevention*. Monsey, NY: Criminal Justice Press.

Clear, T. R. (2001). Has academic criminal justice come of age? ACJS presidential address. *Justice Quarterly, 18*(4), 709–726.

Clear, T. R. (2009). *Imprisoning Communities: How Mass Incarceration Makes Disadvantaged Neighborhoods Worse*. New York, NY: Oxford University Press.

Clear, T. R., & Frost, N. A. (2015). *The Punishment Imperative: The Rise and Failure of Mass Incarceration in America*. New York, NY: NYU Press.

Clinard, M. B. (1951). Sociologists and American criminology. *Journal of Criminal Law and Criminology, 41*(5), 549–577.

Cloward, R. A., & Ohlin, L. E. (1960). *Delinquency and Opportunity*. New York, NY: The Free Press.

Cohen, J. (1983). Incapacitation as a strategy for crime control: Possibilities and pitfalls. *Crime and Justice, 5*, 1–84.

Cohen, A. (2016). *Imbeciles: The Supreme Court, American Eugenics, and the Sterilization of Carrie Buck*. New York, NY: Penguin Books.

Cohen, L. E., & Felson, M. (1979). Social change and crime rate trends: A routine activity approach. *American Sociological Review, 44*(4), 588–608.

Conley, D. (2016). Socio-genomic research using genome-wide molecular data. *Annual Review of Sociology, 42*, 275–299.

Cook, P. J. (1980). Research in criminal deterrence: Laying the groundwork for the second decade. *Crime and Justice, 2*, 211–268.

Cooper, J. A., Walsh, A., & Ellis, L. (2010). Is criminology moving toward a paradigm shift? Evidence from a survey of the American Society of Criminology. *Journal of Criminal Justice Education, 21*(3), 332–347.

Cornish, D. B. & Clarke, R. V. (eds.) (1986). *The Reasoning Criminal: Rational Choice Perspectives on Offending* (Introduction). New York, NY: Springer-Verlag.

Costello, B. (1997). On the logical adequacy of cultural deviance theories. *Theoretical Criminology, 1*(4), 403–428.

Costello, B. J., & Hope, T. L. (2016). *Peer Pressure, Peer Prevention: The Role of Friends in Crime and Conformity*. New York, NY: Routledge.

Costello, B. J., & Vowell, P. R. (1999). Testing control theory and differential association: A reanalysis of the Richmond Youth Project data. *Criminology, 37*(4), 815–842.

Cottle, C. C., Lee, R. J., & Heilbrun, K. (2001). The prediction of criminal recidivism in juveniles: A meta-analysis. *Criminal Justice and Behavior, 28*(3), 367–394.

Cullen, F. T. (2009). Preface. In K. M. Beaver, & A. Walsh (Eds.), *Biosocial Criminology: New Directions in Theory and Research* (pp. xv–xvii). London, UK: Routledge.

Cullen, F. T. (2011). Beyond adolescence-limited criminology: Choosing our future. The American Society of Criminology 2010 Sutherland address. *Criminology, 49*(2), 287–330.

Cullen, F. T. (2013). Rehabilitation: Beyond nothing works. *Crime and Justice, 42*(1), 299–376.

Cullen, F. T., & Wilcox, P. (2013). *The Oxford Handbook of Criminological Theory*. New York, NY: Oxford University Press.

Cullen, F. T., Wright, J., & Blevins, K. (2011). *Taking Stock: The Status of Criminological Theory* (Vol. 1). New Brunswick, NJ: Transaction Publishers.

Currie, E. (1985). *Confronting Crime: An American Challenge*. New York, NY: Pantheon Books.

Currie, E. (1998). *Crime and Punishment in America*. New York, NY: Henry Holt and Company.

Currie, E. (2007). Against marginality: Arguments for a public criminology. *Theoretical Criminology, 11*(2), 175–190.

Daly, K., & Chesney-Lind, M. (1988). Feminism and criminology. *Justice Quarterly, 5*(4), 497–538.

Daly, M., & Wilson, M. (1988). *Homicide.* New Brunswick, NJ: Transaction Publishers.

Daw, J., Guo, G., & Harris, K. M. (2015). Nurture net of nature: Re-evaluating the role of shared environments in academic achievement and verbal intelligence. *Social Science Research*, 52, 422–439.

De Haan, W., & Vos, J. (2003). A crying shame: The over-rationalized conception of man in the rational choice perspective. *Theoretical Criminology*, 7(1), 29–54.

DeLisi, M. (2012). Revisiting Lombroso. In F. Cullen, & P. Wilcox (Eds.), *The Oxford Handbook of Criminological Theory* (pp. 5–21). New York, NY: Oxford University Press.

DeLisi, M. (2017). *Psychopathy as Unified Theory of Crime.* New York, NY: Palgrave-MacMillan.

Dinkelspiel, F. (2010). Remembering August Vollmer, the Berkeley police chief who created modern policing. Berkeleyside. Retrieved from: www.berkeleyside.com/2010/01/27/remembering-august-vollmer-the-berkeleypolice-chief-who-created-modern-policing/.

Ditton, P. M., & Wilson, D. J. (1999). *Truth in Sentencing in State Prisons.* US Department of Justice. Office of Justice Programs. Bureau of Justice Statistics.

Duffee, D. E., & Maguire, E. R. (2007). *Criminal Justice Theory: Explaining the Nature and Behavior of Criminal Justice.* New York, NY: Routledge.

Dugdale, R. (1895). *The Jukes: A Study in Crime, Pauperism, Disease and Heredity.* New York, NY: G. P. Putnam's Sons.

Durkheim, E. (1893/1960). *Division of Labor in Society.* Glencoe, IL: The Free Press.

Durkheim, E. (1897/1951). *Suicide.* Glencoe, IL: The Free Press.

Durkheim, E. (1895/1982). *Rules of Sociological Method.* Edited with an Introduction by Steven Lukes. Translated by W. D. Halls. Glencoe, IL: The Free Press.

Durlauf, S. N., Fu, C., & Navarro, S. (2013). Capital punishment and deterrence: Understanding disparate results. *Journal of Quantitative Criminology*, 29(1), 103–121.

Duwe, G. (2017). *Rethinking Prison: A Strategy for Evidence-Based Reform.* American Enterprise Institute.

Duwe, G., & Donnay, W. (2008). The impact of Megan's Law on sex offender recidivism: The Minnesota experience. *Criminology*, 46(2), 411–446.

Duwe, G., & Rocque, M. (2016). A jack of all trades but a master of none? Evaluating the performance of the Level of Service Inventory–Revised (LSI-R) in the assessment of risk and need. *Corrections*, 1(2), 81–106.

Eggleston, E. P., Laub, J. H., & Sampson, R. J. (2004). Methodological sensitivities to latent class analysis of long-term criminal trajectories. *Journal of Quantitative Criminology*, 20(1), 1–26.

Ehrlich, I. (1975). The deterrent effect of capital punishment: A question of life and death. *The American Economic Review*, 65(3), 397–417.

Einstadter, W. J., & Henry, S. (2006). *Criminological Theory: An Analysis of its Underlying Assumptions.* Lanham, MD: Rowman & Littlefield Publishers.

Elliott, D. S., Ageton, S. S., & Canter, R. J. (1979). An integrated theoretical perspective on delinquent behavior. *Journal of Research in Crime and Delinquency*, 16(1), 3–27.

Ellis, L., & Walsh, A. (1997). Gene-based evolutionary theories in criminology. *Criminology*, 35(2), 229–276.

Farrall, S., & Calverley, A. (2006). *Understanding Desistance from Crime: Theoretical Directions in Rehabilitation and Resettlement.* Maidenhead, UK: Open University Press.

Farrington, D. P. (1986). Age and crime. *Crime and Justice*, 7, 189–250.

Farrington, D. P. (2003). Developmental and life-course criminology: Key theoretical and empirical issues. The 2002 Sutherland Award address. *Criminology*, 41(2), 221–225.

Farrington, D. P. (2007). Advancing knowledge about desistance. *Journal of Contemporary Criminal Justice*, 23(1), 125–134.

Farrington, D. P., & Hawkins, J. D. (1991). Predicting participation, early onset and later persistence in officially recorded offending. *Criminal Behaviour and Mental Health*, 1(1), 1–33.

Farrington, D. P., Ttofi, M. M., & Crago, R. V. (2017). Intergenerational transmission of convictions for different types of offenses. *Victims & Offenders*, 12(1), 1–20.

Farrington, D. P., Ttofi, M. M., Crago, R. V., & Coid, J. W. (2014). Prevalence, frequency, onset, desistance and criminal career duration in self-reports compared with official records. *Criminal Behaviour and Mental Health*, 24(4), 241–253.

Farrington, D. P., & Welsh, B. C. (2007). *Saving Children from a Life of Crime*. New York, NY: Oxford University Press.

Felson, M. (2011). Soft crimes, not criminal. In M. Bosworth, & C. Hoyle (Eds.), *What is Criminology?* (pp. 171–182). New York, NY: Oxford University Press.

Felson, M., & Clarke, R. V. (1998). Opportunity makes the thief. *Police Research Series*. Paper 98.

Fink, A. E. (1938/1962). *Causes of Crime: Biological Theories in the United States 1800–1915*. New York, NY: A. S. Barnes and Company.

Friedrichs, D. O., & Rothe, D. L. (2012). Crimes of the powerful: White-collar crime and beyond. In W. S. DeKeseredy, & M. Dragiewicz (Eds.), *Routledge Handbook of Critical Criminology* (pp. 241–251). New York, NY: Routledge.

Gajos, J. M., Fagan, A. A., & Beaver, K. M. (2016). Use of genetically informed evidence-based prevention science to understand and prevent crime and related behavioral disorders. *Criminology & Public Policy*, 15(3), 683–701.

Gaylord, M. S., & Galliher, J. F. (1988). *The Criminology of Edwin Sutherland*. New Brunswick, NJ: Transaction Books.

Geis, G. (1971). Introduction to the reprint edition. In J. Michael & M. J. Adler (Eds.), *Crime, Law and Social Science* (pp. ix–xi). Montclair, NJ: Patterson Smith.

Geis, G. (2008). Self-control: A hypercritical assessment. In E. Goode (Ed.), *Out of Control: Assessing the General Theory of Crime* (pp. 203–216). Stanford, CA: Stanford University Press.

Gendreau, P., Little, T., & Goggin, C. (1996). A meta-analysis of the predictors of adult offender recidivism: What works! *Criminology*, 34(4), 575–608.

Gibbons, D. C. (1979). *The Criminological Enterprise: Theories and Perspectives*. Englewood Cliffs, NJ: Prentice-Hall.

Gibson, M. (1982). The "female offender" and the Italian School of criminal anthropology. *Journal of European Studies*, 12(47), 155–165.

Gibson, M., & Rafter, N. R. (2006). *Criminal Man*. Durham, NC: Duke University Press.

Giordano, P. C., Cernkovich, S. A., & Rudolph, J. L. (2002). Gender, crime, and desistance: Toward a theory of cognitive transformation. *American Journal of Sociology*, 107(4), 990–1064.

Glueck, S., & Glueck, E. T. (1930). *500 Criminal Careers*. New York, NY: AA Knopf.

Glueck, S. & Glueck, E. T. (1934). *One Thousand Juvenile Delinquents*. Cambridge, MA: Harvard University Press.

Glueck, S., & Glueck, E. T. (1937). *Later Criminal Careers*. New York, NY: The Commonwealth Fund.

Glueck, S., & Glueck, E. T. (1950). *Unraveling Juvenile Delinquency*. New York, NY: The Commonwealth Fund.

Goddard, H. H. (1912). *The Kallikak Family: A Study in the Heredity of Feeble-mindedness*. New York, NY: Macmillan Company.

Goff, C., & Geis, G. (2008). The Michael-Adler report (1933): Criminology under the microscope. *Journal of the History of the Behavioral Sciences*, 44(4), 350–363.

Goring, C. (1913). *The English Convict*. Montclair, NJ: Patterson Smith.

Gottfredson, M., & Hirschi, T. (1986). The true value of lambda would appear to be zero: An essay on career criminals, criminal careers, selective incapacitation, cohort studies, and related topics. *Criminology*, 24(2), 213–234.

Gottfredson, M., & Hirschi, T. (1987). The methodological adequacy of longitudinal research on crime. *Criminology*, 25(3), 581–614.

Gottfredson, M. R., & Hirschi, T. (1990). *A General Theory of Crime*. Stanford, CA: Stanford University Press.

Gottfredson, M. R., & Hirschi, T. (2003). Self-control and opportunity. In C. L. Britt and M. Gottfredson (Eds.), *Control Theories of Crime and Delinquency. Advances in Criminological Theory* (pp. 5–19). New Brunswick, NJ: Transaction Publishers.

Greenberg, D. F. (1975). The incapacitative effect of imprisonment: Some estimates. *Law & Society Review*, 9(4), 541–580.

Guerette, R. T., & Bowers, K. J. (2009). Assessing the extent of crime displacement and diffusion of benefits: A review of situational crime prevention evaluations. *Criminology*, 47(4), 1331–1368.

Hagan, J., Gillis, A. R., & Simpson, J. (1985). The class structure of gender and delinquency: Toward a power-control theory of common delinquent behavior. *American Journal of Sociology*, *90*(6), 1151–1178.

Hagan, J., & Palloni, A. (1988). Crimes as social events in the life course: Reconceiving a criminological controversy. *Criminology*, *26*(1), 87–100.

Hager, E., & Keller, B. (2017). Everything you think you know about mass incarceration is wrong. Or at least misleading, says this contrarian scholar. Here's why it matters. *The Marshall Project*. Retrieved from www.themarshallproject.org/2017/02/09/everything-you-think-you-know-about-mass-incarceration-is-wrong.

Hanson, R. K., & Bussiere, M. T. (1998). Predicting relapse: A meta-analysis of sexual offender recidivism studies. *Journal of Consulting and Clinical Psychology*, *66*(2), 348–362.

Harris, J. R. (2009). *The Nurture Assumption: Why Children Turn Out the Way They Do*. New York, NY: The Free Press.

Hayward, K. (2007). Situational crime prevention and its discontents: Rational choice theory versus the "culture of now". *Social Policy & Administration*, *41*(3), 232–250.

Hawkins, J. D., Kosterman, R., Catalano, R. F., Hill, K. G., & Abbott, R. D. (2005). Promoting positive adult functioning through social development intervention in childhood: Long-term effects from the Seattle Social Development Project. *Archives of Pediatrics & Adolescent Medicine*, *159*(1), 25–31.

Hawkins, J. D., & Weis, J. G. (1985). The social development model: An integrated approach to delinquency prevention. *The Journal of Primary Prevention*, *6*(2), 73–97.

Healy, W. (1915). *The Individual Delinquent: A Textbook of Diagnosis and Prognosis for All Concerned in Understanding Offenders*. Boston, MA: Little, Brown, & Co.

Healy, W., & Bronner, A. (1936). *New Light on Delinquency*. New Haven, CT: Yale University Press.

Helmus, L., Hanson, R. K., Thornton, D., Babchishin, K. M., & Harris, A. J. (2012). Absolute recidivism rates predicted by Static-99R and Static-2002R sex offender risk assessment tools vary across samples: A meta-analysis. *Criminal Justice and Behavior*, *39*(9), 1148–1171.

Henry, S., & Lanier, M. (2006). *The Essential Criminology Reader*. Boulder, CO: Westview Press.

Henry, S., & Milovanovic, D. (1991). Constitutive criminology: The maturation of critical theory. *Criminology*, *29*(2), 293–316.

Hipp, J. R. (2016). General theory of spatial crime patterns. *Criminology*, *54*(4), 653–679.

Hirschi, T. (1969). *Causes of Delinquency*. Berkeley, CA: University of California.

Hirschi, T. (1977). Causes and prevention of juvenile delinquency. *Sociological Inquiry*, *47*(3–4), 322–341.

Hirschi, T. (1979). Separate and unequal is better. *Journal of Research in Crime and Delinquency*, *16*(1), 34–38.

Hirschi, T. (1986). On the compatibility of rational choice and social control theories of crime. In D. B. Cornish, & R. V. Clarke (Eds.), (2014) *The Reasoning Criminal: Rational Choice Perspectives on Offending (105–118)*. New Brunswick, NJ: Transaction Publishers.

Hirschi, T. (1989). Exploring alternatives to integrated theory. In S. F. Messner, M. D. Krohn, & A. E. Liska (Eds.), *Theoretical Integration in the Study of Deviance and Crime: Problems and Prospects* (pp. 37–49). Albany, NY: State University of New York Press.

Hirschi, T. (1996). Theory without ideas: Reply to Akers. *Criminology*, *34*(2), 249–256.

Hirschi, T., & Gottfredson, M. (1983). Age and the explanation of crime. *American Journal of Sociology*, *89*(3), 552–584.

Hirschi, T., & Gottfredson, M. (1985). All wise after the fact learning theory, again: Reply to Baldwin. *American Journal of Sociology*, *90*(6), 1330–1333.

Hirschi, T., & Gottfredson, M. (1986). The distinction between crime and criminality. In T. F. Hartnagel, & R. A. Silverman (Eds.), *Critique and Explanation: Essays in Honor of Gwynne Nettler* (pp. 55–68). New Brunswick, NJ: Transaction.

Hirschi, T., & Gottfredson, M. (1987). Causes of white-collar crime. *Criminology*, *25*(4), 949–974.

Hirschi, T., & Gottfredson, M. (1989). The significance of white-collar crime for a general theory of crime. *Criminology*, *27*(2), 359–371.

Hirschi, T., & Gottfredson, M. (1993). Commentary: Testing the general theory of crime. *Journal of Research in Crime and Delinquency, 30*(1), 47–54.

Hirschi, T., & Hindelang, M. J. (1977). Intelligence and delinquency: A revisionist review. *American Sociological Review, 42*(4), 571–587.

Hobbes, T. (1651/2006). *Leviathan.* New York, NY: Continuum International Publishing Group.

Hulbert, H. S. (1939). Constitutional psychopathic inferiority in relation to delinquency. *Journal of the American Institute of Criminal Law and Criminology, 30*, 3–21.

Jaishankar, K. (2007). Cyber criminology: Evolving a novel discipline with a new journal. *International Journal of Cyber Criminology, 1*(1), 1–6.

Jaschik, S. (2010). Sociology vs. criminology. *Inside Higher Ed.* Retrieved from: www.insidehighered.com/news/2010/06/18/discipline.

Jeffery, C. R. (1979). *Biology and Crime.* Beverly Hills, CA: Sage.

Jewkes, Y. (2005). Men behind bars: "Doing" masculinity as an adaptation to imprisonment. *Men and Masculinities, 8*(1), 44–63.

Joffe-Walt, C. & Spiegal, A. (2012). The psychology of fraud: Why good people do bad things. NPR. Retrieved from www.npr.org/2012/05/01/151764534/psychology-of-fraud-why-good-people-do-bad-things.

Jones, D. A. (1986). *History of Criminology: A Philosophical Perspective.* Westport, CT: Greenwood Press.

Kania, R. R. (1988). Conservative ideology in criminology and criminal justice. *American Journal of Criminal Justice, 13*(1), 74–96.

Kazemian, L. (2007). Desistance from crime: Theoretical, empirical, methodological, and policy considerations. *Journal of Contemporary Criminal Justice, 23*(1), 5–27.

Kennedy, E., Heron, J., & Munafó, M. (2017). Substance use, criminal behaviour and psychiatric symptoms following childhood traumatic brain injury: Findings from the ALSPAC cohort. *European Child & Adolescent Psychiatry, 26*(10), 1197–1206.

Kernsmith, P. D., Comartin, E., Craun, S. W., & Kernsmith, R. M. (2009). The relationship between sex offender registry utilization and awareness. *Sexual Abuse, 21*(2), 181–193.

Kirov, B. (2016). *Karl Marx: Quotes and Facts.* CreateSpace Independent Publishing Platform.

Kobrin, S. (1959). The Chicago Area Project—a 25-year assessment. *The Annals of the American Academy of Political and Social Science, 322*(1), 19–29.

Kornhauser, R. R. (1978). *Social Sources of Delinquency: An Appraisal of Analytic Models.* Chicago, IL: University of Chicago Press.

Kramer, R. C. (2012). Curbing state crime by challenging empire. In W. S. DeKeseredy, & M. Dragiewicz (Eds.), *Routledge Handbook of Critical Criminology* (pp. 442–453). New York, NY: Routledge.

Kraska, P. B. (2004). *Theorizing Criminal Justice: Eight Essential Orientations.* Long Grove, IL: Waveland Press.

Kraska, P. B., & Brent, J. J. (2011). *Theorizing Criminal Justice: Eight Essential Orientations.* Long Grove, IL: Waveland Press.

Kuhn, T. S. (1962). *The Structure of Scientific Revolutions.* Chicago, IL: University of Chicago Press.

Landenberger, N. A., & Lipsey, M. W. (2005). The positive effects of cognitive-behavioral programs for offenders: A meta-analysis of factors associated with effective treatment. *Journal of Experimental Criminology, 1*(4), 451–476.

Langton, L., & Piquero, N. L. (2007). Can general strain theory explain white-collar crime? A preliminary investigation of the relationship between strain and select white-collar offenses. *Journal of Criminal Justice, 35*(1), 1–15.

Laub, J. H. (2002). Introduction: The life and work of Travis Hirschi. In J. H. Laub (Ed.), *The Craft of Criminology: Selected Papers* (pp. vii–xlix). New Brunswick, NJ: Transaction Publishers.

Laub, J. H. (2006). Edwin H. Sutherland and the Michael-Adler report: Searching for the soul of criminology seventy years later. *Criminology, 44*(2), 235–258.

Laub, J. H. (2016). Life-course research and the shaping of public policy. In M. J. Shanahan, J. T. Mortimer, & M. K. Johnson (Eds.), *Handbook of the Life Course* (pp. 623–637). Springer International Publishing.

Laub, J. H., & Sampson, R. J. (1991). The Sutherland-Glueck debate: On the sociology of criminological knowledge. *American Journal of Sociology, 96*, 1402–1440.

Laub, J. H., & Sampson, R. J. (2001). Understanding desistance from crime. *Crime and Justice, 28*, 1–69.

Laub, J. H., & Sampson, R. J. (2003). *Shared Beginnings, Divergent Lives*. Cambridge, MA: Harvard University Press.

Le Blanc, M., & Loeber, R. (1998). Developmental criminology updated. *Crime and Justice, 23*, 115–198.

Lemann, N. (1988). The unfinished war. *The Atlantic Online*. December 1988 [Retrieved June 25, 2017].

Lersch, K. M., & Hart, T. C. (2014). Environmental justice, lead, and crime: Exploring the spatial distribution and impact of industrial facilities in Hillsborough County, Florida. *Sociological Spectrum, 34*(1), 1–21.

Levenson, J. S., & Cotter, L. P. (2005). The impact of sex offender residence restrictions: 1,000 feet from danger or one step from absurd? *International Journal of Offender Therapy and Comparative Criminology, 49*(2), 168–178.

Levenson, J. S., & Hern, A. L. (2007). Sex offender residence restrictions: Unintended consequences and community reentry. *Justice Research and Policy, 9*(1), 59–73.

Levenson, J. S., Brannon, Y. N., Fortney, T., & Baker, J. (2007). Public perceptions about sex offenders and community protection policies. *Analyses of Social Issues and Public Policy, 7*(1), 137–161.

Levitt, S. D. (2004). Understanding why crime fell in the 1990s: Four factors that explain the decline and six that do not. *The Journal of Economic Perspectives, 18*(1), 163–190.

Lipton, D. S., Martinson, R., & Wilks, J. (1975). *The Effectiveness of Correctional Treatment: A Survey of Treatment Evaluation Studies*. Santa Barbara, CA: Praeger Publishers.

Liska, A. E., Krohn, M. D., & Messner, S. F. (1989). Strategies and requisites for theoretical integration in the study of crime and deviance. In S. F. Messner, M. D. Krohn, & A. E. Liska (Eds.), *Theoretical Integration in the Study of Deviance and Crime: Problems and Prospects* (pp. 1–19). Albany, NY: State University of New York Press.

Loeber, R., & Le Blanc, M. (1990). Toward a developmental criminology. *Crime and Justice, 12*, 375–473.

Lombroso, C. (1911a). *Crime, its Causes and Remedies*. Boston, MA: Little, Brown, and Company.

Lombroso, C. (1911b). Introduction. In Ferri, G. L. *Criminal Man: According to the Classification of Cesare Lombroso*. (pp. xi–xx). New York, NY: G.P. Putnam's Sons.

Lopez, G. (2016). Want to end mass incarceration? This poll should worry you. Vox. Retrieved from www.vox.com/2016/9/7/12814504/mass-incarceration-poll.

Lowenkamp, C. T., Latessa, E. J., & Smith, P. (2006). Does correctional program quality really matter? The impact of adhering to the principles of effective intervention. *Criminology & Public Policy, 5*(3), 201–220.

Marks, S. R. (1974). Durkheim's theory of anomie. *American Journal of Sociology, 80*(2), 329–363.

Martinson, R. (1974). What works? Questions and answers about prison reform. *The Public Interest*, (35), 22–35.

Maruna, S. (2001). *Making Good: How Ex-Convicts Reform and Rebuild their Lives*. Washington, DC: American Psychological Association.

Massaro, D. R. (1990). Influence of Cesare Beccaria on the American criminal justice system. *Italian Journal, 4*(2), 29–31.

Massey, D. S. (2015). Brave new world of biosocial science. *Criminology, 53*(1), 127–131.

Massoglia, M., & Uggen, C. (2007). Subjective desistance and the transition to adulthood. *Journal of Contemporary Criminal Justice, 23*(1), 90–103.

Matsueda, R. L. (1982). Testing control theory and differential association: A causal modeling approach. *American Sociological Review, 47*(4), 489–504.

Matsueda, R. L. (1988). The current state of differential association theory. *Crime & Delinquency, 34*(3), 277–306.

Matsueda, R. L. (1997). "Cultural deviance theory": The remarkable persistence of a flawed term. *Theoretical Criminology, 1*(4), 429–452.

Mazzarello, P. (2011). Cesare Lombroso: An anthropologist between evolution and degeneration. *Functional Neurology*, 26(2), 97–101.

McCord, J. (1978). A thirty-year follow-up of treatment effects. *American Psychologist*, 33(3), 284–289.

McCord, J. (1980). The treatment that did not help. *Social Action and the Law*, 5, 85–87.

Mears, D. P., Cochran, J. C., & Cullen, F. T. (2015). Incarceration heterogeneity and its implications for assessing the effectiveness of imprisonment on recidivism. *Criminal Justice Policy Review*, 26(7), 691–712.

Mednick, S. A., Gabrielli Jr, W. F., & Hutchings, B. (1984). Genetic influences in criminal convictions: Evidence from an adoption cohort. *Science*, 224, 891–895.

Merton, R. K. (1938). Social structure and anomie. *American Sociological Review*, 3(5), 672–682.

Messner, S. F., Krohn, M. D., & Liska, A. E. (1989). *Theoretical Integration in the Study of Deviance and Crime: Problems and Prospects*. Albany, NY: State University of New York Press.

Messner, S. F., & Rosenfeld, R. (2013). *Crime and the American Dream*. Belmont, CA: Cengage Learning.

Michael, J. & Adler, M. J. (1933). *Crime, Law and Social Science*. New York, NY: Harcourt, Brace.

Miller, J. (2002). The strengths and limits of "doing gender" for understanding street crime. *Theoretical Criminology*, 6(4), 433–460.

Miller, T. R. (2015). Projected outcomes of nurse-family partnership home visitation during 1996–2013, USA. *Prevention Science*, 16(6), 765–777.

Mocan, H. N., & Gittings, R. K. (2003). Getting off death row: Commuted sentences and the deterrent effect of capital punishment. *The Journal of Law and Economics*, 46(2), 453–478.

Moffitt, T. E. (1993). Adolescence-limited and life-course-persistent antisocial behavior: A developmental taxonomy. *Psychological Review*, 100(4), 674–701.

Moffitt, T. E., & Beckley, A. (2015). Abandon twin research? Embrace epigenetic research? Premature advice for criminologists. *Criminology*, 53(1), 121–126.

Monahan, K. C., Steinberg, L., Cauffman, E., & Mulvey, E. P. (2009). Trajectories of antisocial behavior and psychosocial maturity from adolescence to young adulthood. *Developmental Psychology*, 45(6), 1654–1668.

Morris, A. (1975). The American Society of Criminology: A history, 1941–1974. *Criminology*, 13(2), 123–167.

Mulvey, E. P., Steinberg, L., Fagan, J., Cauffman, E., Piquero, A. R., Chassin, L., & Losoya, S. H. (2004). Theory and research on desistance from antisocial activity among serious adolescent offenders. *Youth Violence and Juvenile Justice*, 2(3), 213–236.

Mustaine, E. E. (2014). Sex offender residency restrictions. *Criminology & Public Policy*, 13(1), 169–177.

Mutua, A. D. (2006). *Progressive Black Masculinities?* New York, NY: Routledge.

Nagin, D. S. (1998). Criminal deterrence research at the outset of the twenty-first century. *Crime and Justice*, 23, 1–42.

Nagin, D. S. (2004). Response to "Methodological sensitivities to latent class analysis of long-term criminal trajectories". *Journal of Quantitative Criminology*, 20(1), 27–35.

Nagin, D. (2005). *Group-Based Modeling of Development*. Cambridge, MA: Harvard University Press.

Nagin, D. S. (2013). Deterrence in the twenty-first century. *Crime and Justice*, 42(1), 199–263.

Nagin, D. S., & Land, K. C. (1993). Age, criminal careers, and population heterogeneity: Specification and estimation of a nonparametric, mixed Poisson model. *Criminology*, 31(3), 327–362.

Nagin, D. S., & Paternoster, R. (1993). Enduring individual differences and rational choice theories of crime. *Law and Society Review*, 27(3), 467–496.

Nagin, D. S., & Piquero, A. R. (2010). Using the group-based trajectory model to study crime over the life-course. *Journal of Criminal Justice Education*, 21(2), 105–116.

Nagin, D. S., & Tremblay, R. E. (2005). Developmental trajectory groups: Fact or a useful statistical fiction? *Criminology*, 43(4), 873–904.

Nicholson, J., & Higgins, G. E. (2017). Social structure social learning theory: Preventing crime and violence. In B. Teasdale, & M. S. Bradley (Eds.), *Preventing Crime and Violence* (pp. 11–20). New York, NY: Springer International Publishing.

Nye, F. I. (1958). *Family Relationships and Delinquent Behavior*. Westport, CT: Greenwood Press.

Olds, D. L. (2006). The Nurse-Family Partnership: An evidence-based preventive intervention. *Infant Mental Health Journal*, 27(1), 5–25.

Olver, M. E., Stockdale, K. C., & Wormith, J. S. (2009). Risk assessment with young offenders: A meta-analysis of three assessment measures. *Criminal Justice and Behavior*, 36(4), 329–353.

Osgood, D. W., Johnston, L. D., O'Malley, P. M., & Bachman, J. G. (1988). The generality of deviance in late adolescence and early adulthood. *American Sociological Review*, 53(1), 81–93.

Panofsky, A. (2014). *Misbehaving Science: Controversy and the Development of Behavior Genetics*. Chicago, IL: University of Chicago Press.

Parcher, J. (1998). The value of debate. *Report of the Philodemic Debate Society*, Georgetown University.

Parmalee, M. (1911). Introduction to the English edition. In Lombroso, C. *Crime, its Causes and Remedies* (pp. xi–xxxii). London, UK: William Heinemann.

Parmalee, M. (1918). *Criminology*. New York, NY: Macmillan.

Paternoster, R. (1987). The deterrent effect of the perceived certainty and severity of punishment: A review of the evidence and issues. *Justice Quarterly*, 4(2), 173–217.

Paternoster, R., & Bushway, S. (2009). Desistance and the "feared self": Toward an identity theory of criminal desistance. *The Journal of Criminal Law and Criminology*, 99(4), 1103–1156.

Paternoster, R., McGloin, J. M., Nguyen, H., & Thomas, K. J. (2013). The causal impact of exposure to deviant peers: An experimental investigation. *Journal of Research in Crime and Delinquency*, 50(4), 476–503.

Paternoster, R., Saltzman, L. E., Waldo, G. P., & Chiricos, T. G. (1983). Perceived risk and social control: Do sanctions really deter? *Law and Society Review*, 17(3), 457–479.

Patterson, G. R. (1982). *Coercive Family Process*. Eugene, OR: Castalia Publishing Company.

Pearson, F. S., & Weiner, N. A. (1985). Toward an integration of criminological theories. *Journal of Criminal Law & Criminology*, 76(1), 116–150.

Pepinsky, H. E., & Quinney, R. (1991). *Criminology as Peacemaking*. Bloomington, IN: Indiana University Press.

Petersilia, J., Greenwood P., & Lavin, M. (1978). *Criminal Careers of Habitual Felons*. Washington, DC: US Department of Justice.

Pfaff, J. (2017). *Locked In: The True Causes of Mass Incarceration—and How to Achieve Real Reform*. New York, NY: Basic Books.

Pinker, S. (2003). *The Blank Slate: The Modern Denial of Human Nature*. New York, NY: Penguin.

Piquero, A. R., Farrington, D. P., & Blumstein, A. (2003). The criminal career paradigm. *Crime and Justice*, 30, 359–506.

Piquero, A. R., Jennings, W. G., & Farrington, D. P. (2010). On the malleability of self-control: Theoretical and policy implications regarding a general theory of crime. *Justice Quarterly*, 27(6), 803–834.

Piquero, A. R., Jennings, W. G., Farrington, D. P., Diamond, B., & Gonzalez, J. M. R. (2016). A meta-analysis update on the effectiveness of early self-control improvement programs to improve self-control and reduce delinquency. *Journal of Experimental Criminology*, 12(2), 249–264.

Pogarsky, G., & Piquero, A. R. (2003). Can punishment encourage offending? Investigating the "resetting" effect. *Journal of Research in Crime and Delinquency*, 40(1), 95–120.

Pratt, T. C., & Cullen, F. T. (2000). The empirical status of Gottfredson and Hirschi's general theory of crime: A meta-analysis. *Criminology*, 38(3), 931–964.

Pratt, T. C., Cullen, F. T., Blevins, K. R., Daigle, L. E., & Madensen, T. D. (2006). The empirical status of deterrence theory: A meta-analysis. In F. T. Cullen, J. Wright, & K. Blevins (Eds.), *Taking Stock: The Status of Criminological Theory* (pp. 367–396). New Brunswick, NJ: Transaction Publishers.

Pratt, T. C., Cullen, F. T., Sellers, C. S., Thomas Winfree, L., Madensen, T. D., Daigle, L. E., Fearn, N. E., & Gau, J. M. (2010). The empirical status of social learning theory: A meta-analysis. *Justice Quarterly*, 27(6), 765–802.

Pratt, T. C., & Turanovic, J. J. (2018). Celerity and deterrence. In D. S. Nagin, F. T. Cullen, & C. L. Jonson. (Eds.), *Deterrence, Choice, and Crime: Contemporary Perspectives—Advances in Criminological Theory*. New York, NY: Routledge.

Pratt, T. C., Turanovic, J. J., Fox, K. A., & Wright, K. A. (2014). Self-control and victimization: A meta-analysis. *Criminology*, 52(1), 87–116.

Quetelet, A. (1831/1984). *Research on the Propensity for Crime at Different Ages*. Cincinnati, OH: Anderson Publishing Company.

Radelet, M. L., & Lacock, T. L. (2009). Recent developments: Do executions lower homicide rates? The views of leading criminologists. *The Journal of Criminal Law and Criminology*, 99(2), 489–508.

Rafter, N. H. (1992). Criminal anthropology in the United States. *Criminology*, 30(4), 525–546.

Rafter, N. (2006). Cesare Lombroso and the origins of criminology: Rethinking criminological tradition. In S. Henry, & M. M. Lanier (Eds.), *The Essential Criminology Reader* (pp. 33–42). Boulder, CO: Westview Press.

Rafter, N. (2008). Criminology's darkest hour: Biocriminology in Nazi Germany. *Australian & New Zealand Journal of Criminology*, 41(2), 287–306.

Rafter, N. (2011). Origins of criminology. In M. Bosworth, & C. Hoyle (Eds.), *What is Criminology?* (pp. 143–156). New York, NY: Oxford University Press.

Rafter, N. H., Posick, C., & Rocque, M. (2016). *The Criminal Brain*. New York, NY: New York University Press.

Raine, A. (2002). Biosocial studies of antisocial and violent behavior in children and adults: A review. *Journal of Abnormal Child Psychology*, 30(4), 311–326.

Raine, A. (2013). *The Anatomy of Violence: The Biological Roots of Crime*. New York, NY: Vintage.

Raine, A., Mellingen, K., Liu, J., Venables, P., & Mednick, S. A. (2003). Effects of environmental enrichment at ages 3–5 years on schizotypal personality and antisocial behavior at ages 17 and 23 years. *American Journal of Psychiatry*, 160(9), 1627–1635.

Rhee, S. H., & Waldman, I. D. (2002). Genetic and environmental influences on antisocial behavior: A meta-analysis of twin and adoption studies. *Psychological Bulletin*, 128(3), 490–529.

Roberts, J., & Horney, J. (2010). The life event calendar method in criminological research. In A. R. Piquero, & D. Weisburd (Eds.), *Handbook of Quantitative Criminology* (pp. 289–312). New York, NY: Springer.

Rocque, M. (2015). The lost concept: The (re) emerging link between maturation and desistance from crime. *Criminology & Criminal Justice*, 15(3), 340–360.

Rocque, M. (2017). *Desistance from Crime: New Advances in Theory and Research*. New York, NY: Palgrave-Macmillan.

Rocque, M. & Paternoster, R. (2012). Positive criminology and positive theories of crime. In D. Schultz (Ed.), *Encyclopedia of American Law and Criminal Justice*. Revised edition, volume ii. (pp. 605–607). New York, NY: Facts on File.

Rocque, M., & Posick, C. (2017). Paradigm shift or normal science? The future of (biosocial) criminology. *Theoretical Criminology*, 21(3), 288–303.

Rocque, M., Posick, C., & Felix, S. (2015). The role of the brain in urban violent offending: Integrating biology with structural theories of "the streets". *Criminal Justice Studies*, 28(1), 84–103.

Rocque, M., Posick, C., Marshall, I. H., & Piquero, A. R. (2015). A comparative, cross-cultural criminal career analysis. *European Journal of Criminology*, 12(4), 400–419.

Rocque, M., Posick, C., & Paternoster, R. (2016). Identities through time: An exploration of identity change as a cause of desistance. *Justice Quarterly*, 33(1), 45–72.

Rocque, M, Posick, C, & Piquero, A. R. (2016). Self-control and crime: Theory, research, and remaining puzzles. In K. D. Vohs, & R. F. Baumeister (Eds.), *Handbook of Self-Regulation: Research, Theory, and Applications* (pp. 514–532). New York, NY: Guilford Press.

Rocque, M., Welsh, B. C., & Raine, A. (2012). Biosocial criminology and modern crime prevention. *Journal of Criminal Justice*, 40(4), 306–312.

Sampson, R. J., & Laub, J. H. (1993). *Crime in the Making: Pathways and Turning Points Through Life*. Cambridge, MA: Harvard University Press.

Sampson, R. J., & Laub, J. H. (2003). Life-course desisters? Trajectories of crime among delinquent boys followed to age 70. *Criminology, 41*(3), 555–592.

Sampson, R. J., & Laub, J. H. (2005a). A life-course view of the development of crime. *The Annals of the American Academy of Political and Social Science, 602*(1), 12–45.

Sampson, R. J., & Laub, J. H. (2005b). When prediction fails: From crime-prone boys to heterogeneity in adulthood. *The Annals of the American Academy of Political and Social Science, 602*(1), 73–79.

Sampson, R. J., & Laub, J. H. (2005c). Seductions of method: Rejoinder to Nagin and Tremblay's developments trajectory groups: Fact or fiction. *Criminology, 43*, 905–913.

Sampson, R. J., Laub, J. H., & Eggleston, E. P. (2004). On the robustness and validity of groups. *Journal of Quantitative Criminology, 20*(1), 37–42.

Sandler, J. C., Freeman, N. J., & Socia, K. M. (2008). Does a watched pot boil? A time-series analysis of New York State's sex offender registration and notification law. *Psychology, Public Policy, and Law, 14*(4), 284–302.

Savelsberg, J. J., & Sampson, R. J. (2002). Introduction: Mutual engagement: Criminology and sociology? *Crime, Law and Social Change, 37*(2), 99–105.

Schlossman, S. (1984). *Delinquency Prevention in South Chicago. A Fifty-Year Assessment of the Chicago Area Project.* Washington, DC: Rand Corp.

Schuessler, K. (1956/1973). *Edwin Sutherland: On Analyzing Crime.* Chicago, IL: University of Chicago Press.

Schur, E. M. (1973). *Radical Non-Intervention: Rethinking the Delinquency Problem.* Englewood Cliff, NJ: Prentice-Hall.

Schwartz, J. A., Connolly, E. J., & Brauer, J. R. (2017). Head injuries and changes in delinquency from adolescence to emerging adulthood: The importance of self-control as a mediating influence. *Journal of Research in Crime and Delinquency.* Online first.

Schwartz, J. A., Connolly, E. J., & Valgardson, B. A. (2017). An evaluation of the directional relationship between head injuries and subsequent changes in impulse control and delinquency in a sample of previously adjudicated males. *Journal of Criminal Justice.* Online first.

Schwartz, M. (1991). The future of criminology. In B. MacLean, & D. Milovanovic (Eds.), *New Directions in Criminology* (pp. 119–124). Vancouver, Canada: Collective Press.

Schwartz, M. D., & DeKeseredy, W. S. (1991). Left realist criminology: Strengths, weaknesses and the feminist critique. *Crime, Law and Social Change, 15*(1), 51–72.

Schwartz, M. D., & Hatty, S. E. (2003). *Controversies in Critical Criminology.* Cincinnati, OH: Anderson Publishing.

Sellin, T. (1938). Culture conflict and crime. *American Journal of Sociology, 44*(1), 97–103.

Shaw, C. (1931). *The Natural History of a Delinquent Career.* Chicago, IL: University of Chicago Press.

Shaw, C., & McKay, H. D. (1972). *Juvenile Delinquency in Urban Areas.* Chicago, IL: University of Chicago Press.

Shepherd, J. M. (2004). Murders of passion, execution delays, and the deterrence of capital punishment. *The Journal of Legal Studies, 33*(2), 283–321.

Sherman, L. W., Gottfredson, D. C., MacKenzie, D. L., Eck, J., Reuter, P., & Bushway, S. D. (1998). *Preventing Crime: What Works, What Doesn't, What's Promising.* Research in Brief. National Institute of Justice.

Shinnar, S., & Shinnar, R. (1975). The effects of the criminal justice system on the control of crime: A quantitative approach. *Law & Society Review, 9*(4), 581–612.

Short, J. F. (1979). On the etiology of delinquent behavior. *Journal of Research in Crime and Delinquency, 16*(1), 28–33.

Shover, N., & Thompson, C. Y. (1992). Age, differential expectations, and crime desistance. *Criminology, 30*(1), 89–104.

Shover, N. (1996). *Great Pretenders: Pursuits and Careers of Persistent Thieves.* Boulder, CO: Westview Press.

Simpson, S. S. (1989). Feminist theory, crime, and justice. *Criminology, 27*(4), 605–632.

Skardhamar, T. (2009). Reconsidering the theory on adolescent-limited and life-course persistent antisocial behaviour. *The British Journal of Criminology, 49*(6), 863–878.

Skardhamar, T. (2010). Distinguishing facts and artifacts in group-based modeling. *Criminology*, *48*(1), 295–320.

Smith, D. (1995). *Criminology for Social Work*. London: Palgrave.

Smith, P., Cullen, F. T., & Latessa, E. J. (2009). Can 14,737 women be wrong? A meta-analysis of the LSI-R and recidivism for female offenders. *Criminology & Public Policy*, *8*(1), 183–208.

Smith, P., Gendreau, P., & Swartz, K. (2009). Validating the principles of effective intervention: A systematic review of the contributions of meta-analysis in the field of corrections. *Victims and Offenders*, *4*(2), 148–169.

Snodgrass, J. (1973). The criminologist and his criminal: The case of Edwin H. Sutherland and Broadway Jones. *Issues in Criminology*, *8*(1), 1–17.

Sorenson, A. M., & Brownfield, D. (1995). Adolescent drug use and a general theory of crime: An analysis of a theoretical integration. *Canadian Journal of Criminology*, *37*, 19–37.

Sparks, R. F. (1980). A critique of Marxist criminology. *Crime and Justice*, *2*, 159–210.

Spelman, W. (2000). The limited importance of prison expansion. In A. Blumstein, & J. Wallman (Eds.), *The Crime Drop in America* (pp. 97–129). Cambridge, MA: Cambridge University Press.

Spitzer, S. (1975). Punishment and social organization: A study of Durkheim's theory of penal evolution. *Law & Society Review*, *9*(4), 613–638.

Steffensmeier, D. (1989). On the causes of white-collar crime: An assessment of Hirschi and Gottfredson's claims. *Criminology*, *27*(2), 345–358.

Steffensmeier, D., & Allan, E. (1996). Gender and crime: Toward a gendered theory of female offending. *Annual Review of Sociology*, *22*(1), 459–487.

Steinberg, L. (2010). A dual systems model of adolescent risk-taking. *Developmental Psychobiology*, *52*(3), 216–224.

Steinberg, L., & Cauffman, E. (1996). Maturity of judgment in adolescence: Psychosocial factors in adolescent decision making. *Law and Human Behavior*, *20*(3), 249–272.

Stith, K., & Koh, S. Y. (1993). The politics of sentencing reform: The legislative history of the federal sentencing guidelines. *Wake Forest Law Review*, *28*, 223–290.

Stolzenberg, L., & D'alessio, S. J. (1997). "Three strikes and you're out": The impact of California's new mandatory sentencing law on serious crime rates. *Crime & Delinquency*, *43*(4), 457–469.

Sullivan, C. J., McGloin, J., Pratt, T. C., & Piquero, A. R. (2006). Rethinking the "norm" of offender generality: Investigating specialization in the short-term. *Criminology*, *44*(1), 199–233.

Sullivan, C. J., & Piquero, A. R. (2016). The criminal career concept: Past, present, and future. *Journal of Research in Crime and Delinquency*, *53*(3), 420–442.

Sutherland, E. H. (1934). *Principles of Criminology*. Philadelphia, PA: Lippincott.

Sutherland, E. H. (1937). *The Professional Thief*. Chicago, IL: Chicago University Press.

Sutherland, E. H. (1939). *Principles of Criminology*. Philadelphia, PA: Lippincott.

Sutherland, E. H. (1947). *Principles of Criminology*. 4th ed. Philadelphia, PA: Lippincott.

Sutherland, E. H. (1949). *White Collar Crime*. New York, NY: Holt, Rinehart, and Winston.

Sykes, G. M., & Matza, D. (1957). Techniques of neutralization: A theory of delinquency. *American Sociological Review*, *22*(6), 664–670.

Tarde, G. (1903). *Laws of Imitation*. New York, NY: Henry Holt and Company.

Tarde, G. (1912). *Penal Philosophy*. Boston, MA: Little, Brown, and Company.

Taylor, M. P., Forbes, M. K., Opeskin, B., Parr, N., & Lanphear, B. P. (2016). The relationship between atmospheric lead emissions and aggressive crime: An ecological study. *Environmental Health*, *15*(23), 1–10.

Thomassen, B. (2012). Émile Durkheim between Gabriel Tarde and Arnold van Gennep: Founding moments of sociology and anthropology. *Social Anthropology*, *20*(3), 231–249.

Thornberry, T. P. (1989). Reflections on the advantages and disadvantages of theoretical integration. In S. F. Messner, M. D. Krohn, & A. E. Liska (Eds.), *Theoretical Integration in the Study of Deviance and Crime: Problems and Prospects* (pp. 51–60). Albany, NY: State University of New York Press.

Thornberry, T. P. (2012). Criminological theory: Past achievements and future challenges. In R. Loeber, & B. C. Welsh (Eds.), *The Future of Criminology* (pp. 46–55). New York, NY: Oxford University Press.

Thornberry, T. P., Freeman-Gallant, A., Lizotte, A. J., Krohn, M. D., & Smith, C. A. (2003). Linked lives: The intergenerational transmission of antisocial behavior. *Journal of Abnormal Child Psychology, 31*(2), 171–184.

Tittle, C. R. (1988). Two empirical regularities (maybe) in search of an explanation: Commentary on the age/crime debate. *Criminology, 26*(1), 75–85.

Tittle, C. R. (1989). Prospects for synthetic theory: A consideration of macro-level criminological theory. In S. F. Messner, M. D. Krohn & A. E. Liska (Eds.), *Theoretical Integration in the Study of Deviance and Crime: Problems and Prospects* (pp. 161–178). Albany, NY: State University of New York Press.

Toby, J. (1957). Social disorganization and stake in conformity: Complementary factors in the predatory behavior of hoodlums. *Journal of Criminal Law and Criminology, 48*(1), 12–17.

Todd, B. K., Barry, J. A., & Thommessen, S. A. (2017). Preferences for "gender-typed" toys in boys and girls aged 9 to 32 months. *Infant and Child Development, 26*(3), 1–14.

Trulson, C. R., Haerle, D. R., Caudill, J. W., & DeLisi, M. (2016). *Lost Causes: Blended Sentencing, Second Chances, and the Texas Youth Commission*. Austin, TX: University of Texas Press.

Turkheimer, E., & Harden, P. (2014). Behavior genetic research methods: Testing quasi-causal hypotheses using multivariate twin data. In H. T. Reis, & C. M. Judd (Eds.), *Handbook of Research Methods in Social and Personality Psychology* (pp. 159–187). Cambridge, MA: Cambridge University Press.

Tyler, T. R. (2003). Procedural justice, legitimacy, and the effective rule of law. *Crime and Justice, 30*, 283–357.

Uggen, C., & Kruttschnitt, C. (1998). Crime in the breaking: Gender differences in desistance. *Law and Society Review, 32*(2), 339–366.

Unnever, J. D., & Gabbidon, S. L. (2011). *A Theory of African American Offending: Race, Racism, and Crime*. New York, NY: Routledge.

Vargas, E. V., Latour, B., Karsenti, B., Aït-Touati, F., & Salmon, L. (2008). The debate between Tarde and Durkheim. *Environment and Planning D: Society and Space, 26*(5), 761–777.

Vaske, J. C. (2017). Using biosocial criminology to understand and improve treatment outcomes. *Criminal Justice and Behavior, 44*(8), 1050–1072.

Vaske, J., Galyean, K., & Cullen, F. T. (2011). Toward a biosocial theory of offender rehabilitation: Why does cognitive-behavioral therapy work? *Journal of Criminal Justice, 39*(1), 90–102.

Walsh, A., Johnson, H., & Bolen, J. D. (2012). Drugs, crime, and the epigenetics of hedonic allostasis. *Journal of Contemporary Criminal Justice, 28*(3), 314–328.

Walsh, A., & Yun, I. (2017). Examining the race, poverty, and crime nexus adding Asian Americans and biosocial processes. *Journal of Criminal Justice*. Online first.

Warner, B. D. (2003). The role of attenuated culture in social disorganization theory. *Criminology, 41*(1), 73–98.

Warr, M. (1998). Life-course transitions and desistance from crime. *Criminology, 36*(2), 183–216.

Watson, J. B. (1945). *Behaviorism*. London, UK: Transaction Publishers.

Weisburd, D., Bushway, S., Lum, C., & Yang, S. M. (2004). Trajectories of crime at places: A longitudinal study of street segments in the city of Seattle. *Criminology, 42*(2), 283–322.

Weisburd, D., Maher, L., Sherman, L., Buerger, M., Cohn, E., & Petrisino, A. (1993). Contrasting crime general and crime specific theory: The case of hot spots of crime. In F. Adler, & W. S. Laufer (Eds.), *Advances in Criminological Theory* (pp. 45–70). Piscataway, NJ: Transaction Publishers.

Weisburd, D., & Piquero, A. R. (2008). How well do criminologists explain crime? Statistical modeling in published studies. *Crime and Justice, 37*(1), 453–502.

Welsh, B. C., & Farrington, D. P. (2009). Public area CCTV and crime prevention: An updated systematic review and meta-analysis. *Justice Quarterly, 26*(4), 716–745.

Welsh, B. C., & Farrington, D. P. (2012). Science, politics, and crime prevention: Toward a new crime policy. *Journal of Criminal Justice, 40*(2), 128–133.

Welsh, B. C., & Rocque, M. (2014). When crime prevention harms: A review of systematic reviews. *Journal of Experimental Criminology, 10*(3), 245–266.

Welsh, B. C., Zane, S. N., & Rocque, M. (2017). Delinquency prevention for individual change: Richard Clarke Cabot and the making of the Cambridge-Somerville Youth Study. *Journal of Criminal Justice, 52*, 79–89.

Wilson, J. R. (2016). The word criminology: A philology and a definition. *Criminology, Criminal Justice Law, & Society, 16*(3), 61–82.

Wilson, J. Q. (1985). *Thinking About Crime*. New York, NY: Vintage.

Wilson, M. S. (1954). Pioneers in criminology I—Gabriel Tarde (1843–1904). *Journal of Criminal Law and Criminology, 45*(1), 3–11.

Wirth, L. (1931). Clinical sociology. *American Journal of Sociology, 37*(1), 49–66.

Wolfgang, M. E., Figlio, R. M., & Sellin, T. (1987). *Delinquency in a Birth Cohort*. Chicago, IL: University of Chicago Press.

Wright, J. (2009). Inconvenient truths: Science, race and crime. In K. M. Beaver, & A. Walsh (Eds.), *Biosocial Criminology: New Directions in Theory and Research* (pp. 137–153). New York, NY: Routledge.

Wright, J. P., Barnes, J. C., Boutwell, B. B., Schwartz, J. A., Connolly, E. J., Nedelec, J. L., & Beaver, K. M. (2015). Mathematical proof is not minutiae and irreducible complexity is not a theory: A final response to Burt and Simons and a call to criminologists. *Criminology, 53*(1), 113–120.

Wright, J. P., Beaver, K. M., DeLisi, M., Vaughn, M. G., Boisvert, D., & Vaske, J. (2008). Lombroso's legacy: The miseducation of criminologists. *Journal of Criminal Justice Education, 19*(3), 325–338.

Wright, J. P., & Boisvert, D. (2009). What biosocial criminology offers criminology. *Criminal Justice and Behavior, 36*(11), 1228–1240.

Wright, J. P., & DeLisi, M. (2016). *Conservative Criminology: A Call to Restore Balance in the Social Sciences*. London, UK: Routledge.

Wright, J. P. & DeLisi, M. (2017). What criminologists don't say and why: Monopolized by the Left, academic research on crime gets almost everything wrong. *City Journal,* Summer 2017. Retrieved from www.city-journal.org/html/what-criminologists-dont-say-and-why-15328.html.

Young, J. (1988). Radical criminology in Britain: The emergence of a competing paradigm. *British Journal of Criminology, 28*, 159–183.

Young, J. (2004). Voodoo criminology and the numbers game. In J. Ferrell, K. Hayward, W. Morrison, & M. Presdee (Eds.), *Cultural Criminology Unleashed* (pp. 13–27). London, UK: Routledge.

Young, J. (2011). *The Criminological Imagination*. Cambridge, UK: Polity Press.

Zane, S. N., Welsh, B. C., & Zimmerman, G. M. (2016). Examining the iatrogenic effects of the Cambridge-Somerville Youth Study: Existing explanations and new appraisals. *British Journal of Criminology, 56*(1), 141–160.

Zehr, H. (2005). *Changing Lenses: A New Focus for Crime and Justice*. Scottdale, PA: Harold Press.

Index

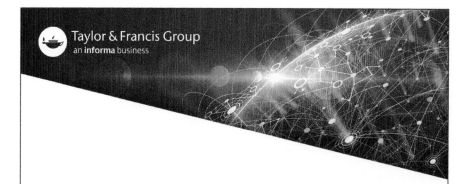